DIGGING UP THE PAST

An Introduction to

Archaeological Excavation

John Collis

SUTTON PUBLISHING

First published in the United Kingdom in 2001 by
Sutton Publishing Limited · Phoenix Mill
Thrupp · Stroud · Gloucestershire · GL5 2BU

British Library Cataloguing in Publication Data
A catalogue record for this book is available from the British Library.

ISBN 0-7509-2737-2

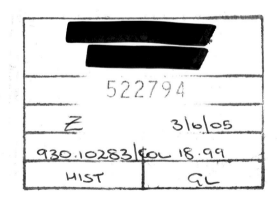
Typeset in 10/13pt Sabon.
Typesetting and origination by
Sutton Publishing Limited.
Printed and bound in England by
J.H. Haynes & Co. Ltd, Sparkford.

CONTENTS

FOREWORD

I have now spent more than forty years of my life on archaeological excavations. On the one hand there is much that I have learnt, on the other there is much that I simply take for granted, so that it is difficult for me sometimes to communicate the obvious to people who are taking part in their first excavation. There is so much that a new volunteer or student needs to know, but so much that is totally meaningless until one actually does it. As a director of an excavation I will talk to people about what they should do on site, but inevitably I will forget to say something, or the people I am talking to can only absorb so much at one time, so that inevitably things go wrong. The eventuality that one had not expected, the exceptional find or unusual occurrence, may happen to someone who simply doesn't have the experience to cope with the situation. This book is aimed at giving new excavators as much information as possible in a form they can absorb or go back to refer to, so that they will not only be ready to work on site, but also be confident that they are not likely to cause some disaster. It aims to tell the digger what is expected of him or her, and also tries to explain what else is (or should be) going on around on the project, and to show how often directing an excavation involves compromises or choices.

But it is also aimed at those who have to teach, and at supervisors and directors who may themselves lack the experience of teaching something that they learnt so long ago that they have forgotten what it is like to be ignorant. In the last couple of decades archaeology has become more professional, with more people earning their living from digging, whereas in the 1950s and 1960s, when I came into archaeology, the professional was the exception, and most of us were amateurs, spending our holidays and weekends on excavations. The opportunities to start while still at school, especially as I did at the age of eleven, are perhaps now less available, but it is still pleasing, when interviewing potential students, to find how many of them already have some experience of excavation from school. I do not advocate a return to the bad old days when large-scale excavation of complex urban sites was the domain of large numbers of semi-skilled or unskilled volunteers. Young professional archaeologists should be adequately paid for their work, and should also have a proper career structure. But, on the other hand, archaeology is becoming an accepted leisure activity, and if its skills are not communicated to the public at large it becomes a pointless exercise. Part of our professionalism should be in teaching and communicating. But this requires both skill on the part of the professional, and understanding of his or her limitations by the amateur, so that both will strive towards higher standards of research and results. There are certain sorts of site which should be left to the skilled – which usually, though not inevitably, means the professional; there are other sites which can only be excavated on a large scale by amateurs, and where simply by employing large numbers of people, or by taking the site slowly over a long period of time, higher standards may be achieved than would be the case if using a small professional team over a short period of time.

This book is intended for students, at all levels, and volunteers who want to gain some experience in something that will enrich their lives, or which may be of peripheral use when they go into another profession such as teaching. It is also aimed at teachers and professionals – those of us who are concerned with training in universities and evening classes, and who see archaeology as a subject that is relevant to our own society and has something to say to the world at large. Though in Britain the majority of archaeology takes place in rescue situations, with a small group of professionals carrying out the work, much of what I am writing is addressed to those who are not professionals, or have not yet achieved that hallowed status. I am assuming that they will usually be working on research projects organised by universities or other groups, and they may be working anywhere in Europe. Thus, I am not assuming that they will necessarily be faced with 'single context recording' which is the norm in professional circles in Britain, or indeed will encounter what I would consider the ideal of 'open area excavation', though I shall be emphasising these methodologies. So, it is possible to find the 'Wheeler grid' or the 'Bersu Schnitt' methods still the norm in parts of Europe; students may well encounter them and thus should be aware of how they function. At the same time I am taking the opportunity to criticise some aspects of modern practice, so that students realise that there are alternative ways of doing things, some of which may be better than what is common practice, and also to increase awareness that what they are being taught on one particular project may not be best practice. In general, by increasing awareness, I hope we can improve standards.

I was brought up on two textbooks. The first was Sir Mortimer Wheeler's *Archaeology from the Earth*, a stimulating book that provided inspiration for a generation of archaeologists, telling us what archaeology was like and how high our standards should be, and was written in an entertaining and witty style. The second was Kathleen Kenyon's *Beginning in Archaeology*, which was more prosaic and down-to-earth, but with many practical hints of what to do, and what not to do. It is this sort of book which I feel is now lacking, and I hope this book will go some way towards filling the gap. In recent years there has been a number of books on techniques, but either they have been aimed at the professional market, for instance Phil Barker's influential *Techniques of Archaeological Excavation*; or they have become dated, like Graham Webster's *Practical Archaeology*, which in many ways was the successor of Kathleen Kenyon's book; or they have aimed at explaining archaeology to an interested public, for instance Kevin Greene's *Archaeology: an Introduction*, or Phil Barker's *Understanding Archaeological Excavation*. None, however, describes what it is like to participate on an excavation or how one should excavate a burial, or the almost military discipline that is necessary for a site to function properly. Colin Renfrew and Paul Bahn's *Archaeology: Theory, Methods and Practice* is a very useful textbook which gives a wide perspective of the aims, theory and methodology of archaeology, but of necessity it does not go into the details of excavation techniques. I can also recommend Peter Drewett's *Field Archaeology: an Introduction* which covers the whole range of fieldwork. While my book was in press, Stuart Roskam's *Excavation* appeared, giving another excavator's perspective on excavation technique. I hope, thus, that this book will complement these other publications.

ACKNOWLEDGEMENTS

I would like to thank the commentators on the earlier versions of this book, Phil Barker and the anonymous reviewer for Sutton's, and especially Geoff Carver for his detailed criticism. Many of their thoughts have been incorporated, but I am especially thankful for their encouraging remarks at times when the project was grinding to a halt.

I would like to thank all those many excavators and students who have contributed ideas, many of which I have shamelessly adopted. For help with the illustrations I would like to thank Irene Luis de la Cruz for assistance with some of the original drawings. I acknowledge the following for the drawings and photographs: 1.1, reproduced by kind permission of the Wiltshire Natural History and Archaeological Society; 1.2a–b, after Clark 1954, by permission of the University of Cambridge; 1.3c, Salisbury & South Wiltshire Museum; 1.4a, Allen Collection no. 768, reproduced by courtesy of the Visitors of the Ashmolean Museum, Oxford; 1.4b and 6.6a–b, after Wheeler 1943, by permission of the Society of Antiquaries of London; 1.5a–b, from Wheeler 1954, by permission of the Society of Antiquaries of London; 1.6a, after Krämer 1957, by permission of the Bayerisches Landesamt für Denkmalpflege, Ausgrabung Manching 1955; 1.6b, after Krämer 1957; 1.7, after Grimes 1960; 1.8, John Hampton, National Monument Record; 1.9, after Barker 1969 and http://www.tandf.co.uk/journals, © and by permission of Taylor and Francis; 2.1, after Redman 1986; 2.2, Dept of Archaeology and Prehistory, University of Sheffield; 2.3, 2.7, 3.4, 3.5, 6.4, 6.6a, 6.7, 7.1, 9.4, 10.4c, 10.8, 11.1c and 11.4b, Association pour la Recherche sur l'Age du Fer en Auvergne; 2.5a–b, 8.5, 9.7a, 9.7b, 10.1a, 10.1b and 10.2, Exeter City Museums; 2.10, Steve Marsden; 4.2, John Coles, © Somerset Levels Project; 5.3, after Harris 1989, courtesy of Edward C. Harris; 6.2a, © Museum of London Archaeological Service, from MoLAS 1994; 8.1, based on R. Parrenti in Frankovitch et al. 1983; 8.4a, reproduced by permission of Rescue, from Rescue slide-set; 6.6d and 9.2, from Bersu 1940; 9.2c and 9.3a–b from Musson 1970, by permission of C. Musson; 9.5a–b, based on Richmond 1961; 9.6a–d, based on Hope-Taylor 1977; 9.8a–b, after Beresford and Hurst 1992, courtesy of the Wharram Research Project, drawings by Chris Philo; 9.9, after B. Soudský 1966; 10.4a, from Reynolds 1974; 10.6, from Dimbley 1965, by permission of the Experimental Earthworks Committee; 10.10, Graeme Guilbert; 12.1, John Warbis.

While this book was in the final stages of preparation, Phil Barker and Brian Hope-Taylor, two of the greatest excavators of the later twentieth century, died, and I would like to dedicate this book to their memory.

ONE

PARADIGMS

There are two schools of thought about the development of archaeological technique. One, the usually accepted view in Britain, sees the development and improvement of excavation techniques as something technical – we devise better methods and techniques, and so can better understand and get more information from excavations. The other viewpoint, which I wish to put forward here, is that the best archaeological excavators have always been efficient, it is merely that the aims of excavation have changed. I was once asked to play the part of Thomas Bateman, one of the best of the nineteenth-century antiquarians, and to argue in public against my students that in fact modern excavators waste a lot of time recording irrelevant information – and I won the argument, not because Bateman could excavate better, but he was clearer in his mind about what he wanted to achieve. Excavation is very much a matter of deciding what one wants to know or obtain, and setting about finding it, even though what one finds may refute the original hypothesis, and this should be as true for rescue excavations as it is for pure research projects.

This view of archaeology is akin to the general approach to science, which argues that science is based not so much on observed 'facts' but on the logical framework within which we place those facts. This is what scientists refer to as a 'paradigm', and in archaeology we can demonstrate that methods of excavation have been dominated by the prevalent paradigm in society at large. However, as I shall discuss later, this is very much the purist, academic, view of archaeology, and the reality of modern excavation is that we are driven by events as much as by research. Increasingly we recognise that archaeological sites are precious documents, and that digging a site is like a historian reading a unique document, but tearing it up as part of the process of reading, so that no one else will ever be able to read it again. For unique and special sites such as Stonehenge, this is obvious, but it is also true for more mundane sites – there may be many farms or town houses from which we may draw generalisations about architectural, social or economic history, but each site has its own unique history.

This attitude has now been enshrined in a number of international agreements, notably the Treaty of Malta (or Valetta Convention) which the British government has just signed; indeed, this lays down the legal and ethical framework for the archaeology carried out in all countries in Europe which are signatories to it. It states that the archaeological resource is limited and is rapidly being diminished; once it is destroyed, it is gone for ever, so it should be preserved as far as possible. So, although there are still excavations which are carried out for research or for social reasons (for example to display a site to the public), most excavations occur because the site is threatened by development. It is therefore up to developers to preserve the archaeology by avoiding sites or, where that is not possible, either to minimise the site destruction or to ensure its preservation 'by record' – that is, to pay for an excavation to take place. There is a lively debate, which I shall come back to in the last chapter, about how far such 'rescue' excavations are, or should be, dictated by research problems, and to what extent we are merely trying to record even when we have no research questions to ask. Should only threatened sites be excavated, or should some excavation be carried out for research reasons? Whatever, excavation is a privilege, and we need to accept that we are privileged in a way that future generations will not be; once the majority of sites have been irreparably damaged or destroyed, excavation may well be the exception.

TREASURE HUNTING

Though there are occasional records of people digging holes to obtain information in the classical and medieval periods, essentially early excavation was intended only to find treasure. In Britain until recently we were hampered by the concept of 'Treasure Trove' and the conflicting rights of the finder, the landowner and the state. This concept still exists in the financial rewards given to people who find valuable objects which are declared to be the property of the state; it is also reflected in the flourishing trade in antiquities which has led to conflicts between archaeologists and the art world about the display of objects known to have been dug up clandestinely and sold. Many objects such as coins come from the work of 'treasure hunters', some of whom work closely with archaeologists so that their finds can be given greater meaning; others do it merely for money, and disguise the true origin of their finds if they have been removed illegally.

On some excavations in Britain you will be asked to sign a disclaimer to any gold or silver objects you may find, as sometimes coroners' inquests have found in favour of the person who actually discovered the object, including in one case a volunteer on an excavation. In other countries the right of the state to all antiquities is better established. The general view of archaeologists is that objects removed from their context lose much of their scientific value, and equally that they should be preserved somewhere where they will be available for other people to study and look at – so do not pocket anything you find on an excavation, even pot-sherds from the dump, without prior consultation with the person in charge. You may find that even (s)he does not have the right to give you that permission, as in most countries finds are the property either of the State or of the landowner.

THE ANTIQUARIANS

It was in the eighteenth and early nineteenth centuries in Britain that the first excavations took place, the results of which can still be used by modern archaeologists. The aim of these excavators was simply to acquire objects for their private cabinets, be they of classical or local origin, and in certain circles an interest in antiquities was an indication of a cultivated and educated person. Finds from the classical world had greater prestige, given the debt that Europeans from the Renaissance onwards ascribed to their Greek and Roman predecessors, but by the nineteenth century this value was extended to other civilisations of the Near East, as well as India and China, and it is these values which still form the foundation of the monetary worth ascribed to objects by the antiquities market. The best objects, then as now, could be obtained either by excavating in ancient tombs or by pillaging monumental buildings of inscriptions and sculptures. This activity was very much an upper-class activity, though in general those who did the actual pillaging were, and often are, local peasant farmers.

The best of the early excavators, like William Stukeley, Sir Richard Colt Hoare and William Cunnington, recorded in addition the place where these objects were found, and published illustrated descriptions of the finds and the circumstances of discovery. Items found together with an individual burial would also be noted, and sometimes the associated material and stratigraphy (a concept of a chronological sequence of deposits taken over from geologists such as William 'Strata' Smith) deserved comment; for example John Frere observed in 1797 that hand axes occurred with the bones of extinct animals in the gravels of Hoxne. Since complete or well-preserved objects worthy of display were required, in Britain burials were the favourite hunting ground of the early antiquarians, especially where these were observable on the surface as barrows. Burials tend to be in the centre of the mound, so the most efficient form of recovery was to dig a hole in the middle (Fig. 1.1).

RACIAL ORIGINS

In the early nineteenth century Colt Hoare was already attempting to assign greater meaning to his objects, by dating them and assigning them to different peoples in the past, though he himself remarked how difficult this was for the period before written records. One major interest in the early to mid-nineteenth century was the question of racial origins, and of the peoples who made up the nation state, as well as those who populated the less civilised parts of the world. One solution to the problem, advocated by the Danish

1.1. Antiquarian excavation has often been dismissed as being a disastrous loss of information from poor excavations. In fact for what these early excavators wanted – specimens of artefacts or skulls for collections – it was on the whole very efficient. The easiest way to get complete prehistoric pots is to dig a hole in the middle of a burial mound, as William Cunnington is doing in this picture. The problem was that the questions being asked were too limited, and modern excavation can tell us much more about the context in which the objects were buried.

anthropologist Daniel Friedrich Estricht, was the study of skulls, especially their dimensions and shape. By 1850 the Derbyshire antiquarian Thomas Bateman had started to collect skulls in addition to the artefacts, and this led on to the detailed publication of skulls by Joseph Davis and John Thurnam in *Crania Britannica*. Details of pottery styles and burial rites were linked to the supposed racial groups (long-headed people buried in long barrows, and round-headed in round barrows), and these were assigned to specific 'peoples', usually defined by their language – the change of head shape from 'long' to 'round' was often interpreted as the replacement of pre-Indo-Europeans with Indo-European-speaking people! These questions increased the need for recording, with plans of burials and sections appearing in published reports, but these were minimal and idealised, usually done after the excavation and for purposes of description only. Excavation of barrows began to be more systematic, like Thurnam's clearing out of the eastern chamber and passage of the West Kennett long barrow to obtain human skeletons.

THE TECHNOLOGICAL PARADIGM

Christian Thomsen's concept of the Three Age System for the first time provided a chronological framework into which these antiquarian discoveries could be placed, linked with the concept of technological advancement, as first stone, then bronze and finally iron were adopted by prehistoric man. This idea of technological advance was to be a dominant theme throughout the nineteenth century, so again archaeology was merely reflecting the interests of society at large. It was another Dane, J.J.A. Worsaae, who first applied the concept to field observations, recording the different types of artefact turning up in the shell middens and the megalithic tombs, and so building a basic chronology. Sophus Müller, a later Director of the National Museum in Copenhagen, noted that Stone Age graves tended to be the deepest in barrows, with graves inserted later occurring at depths varying according to their relative age – a simple form of stratigraphy – and this chronology was later confirmed by finds from the Danish bogs where the associated plant remains could be studied.

By the time these ideas had become generally disseminated in the mid- to late nineteenth century the concept of evolution was becoming widely accepted. This could be applied to objects as well as to living creatures, and the Swedish prehistorian Oscar Montelius developed the concept of typology, by which objects such as bronze axes could be demonstrated to change over time, becoming more efficient in design, especially as better technology became available. To demonstrate his thesis Montelius used a modern analogy: the evolution of the railway carriage from the stagecoach. His use of association of objects in hoards and graves required greater precision in observation and publication, firstly to demonstrate how the typologies of different artefacts could be tied together (e.g. axes and swords), and secondly to link the chronologies of northern Europe with the historically dated sequences of the Near East by cross-dating (by studying the context of exports from one part of Europe to another, and so linking the sequences in the two areas). Though modern methods such as dendrochronology give us much greater precision, Montelius's basic chronology for the later phases of prehistory is still right in its general outlines. It also allowed greater potential in dating archaeological sites. This in turn placed a greater emphasis on field recording, noting the associations of objects with one another in burials or in hoards, and, where possible, making stratigraphical observations in burial mounds.

CLIMATIC CHANGE

Charles Lyell's publication in 1830–3 of the *Principles of Geology* opened up for archaeologists the possibility not only of using stratigraphy and type fossils for dating different strata but also of finding remains of early man in association with extinct animals, indicating climates very different from the modern. In 1859 the various observations which had been made about such associations, such as Frere's notes at Hoxne, or Jacques Boucher de Perthes's discoveries in the gravels of the Somme around Abbeville, were brought together by Sir John Evans and Joseph Prestwich. This triggered excavations not only in river gravels, but also in French caves and Danish bogs. In both bogs and caves stratigraphy can be complex and difficult, so considerable precision is needed if artefacts and other finds are to be correctly located – in the case of the caves with animal bones, in the bogs with macro-fossils of plants (later, at the beginning of the twentieth century, it was recognised that pollen also survived, and was a better indicator of climatic change). The excavation techniques which evolved laid a great emphasis on detailed stratigraphy, coupled with detailed plans of bones and artefacts *in situ*.

The methodology was to excavate slices of the deposits, and this was gradually systematised into excavation in one- or two-metre squares, each with a series of superimposed plans, and a series of drawn sections, which in this book I shall call the 'squares' method. Only rarely was a surface of more than a few metres square opened up, and each square was treated as a separate unit. It allowed the collection of the artefacts by the metre square, and so allowed density of finds to be plotted – useful in studying, for instance, camp sites of hunter gatherers; this became the standard technique in the 1930s for the excavation of Mesolithic sites in Britain. The classic example of this kind was Grahame Clark's excavation of Star Carr in the 1950s (Fig. 1.2). However, attempts by French archaeologists to employ this technique on more complex sites, riddled by pits and ditches, such as my French colleague's excavation at Aulnat in the 1960s, were less successful, and despite the detail of their recording it is now very difficult to assign finds to individual features, and especially to identify groups of associated finds.

SOCIAL EVOLUTION

Evolution was also applied to the development of society as a whole, with the realisation that society had become more complex as mankind had developed. Perhaps the concepts of anthropological and sociological writers such as Morgan and Engels were not immediately applied to archaeology – that was the impact of Gordon Childe a generation or more later – but the awareness that societies other than our own had lived on the same land, had used it and left traces of their activity in the soil led to a marked change in excavation technique. In Britain this change is usually associated with General Pitt Rivers, the 'father of British archaeology', but in fact he enjoys this reputation more because of his excavation technique than because of the conceptual framework that lay behind it. His museum at Farnham in Dorset contained not only an exhibition of the finds and excavations he had carried out on his estate on Cranborne Chase, but also a large ethnographic collection demonstrating technological evolution on a world-wide basis.

Pitt Rivers and his contemporaries were trying to demonstrate the life-style of previous inhabitants of this country. Thus the emphasis shifted from the discovery of individual objects (and thus an emphasis on burials) to settlement archaeology and a concern with the

1.2. Star Carr. Grahame Clark's excavations contrasted strongly with the dominant methods prevalent in Britain in the 1950s. Though he was digging in trenches to remove the overburden and get down to the archaeological deposits (Fig. 1.2a), the occupation levels, once located, were excavated in one yard squares, a methodology originally developed for French caves and for bog sites similar to Star Carr excavated in Scandinavia. It allowed finds to be tied in very closely with the environmental data, especially with the pollen sequence. However, it also allowed Clark to look at densities of finds, and so locate activity areas, and calculate the size of the site (Fig. 1.2b).

more prosaic elements of life – what sort of animals did they keep, what sort of pottery did they use, what sort of ornaments did they wear? Excavation was on a large scale, with complete excavation of settlements where possible (Fig. 1.3), and detailed descriptions of the finds. Excavation was still the domain of the rich middle and upper classes, but it was no longer simply an enjoyable way to spend a weekend; instead it became a seasonal activity, with workmen employed full-time over a period of weeks, if not months.

Authors such as Wheeler, who see the evolution of excavation technique as essentially technical, have often contrasted Pitt Rivers's excavations on Cranborne Chase with those carried out at the same time at Silchester, and they express surprise that Pitt Rivers, though he visited Silchester as the first Inspector of Ancient Monuments, passed no comment on the limitations of the excavation techniques employed there. At Cranborne Chase every find was measured in, its stratigraphical position recorded, and all significant finds were illustrated and published. At Silchester the aim was to discover the plans of buildings, so that walls were followed, with little concern to study finds within their stratigraphical context. However, the difference was in many ways one of scale. The quantities of finds at Silchester were huge compared to those found by Pitt Rivers, and no excavators then understood the complexities of stratigraphy or were able to identify the ephemeral traces of timber buildings. Both were trying to do the same thing – to describe the societies they were

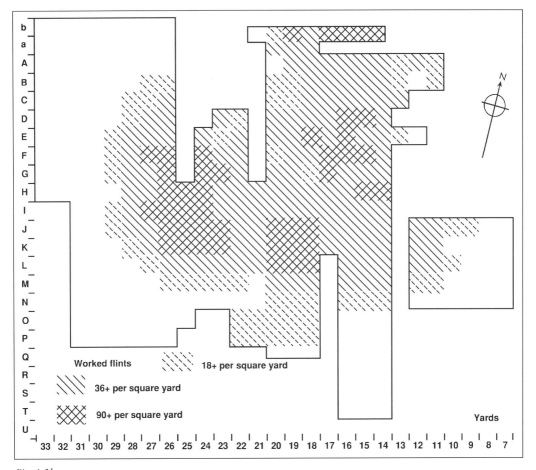

Fig. 1.2b

excavating, and place them within their evolutionary context. For Pitt Rivers on Cranborne Chase it was the peasant farmers of the prehistoric and Roman periods; for Fox and St John Hope at Silchester it was the inhabitants of a Roman town. What they did not realise was that they were dealing with several towns one on top of the other, and that the Roman town did not remain static through the four hundred years of Roman occupation.

For later periods the description of life-styles was less often attempted (that could be done to a certain extent by using written sources, or so it was believed); rather, there was an interest in artistic and architectural development. Excavations were carried out to elucidate the plans of castles and abbeys, with little concern for the chronological aspects of the site or for the stratification of the finds. Thus Sir Charles Piers's excavations at Whitby Abbey in the 1920s have left us a legacy of tantalising finds of Saxon date, which *must* come from the earliest Saxon foundation recorded by Bede – but we know nothing of their context. As late as the 1960s Roman archaeologists were more concerned with understanding the architectural history of the Roman villas, as a perusal of Collingwood and Richmond's *Archaeology of Roman Britain* shows, than with understanding what villas actually were and how they functioned. This concern with architecture and art history reflects upper-class interests, and there was little interest in the sites where the majority of the population lived.

1.3. General Pitt Rivers at Wor Barrow. Using the extensive finances generated by the family estate on Cranborne Chase, Pitt Rivers was able to employ workmen to carry out excavation on a large scale, including the complete stripping of the Neolithic Wor Barrow and the total clearance of several Bronze Age, Iron Age and Roman settlements. The plans of settlements he produced were not to be equalled until the 1960s. However, he did not fully understand the structures he encountered, such as traces of timber buildings, and re-excavation of one of his sites has shown that he commonly missed smaller features such as post-holes. His aim was not to find spectacular objects, but to provide a description of the life-styles of earlier people. Any significant objects, including small pieces of pottery, he considered should be published, and this was done in a series of volumes, Excavations on Cranborne Chase, *which remains one of the classics of British archaeology, and is a mine of useful information. The objects, with plans and models of the sites, were exhibited in his museum at Farnham, and he used to hold dances on Sundays to encourage local people to come and see the collection, and report finds to him. My grandmother was invited to one by a boyfriend, but refused to go, as it was not considered quite respectable – a problem archaeologists have always suffered from!*

However, the approach also survived for a long time in the Marxist archaeology of central and eastern Europe. Large amounts of money were expended by the state on large-scale excavations of typical sites of various periods, which could then be used to illustrate the various phases of social development as laid out in the works of Engels. In Russia the most famous excavation was of the early medieval trading site of Novgorod. In Czechoslovakia such research excavations included the Palaeolithic site of Dolní Věstonice, the Neolithic *Bandkeramik* settlement of Bylany, the excavation of various Iron Age oppida such as Hrazany and Závist, and the medieval settlements of Mikulčice and Staré Město–Velehrad, on a scale which could not be matched in western democracies. In the National Museum in Prague the results of these excavations were laid out strictly according to Marxist theories of social evolution.

THE CULTURE-HISTORICAL PARADIGM

The tradition of Pitt Rivers continued into the early part of the twentieth century with excavators such as Bushe Fox, St George Gray, Bulleid and Toms, but gradually the aim of excavation was changing from the description of ancient societies to an understanding of the dynamics of change. The stimulus for this came mainly from prehistory, with the desire to understand the changes in ceramic types, burial traditions and so forth: the history of culture-groups as conceived by the German scholar Gustav Kossinna and developed by Gordon Childe. These culture groups were then equated with ancient peoples, and were used, for instance, to document the supposed origin and spread of the Germans, a methodology which underpinned claims over territory. (This false approach is still used today in political conflicts.) The catalyst for change was essentially seen in external influence, usually in the form of invasions – what Grahame Clark was later to term the 'invasion hypothesis'. In Roman archaeology a parallel process was especially concerned with military and political changes, such as the details of the conquest of Britain. In both cases the emphasis was on short-term changes, with a need for precise dating.

In terms of excavation technique this meant a change from horizontal to vertical recording. The section demonstrating the stratigraphical sequence became more important than the plan, and excavation strategies changed accordingly from area excavation to trenches and similar forms of excavation. However, unlike the parallel development that I have noted under 'Climatic Change', where excavations were small-scale and conducted by students and specialists, the culture-historical paradigm dealt with complex societies, for which a larger scale of excavation was needed, which generally involved employing unskilled workmen. The approach is nowhere more vividly demonstrable than in Wheeler's excavations at Maiden Castle (Fig. 1.4a). Virtually all excavation was directed towards the sequence of defences, especially the gateways, and information about the interior of the Iron Age hill-fort is largely incidental, from the excavation of the Roman temple. At the same time the precise stratification of a specific find could be vital, so greater control was needed in the recording of the excavation.

The trench gave this control, but in addition Wheeler introduced on to his excavations a hierarchical organisation of trained supervisors whose responsibility it was to label finds, to label and draw sections, and to keep written records in a site note-book linking this information together with numbering and descriptions of the layers. The actual excavation was still largely the domain of the paid workman, though supervisors were expected to dig as well – indeed, this was part of their training. The use of the trench meant that diggers could be broken down into small groups and their work closely monitored.

This did not mean that interest in the plan totally disappeared, but to obtain a useful plan view meant an adaptation of the trench strategy to an area. There were two main solutions. The best known is Wheeler's 'grid' (or 'box') method which consisted of a grid of squares divided by baulks (Fig. 1.4b), which could be used for access to any part of the area without trampling on any excavated surfaces. It gave rigid control over the individual excavators, as well as stratigraphical control, with a large number of sections crossing the area in both directions. It also had flexibility as it could be expanded in any direction as time and funds allowed, and following the areas with most significant results. After recording, the baulks could be removed, as was done at Maiden Castle to expose the 'war cemetery' or at Stanwick in the 1950s (Fig. 1.5). This system became Wheeler's hallmark, and was introduced by him (or his trainees) into other countries such as India.

The other solution was to dig a series of parallel trenches, preferably alternating with blank areas where the spoil could be dumped. After recording the sections, the trenches were filled in and the blank strips excavated to give a total plan. This allowed greater efficiency in keeping the movement of soil down to a minimum, but had the disadvantage that all the sections were essentially in one direction. I have always referred to this as the 'Schnitt' method (Schnitt is the German word for trench), as it was primarily developed in

1.4. Wheeler at Maiden Castle. Sir Mortimer Wheeler produced a number of innovations, and popularised archaeology for a wide public. However, in the realm of excavation technique, he imposed standards of organisation and control which form the basis of those in force today. Trenches were cut vertically and exactly, layers were numbered, sections labelled and drawn, and finds carefully labelled. The emphasis was on sequence, so the vertical record was important, and on the detailed stratigraphy of individual finds. This also involved cleanliness on site to prevent deposits and groups of finds becoming contaminated. Wheeler's excavations concentrated on the sequence of the ramparts to obtain a cultural sequence, with less concern for the interior (Fig. 1.4a). Where more was needed to obtain a plan, for instance of the entrances or of the 'war cemetery', he developed his grid method which gave considerable control not only over the stratigraphy, but also over the work force (Fig. 1.4b).

Germany, a classic example being Werner Krämer's excavations at the Iron Age site of Manching in the 1950s (Fig. 1.6). The main innovator was Gerhard Bersu. The leading archaeologist in Germany in the 1930s, he was forced to emigrate for political reasons; he introduced the technique to Britain, and used it on the Iron Age settlement of Little Woodbury and also on his excavations in the Isle of Man where he was interned during the war. I have found the system useful in situations where there is a small labour force but the topsoil has to be removed by hand, for example at the cemetery at Owslebury, where finds disturbed by deep ploughing were still in the topsoil, and where an overall view of the site was not essential (Fig. 2.4). In Germany, especially on the löss soils, stratigraphy might not always be clear, and stratigraphical excavation in the style employed by Wheeler and others did not appear until the 1960s, so often the '*Schnitte*' were dug in spits, as Bersu did on the Isle of Man, a method often referred to as the 'planum' method. As each horizontal surface was cleaned and planned, features of soil

Fig. 1.4b.

changes would be marked, and the diggers instructed to keep the finds from them separate from the rest; thus some stratigraphy was introduced into the system.

Both these techniques of excavation appear in modified form in various contexts. For instance Sir Cyril Fox applied the '*Schnitt*' method to round barrow excavation, but more commonly used was the 'quadrant method', an adaptation of the grid, whereby four squares were laid out centred on the round barrow, giving sections across the mound in two different directions. In various forms this technique dominated barrow excavation in the 1950s despite the inconvenience of the baulks usually masking the central burial!

Other methods were employed. From 1953 to 1961 early urban excavation in Winchester consisted of digging a trial trench through the deposits and then opening up an area adjacent to the trench once the stratigraphy had been tested. The areas were dug piecemeal and lacked proper control, so this was not true 'open area' excavation (it was more akin to that described under 'Climatic Change'). At Verulamium, Shepard Frere found the traditional 3m (10ft) square trenches too small, and opened up larger ones, specifically to deal with the extensive timber buildings.

THE SOCIO-ECONOMIC PARADIGM

The revolution, when it reached Britain in the 1950s, came from an unexpected quarter. Medieval archaeology had trailed behind other periods, being largely concerned with art and architectural history or simply with exposing sites for public display. In Britain two excavations from the 1950s stand out: those at the deserted medieval village of Wharram Percy and the Saxon palace site at Yeavering. Wharram Percy was instigated by the social and economic historian Maurice Beresford, who was himself one of the catalysts for changing the paradigm in medieval archaeology, by asking questions about the causes of

1.5. Wheeler at Stanwick. The grid excavation method had its problems. The baulks often masked important features and relationships, perhaps even complete walls. It also made an overall appreciation of the features difficult even on a relatively simple site such as Stanwick. On multi-period sites, the various trenches might be at different levels, and also the baulks prevented communication between the excavators in each square (Fig. 1.5a). In this case, by the time the baulks had been removed, the relationships between the various gullies had been destroyed, and one searches in vain in the report for a discussion of the phasing of the different structures (Fig. 1.5b).

desertion and, later, about the origins of villages such as Wharram Percy. The early attempts at excavation were disastrous: normal trench excavation was totally unsuitable for peasants' dwellings where often only a trace remained of the ephemeral structures, unlike the substantial remains on castle and church sites. Jack Golson and John Hurst, who had some training in the Danish methods pioneered by Gudmund Hatt of 'open area excavation' of occupation sites, suggested that this technique should be applied at Wharram Percy. The point to make is that the change of paradigm caused a different sort of site to be excavated, and it was the problems these sites caused which then forced a change in excavation method. Brian Hope-Taylor, who excavated the timber buildings at Yeavering, was also familiar with Scandinavian techniques and he excavated complete buildings rather than attempting to trench the features that showed up on the aerial photographs. The reason why Scandinavian archaeology was more advanced was in part due to the political and social climate of pre-war Denmark, a country dominated by small farmers who had a great interest in settlement and environmental history, in contrast to the imperial and colonial aspirations of Britain which emphasised progress and change through conquest and colonisation.

But during the Second World War 'open area' excavation had already appeared, in the form of the rescue excavations by W.F. Grimes (arguably the first professional field archaeologist in Britain) on round and long cairns in the Cotswolds. His aim was purely practical: to interpret aspects of barrow construction which he felt could not be tackled in small trenches, as had been attempted up to that time (Fig. 1.7). Though these were classic excavations, few

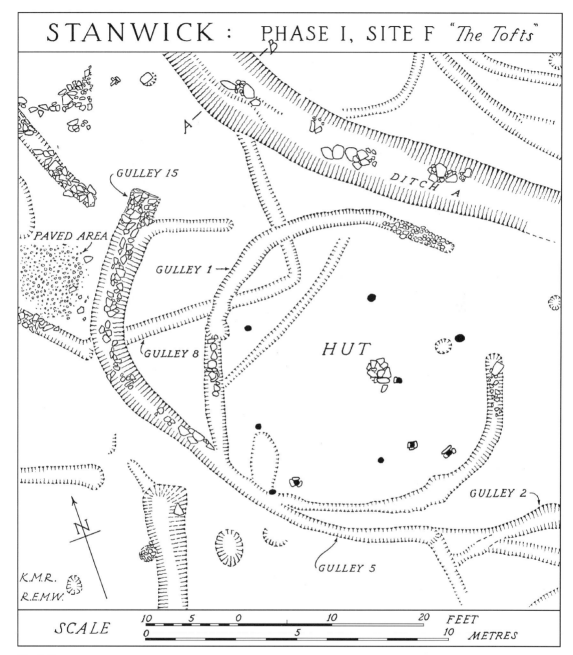

STANWICK : PHASE I, SITE F "The Tofts"

GULLEY 15

PAVED AREA

DITCH A

GULLEY 1

GULLEY 8

HUT

GULLEY 2

GULLEY 5

N

K.M.R.
R.E.M.W.

SCALE

10   5   0   10   20   FEET
0   5   10   METRES

Fig. 1.5b.

followed his example (Dudley Waterman on the barrow at Quernhow in Yorkshire and on the Navan Fort in Ulster), largely because the excavations were not published until 1961, but also because the climate of academic thought was not yet ready to adjust.

Other changes were going on elsewhere. Prehistoric archaeologists had long taken an interest in economic interpretations of their sites, as had Bersu at Little Woodbury and Grahame Clark at Star Carr. But more important was Clark's attempt to quantify the animal remains from Star Carr to reconstruct evidence for seasonal activity and diet, and

1.6. Manching. This huge site (measuring 2km across) was threatened by the construction of a new airfield after the war, and then by road and factory construction. To define the areas that it would be most profitable to excavate, the director Werner Krämer dug trial trenches across the area, locating the zones of densest occupation. These were then cleared by hand, using the 'Schnitt' style of excavation, whereby series of parallel trenches were excavated and planned (Fig. 1.6a). These were then filled in, and the areas in between excavated, thereby giving a complete plan of the area (Fig. 1.6b). The trial trenches incidentally also gave some interesting information on the size and density of the occupation within the defended area, something we do not possess for any other contemporary site.

also to use evidence of pollen and soils to reconstruct the environment – another area of Scandinavian influence.

A third revolution that started in the 1950s was the arrival of the mechanical excavator. This was a mixed blessing: it increased the destruction of archaeological sites, but also helped archaeologists to undertake larger-scale excavations. Early examples of the use of mechanical excavators include Werner Krämer at Manching who in 1955 dug trial trenches up to a kilometre long to define the main nucleus of occupation inside the Iron Age oppidum, where areas were then opened up by hand; and Martin Biddle in Winchester who in 1961 removed great depths of overburden to reach stratified Saxon and Roman archaeological deposits over a wide area. (It is interesting to note that he reverted the following year to hand excavation using a Wheeler-style grid, before turning to open area excavation in the mid-1960s.) It was on sites with no stratigraphy that the mechanical excavator came into its own, because here one could strip to the bedrock and then excavate the features cut into it. This became common from the mid-1960s onwards, as on my excavations at Owslebury, Hants (Fig. 1.8).

Fig. 1.6b.

The fourth revolution had happened within British society as a whole with the opening up of higher education to larger sections of the population, producing an educated and skilled student body happy to work on summer excavations for little or no return. Large-scale use of student volunteers started on urban sites such as Verulamium and Cirencester, and reached its peak in the massive excavations at Winchester in the 1960s where up to 180 people might be working at any one time. The application of the techniques of 'open area' excavation, pioneered in medieval archaeology, to Roman urban sites, most notably Phil Barker's excavation at Wroxeter, demonstrated vividly the failure of the Wheeler style of excavation (Fig. 1.9).

These massive excavations produced large quantities of finds and data that needed processing. This in its turn produced a need for full-time co-ordinators and specialists, and again Winchester led the way in Britain in setting up the first 'Archaeological Unit' to deal with excavation, recording and publication, and this formed a model for the numerous units that sprang up in the early 1970s as money became available from local and central government to deal with the crisis of destruction, as city centres were reconstructed, and housing estates, industrial development and roads spread into the countryside. My own experiences at Exeter, excavating the complex deposits of the Roman and medieval city, suggested that the solution lay not in the short summer seasons with a large body of generally inexperienced volunteers, but in a small professional team which could work the whole year round, supplemented by a small amount of additional labour in the major digging seasons. Such small professional teams became widespread in the 1970s, usually working for local government, especially in museums and planning departments.

The other great need was to find ways of manipulating the data quickly and efficiently. By its very nature archaeology produces large quantities of minute details which may or may not be relevant to what the excavator wants to know. Attempts to input this on to mainframe computers proved costly, and computer accessibility is not adequate when one is out in the field. The advent of battery-operated micros with large memories is changing this, but is also altering the way in which we conceive and record data. Recording has to be more systematised to fit in with pre-set programmes, but these are not always flexible enough to deal with the ambiguities often met in excavation data.

A further change has been the shift from 'single site' archaeology to a regional view. Thus when I started the excavation of the Iron Age and Roman farm at Owslebury in the early 1960s the aim was purely economic: a reconstruction of the changing farming economy of the settlement. But it rapidly became clear that this could only be done in terms of relationships with neighbouring settlements, to establish the size of its territory, or, for instance, by a comparison of the relative wealth of burials and other finds. The site was producing a surplus from the Iron Age onwards and importing wine from Italy a century or more before the Roman conquest, so what was its relationship with hill-forts and later Roman towns, or with port sites such as Hengistbury Head? At this period geography had a major impact on archaeology, with theories dealing with problems of land use, settlement hierarchies, central places, etc. This led on to a more systematic approach to the results of aerial photography, and more especially to the systematic recovery of data from field-walking, which was the boom industry in archaeology in the 1980s; all this was aimed at gaining some idea of the full range of settlements for each period, which could then be followed by selective excavation.

*1.7. **Burn Ground, West Hampnett.** During the war W.F. Grimes excavated a number of sites threatened by airfield construction, including the barrows at Burn Ground in the Cotswolds. One of the problems with Neolithic long barrows was the nature of the 'extra-revetment' material – had it been deliberately dumped, or had it merely slipped off the mound as it collapsed? Grimes argued that this could only be seen in plan, not in section as had generally been attempted. To achieve this, and to understand how the mound had been constructed, the whole area was stripped, every stone planned and its angle of rest recorded. Grimes was able to demonstrate in detail the process of construction, and showed that the extra-revetment material represented the final phase of activity: the deliberate 'closing' of the mound for burial. Inadvertently he pre-empted the techniques of open area excavation in Britain by over a decade.*

THE IDEOLOGICAL PARADIGM

This socio-economic approach (often labelled the 'New Archaeology' or 'Processual Archaeology', though the equation is not exact) largely worked on the assumption that we can study ancient societies according to our own rationality; settlements will be located in the situation best suited for the prevailing economic, technological and sociological conditions – near water, in good defensive positions, on trade routes, etc. It also assumes that the sort of material we excavate will largely represent rubbish discarded and disposed of in ways which we would consider sensible. However, it is clear from the archaeological record that this may not always be the case, and that there may be a logic other than our own, for instance, in the deposition of animal bones. Expressions such as 'structured deposition' are used to describe material which has been discarded in some way which implies a set of beliefs laying down norms on how material can be discarded – certain types of material can, or cannot, appear in certain contexts, even on habitation sites. To give us further insight, we need to reconstruct, as far as we can, the daily round of activities of the inhabitants of a site and their experiences, and to look at the 'environment as lived in' or 'experienced'.

In many ways the excavation techniques are those used for the socio-economic approach, except that more detailed recording is needed. The detailed location of pottery and bones needs to be studied in context; we need to know as much as

1.8. Owslebury in 1966 was one of the first large-scale excavations carried out using a mechanical excavator to strip off the surface plough soil down to the natural rock surface. The hope was to find the plans of buildings cut into the chalk subsoil, but also to expose great lengths of ditches which would produce large quantities of animal bones and pottery for analysis to reconstruct the site's economy. This aerial view shows the 1967 area cleared by mechanical excavator. Excavation has not yet started on the right. In the centre, the initial metre wide cuts are being made in the ditches to check the stratigraphy, while to the left 'total' excavation has started, removing all but the 25cm baulks across the ditch for recording the stratigraphy (see Chapter 10). At this stage the complex ditch intersections have not been tackled, so that the maximum of information has been obtained beforehand.

possible about the way movement on a site was organised, what activities were carried out where; chemical and physical analysis of soils becomes more important, using phosphate analysis, magnetic susceptibility, occurrence of phytoliths (see Chapter 12) and so on. Indeed, generally we should be looking for other ways to characterise what we are digging up – one excavation project has tried to do this in terms of the senses (sight, smell, touch, hearing) rather than in terms of pits, animal bones, houses, etc.

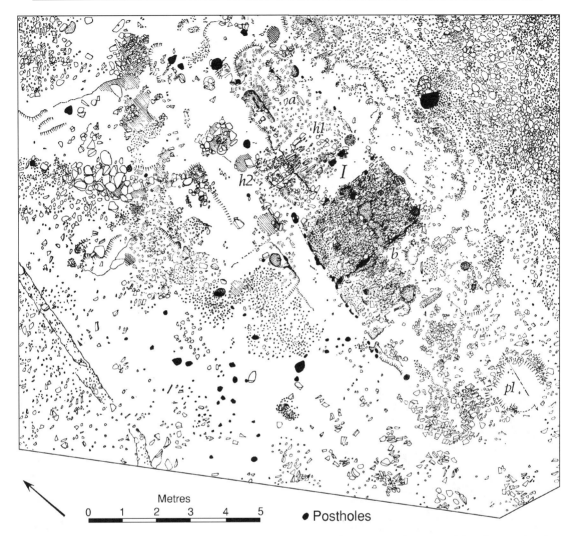

1.9. Wroxeter. *In the excavation of the baths area of the Roman town of Wroxeter in the 1960s, Phil Barker introduced the techniques of medieval rural excavation into a Roman urban context. Previous trench excavations had located the massive walls of the Roman basilica, overlain by the rubble from the collapse of the building. By employing 'open area' excavation, Barker was able to demonstrate that the rubble was in fact the foundations for substantial wooden buildings, and indeed, where previous excavators had identified only one building, he recognised about 150! The later phases of Wroxeter, indeed of many Roman towns, had been rewritten, and Roman archaeology was never the same again.*

CONSERVATION

In Europe a directive from the European Union has decreed that developers must have proper concern for the environment, and should mitigate as far as possible against any damage development may cause. This is extended to the historical environment, so that sites which will be damaged or destroyed need to be explored at the cost of the developer. This directive has been interpreted differently from one country to another. In France, for example, a central agency (AFAN) has been set up, which uses the funds raised from developers to carry out large-scale excavation, for instance on the routes of motorways and new railways, though smaller threats may simply be ignored. In Britain, in contrast, it has been interpreted as meaning that sites should be preserved as far as possible, and excavation should be the last resort, and on as small a scale as possible. In some countries archaeologists only have the right of intervention if something important appears once development has already started; in countries such as France and Britain consideration of the archaeology starts at the planning stage, and an environmental impact study must be made first, backed up by small-scale excavation to define the extent of the potential damage. Only then are decisions made on whether to excavate or relocate the development to a less sensitive area. At first sight this conservation policy may not seem to be a paradigm, but it does in fact incorporate new theoretical and ideological attitudes to our past.

In terms of excavation techniques, in Britain this approach has led to a return to the use of the trench as the primary means of investigation. This might, in any case, have been the trend within excavation of certain periods as research questions become more specific, and where large-scale excavations may not provide much new information. In Britain there is a greater concern for the conservation of ancient landscapes, not just a few spectacular sites; thus, the excavations of the Iron Age hill-fort at Danebury have been followed up by a consideration of the surviving ancient landscape surrounding it, encompassing field systems and linear boundaries as well as other types of settlement. To understand this landscape, some major excavations may still be needed of types of sites which have never been investigated, but often small-scale excavation is all that is needed to define a chronology, or to illustrate key elements or relationships in the landscape.

SUMMARY

This introductory historical chapter has, I hope, demonstrated that, as Wheeler said, there is no right way to excavate a site, but there are many wrong ways. Very often we are forced into the wrong way, because time, money and personnel are not sufficient to do all we wish, so very often the director has to make choices about what is most important. Different sites demand different techniques; thus, the excavation of Star Carr belonged to a tradition foreign to the mainstream in Britain, nor was it one which we would readily adopt nowadays, but none the less it is considered a classic of its kind. The social context of the excavation may also be important – is it professional, or are amateurs going to be used, or perhaps paid workmen? In Greece, for instance, some permits for research excavations insist on the employment of a local workforce, who may become very skilled by working on a project over many years; in Germany local workmen are also usually employed on rescue excavations, but legal restraints mean that often they can only be employed short-term; there is also a separate class of technicians who organise the practical aspects of the excavations, while these can only be directed by archaeologists with academic degrees. There are thus many different styles of excavation, good and bad, which the digger may encounter, and it is important to know the background to the excavation to understand why things are done in the way they are. However, for this book, I shall take 'open area' excavation as the ideal, though I shall also discuss other ways of doing things, as open area excavation presents problems of its own.

Two

Site Preparation

Before an excavation takes place, a lot of decisions have to be made which will affect what happens; these are the domain of the project director and his planning team, but any good director informs the team of what the context of the excavation is, why it is taking place, and the choices that have had to be made. It is important that the team should be aware of the context of what they are doing as part of their site training, as it gives a greater sense of belonging to a team, and therefore greater motivation. The reasons for the choices that have been made should be openly discussed and transparent.

First and foremost in the director's mind should be the aims of the excavation. This is not only true for research excavations where there is an academic agenda, but should also be applicable to all excavations. If someone is paying for an excavation, be it the public (via the state or local government) or a developer, we as archaeologists are answerable for what we do with that money, and it will not serve us in the longer term simply to claim that because the archaeology is there it must be dug. We must be able to demonstrate that what we are doing will end in a worthwhile product, even for a small excavation recording a common type of feature. For this there needs to be a research statement, and this will then inform the way the work is carried out, and define what is deemed important to be recorded. As I have tried to demonstrate in the first chapter, the purpose and aims of excavations are many and varied. Many finds are not particularly meaningful in themselves, but they form part of a larger picture, and it is this larger picture, often within a regional context, which must be understood and expressed. It should also inform all those taking part in the project, though because of the very nature of archaeology it will certainly need modification as the excavation progresses.

REASONS FOR EXCAVATION

There are three main reasons why excavations take place:

1) *Rescue excavations*. The vast majority of excavations since the 1950s have been carried out because sites are threatened, either by activities such as housing, agriculture, road building and urban renewal, or occasionally through natural causes such as coastal erosion. From the 1950s much of this rescue work in Britain was funded either by central government, or by local government through museums, or through voluntary work. From the 1970s local government took on much of the burden of organising and underwriting this, though still with substantial state subventions. In the early 1990s, the burden was shifted on to the developer to fund excavations and to minimise damage caused during redevelopment, and in Britain excavation was largely privatised. The result has been a vast increase in the quantity of excavation undertaken, and the level of funding.

2) *Research excavations.* These are mainly carried out through universities, and are supposedly aimed at answering questions of academic debate. Funding for these is much more limited, and they often rely on student labour (under the guise of 'training excavations'), but some attract funding from national societies or local government, or from research organisations such as the British Academy. They tend to be long term, running over several years, but with only a few weeks in the field each year. For many students these provide the first experience of field archaeology.

3) *Social excavations.* These tend to be of two main types. In the first type, excavations are organised as part of the preparation of a site for public presentation. In Europe such work is often carried out in work camps organised for the restoration of castles and other monuments, and such work can be of variable quality, but organisations such as English Heritage have public display as part of their remit and so carry out excavations on scheduled monuments. The second type comprises the excavations carried out for reasons of education or leisure. Commonly in Britain they are organised by local societies for their members, often running at weekends or for a few weeks during holiday periods, and these projects are another important place for young people to gain their first experience in archaeology (as I did myself). The problems of such excavations relate to the scientific analysis and publication of the work, as usually it is easy to find people willing to find things, but less common for people with the necessary interest and skills to prepare them for publication. In Britain this has produced two completely contrasting reactions from the professional world: one follows the German line, and sees archaeology as a purely professional pursuit, leading to the suppression of this amateur component; the second tries to get professionals and amateurs to work in close collaboration, with the professionals providing technical support and advice. In Britain it is the latter attitude which is coming back into favour, especially as there is now potentially extensive National Lottery funding for projects involving the public.

In fact there are more and more projects which try to combine various of these aspects. For instance, work organised by the Peak National Park regularly involves local professionals from the museums and universities, but uses both student and volunteer labour on projects which are given a high public profile (thus encouraging visitors to the site) to make people more aware of the history of the landscape. The international research project based at Mont Beuvray in France depends on research collaboration between teams from a number of countries, each bringing students to work on the project; in addition, one site is organised specifically for training younger people who are still at school. As awareness has increased among archaeologists of the social role of archaeology, and of the importance of our relationship with a wider public (who inevitably pay for us to work), so such multi-faceted projects have become more common. Part of being a professional archaeologist involves communicating with and involving the wider public.

DESK-TOP SURVEY

The process for evaluating threatened sites is more formalised than that for research and social excavations, though these excavations should pass through a similar process of development. So I shall use the sequence for rescue excavations to illustrate how decisions about strategy may be made. In Britain any plans for development pass through the local planning department, where they should be scrutinised by an archaeologist concerned with Development Control (the 'Curator', usually the County Archaeologist or one of his or her team), to see if there are any archaeological implications. If there are, the first stage is to carry out a 'desk-top survey'. As the name implies, this is carried out indoors, and involves the gathering together of any information which has already been recorded about the site. A summary of such information will already be held by the planning department in the form of the 'Sites and Monuments Record' (SMR), ranging from casual finds or documentary evidence to information on previous work on the site. Additional information will be collected from sources such as maps, aerial photographs, historical archives or personal recollections of people who have worked there previously, as well as, in Britain, from the National Monument Record at Swindon. All this information is brought together to identify the archaeological potential of the site.

ENVIRONMENTAL IMPACT STUDY

The desk-top survey may result in three main decisions. First, the site may have no potential and therefore can be ignored, or perhaps subject to a 'watching brief' – that is, an archaeologist will visit the site during development to check that nothing turns up. Secondly, the site may have potential, but nothing is known about it. In this case the decision may be made to carry out some form of sampling (for example digging trial pits to see if there is any archaeology). Thirdly, the site may have definite evidence of occupation, and this may vary from a few chance finds to cases where considerable information is already known (such as the layout of a settlement visible on aerial photographs). If enough is not known, some attempt will be made to increase knowledge by carrying out fieldwork on the site to study the environmental impact; the more precise the information an archaeologist has about the site, the more efficient can be the excavation. Any fieldwork, in the British rescue context, will be put out for tender.

SITE DEFINITION

The first thing that has to be done is for a recording framework to be laid out so that any finds or information can be relocated at a future date, and related to subsequent finds; this is discussed below. The main preliminaries that may have to be done on site include:

1) *Surface survey*. It is essential to do a contour survey of the site if there are above-ground features; even if not much is apparent, micro-contouring may reveal features not visible to the naked eye.
2) *Field-walking*. If a site has been ploughed, finds may appear on the surface. These can be collected and plotted, with as much precision as the director feels may be necessary.
3) *Geophysical survey*. Various techniques are available: resistivity involves passing an electric current through the soil, the resistance being greater where there are dry structures such as walls, and less where there are damp features like ditches; magnetometry measures concentrations of the earth's magnetic field indicating areas of burning, such as hearths or kilns (iron objects act as a magnet, and so give high readings, and even ditch and pit fills can do the same); penetrating ground radar which can give information about buried surfaces and features, especially on deeply stratified sites. All these techniques cost time and money, and many excavators choose to do

without them. If the topsoil is likely to be removed mechanically, but may contain metal finds such as coins, a preliminary search with metal-detectors can prove fruitful.

4) *Chemical traces*. Phosphates are concentrated on sites occupied by humans and animals, and can be measured chemically. Magnetic susceptibility can pick up concentrations of phosphates, but is especially good at detecting soils that have undergone some burning. Such surveys should be undertaken as a matter of course on shallow sites, as the topsoil may contain information which has otherwise disappeared, and so will not show up during the excavation (for example the location of hearths and middens).

5) *Trial trenches*. Digging small pits and trenches, or even coring, to locate the areas of archaeological interest is a common strategy. Where nothing is known about the site, some form of statistical sampling strategy will be adopted: either a number of small trenches will be dug systematically or at random, or a long trial excavation (transect) will be dug on the edge, or through the middle, of the area likely to be of interest (sampling techniques are discussed below). But where a fair amount is already known, then a judgement sample is better, for example trenching features visible on aerial photographs. Trial pits are useful for locating ditches and walls, but even hand-digging of trial trenches on deeply stratified sites can prove destructive, so the strategy should be to do the minimum of work to get the information needed, and often simply opening up pits to expose features rather than digging them may be all that is needed.

In addition, the director will be trying to find out what hazards there may be on the site, such as live sewers or electrical cables, especially on an urban site. However, especially if such hazards were installed a long time ago, the planners may ask the archaeologists for information. One of the most famous discoveries on a London excavation was the Underground!

EXCAVATION STRATEGY

If the decision is made to progress further with a large-scale excavation the County Archaeologist will prepare a research design, with details of the work to be done, including requirements for sampling, etc.; this will then be put out to tender to professional archaeological units, and a team chosen – often on the basis of the lowest bid, but not necessarily, as quality of the work to be done and the reputation of the unit will also be key factors. The County Archaeologist is responsible for ensuring that the quality of work is adequate, and that the terms of the contract are met. For research and social excavations, the research design will be prepared by the project director, usually in the context of requests for money or for permission to excavate if it is a scheduled monument.

All projects work under constraints, be it only the state of our knowledge at the time the excavation takes place. However, all archaeologists find that usually there are two major, closely inter-related constraints: money and time. Modern professional archaeology has to work within strictly defined parameters. How long does it take to excavate a cubic metre of soil in a certain way? How much soil will have to be removed, in what way? What sampling will have to be done to extract information which will not normally be recorded on site (such as phosphate content, seeds, mollusca); who will do this, and how much will it cost; can the expense be justified within the research statement? What sort of people need to be employed, how many, and what skills will they need? How should they be deployed on site? What training must be provided for staff? Will the site require equipment, such as surveying equipment, seed machines or water pumps? All these need to be carefully budgeted, especially if, as in Britain, it is part of a bid to be compared with other archaeologists competing for the work.

The type of site is also vital in planning. Is it a multi-period site with complex stratigraphy? – in which case it will cost much more to excavate than a simple site with discrete features such as pits and post-holes. Is it a waterlogged site? – where there is not only the problem of digging under the water-table, but also a wealth of information may be preserved, such as wood, plant remains, insect remains, etc., which will need to be stored in such a way that they will not deteriorate. Decisions have to be made on the methods of excavation to be used: trenches, area excavation, the systems of vertical and horizontal recording, the paper and electronic records to be made and their format, and the labelling and treatment of finds. Though the decisions on these matters have to be made by the director, it is for the site personnel to carry them out, and so they will form a major element in this book.

A key concern must also be site safety. Owing to disasters that have happened in the past, laws covering Health and Safety have become increasingly restrictive, and directors now have the legal duty to instruct their staff on site discipline. The days of happily wandering around sites wearing only sandals, or digging in unshored trenches, or digging small holes on construction sites, as I did in my early days, are long past. One or two friends have been killed on excavations because they broke the rules – during one lunchtime, when no one else was on site, one went down a deep, unshored trench which had been dug by a mechanical excavator. Everyone on site has their responsibilities, but ultimately it is the director who needs to know the law, as well as use his/her common sense.

SAMPLING

Excavation is a form of sampling, as we can never hope to excavate the whole of any archaeological site to the level of detail that we would like, especially if we are dealing with a landscape, for instance an area threatened by open-cast mining. Decisions have to be made about what bits to dig in which way, and which bits not to excavate at all. Rarely do we have the choice to excavate just what and where we wish; sites will be partially covered by modern buildings, roads, trees and woodland, or may be unavailable for a multitude of reasons. Often the excavation is taking place within strict limits because it is the area threatened by a redevelopment. But first we will look at the ideal.

There are four main approaches to sampling, which we will encounter at other points in this book:

Random sampling. This uses strict statistical methods to decide where the sample points should lie (Fig. 2.1). One simple method is to lay out a grid on the site, and throw a dice to decide which squares should be excavated. There are computer-generated random number tables which can be consulted, the advantage of which is that we have no preconceptions that may bias our choice of areas. Thus, if we were sampling an ancient town, and the number of sample areas is large enough, we might reasonably expect to end up excavating a selection of areas: rich and poor, habitation and business, cemeteries and settlement. The disadvantage is that we may be missing key areas, such as the ramparts or public buildings.

The other problem is that there is no point in digging lots of little holes across a site if we cannot understand what it is we are sampling, and many advocates of random sampling have not taken into account the advantages of open area excavation. It can, however, be useful if we are investigating a landscape (e.g. looking at the density of artefacts in the ploughsoil where there is little or no stratigraphy and few, if any, structures).

Systematic sampling. This involves laying out a grid in which the areas to be excavated are at regular distances from one another. Thus, an area could be divided up into 10 metre squares, and a one metre square be dug in the south-west corner of each square (Fig. 2.2). This system is much easier to lay out than random sampling, but can be affected by regularities in what we are sampling; for instance we could lay out our trenches parellel to the line of a straight road or ditch, but miss the main features, or lay out the trenches along the feature and miss what was happening on either side of it.

Judgement or purposeful sampling. This is the norm with archaeological excavation (Fig. 2.1). We choose an area to excavate because there is something which makes it more important than other areas. It could be influenced by the ancient situation: we want a sample of human skeletons, so we choose a cemetery, especially one where bone preservation is likely to be good. Alternatively, the sampling may be imposed by modern conditions: we want to know about an ancient city which underlies a modern one, but we can only excavate in areas that are devoid of modern buildings, or that are in the process of being redeveloped.

Haphazard sampling. Often confused with random sampling, haphazard is when there is no defined strategy. It has no statistical value.

Within these sampling techniques there are additional variations:

Nested or hierarchical sampling. Some areas are likely to be more informative than others so, whatever sampling technique we employ, we usually bias our sampling towards these more informative areas. Within the context of excavating a site, it is normal to concentrate on the 'richest' areas in terms of finds. On a farming settlement, for instance, we would concentrate on the farmhouse and its subsidiary buildings as the main priority; next, we would look at the enclosures around the farm used for livestock and perhaps intensive cultivation, then at the fields, and lastly, and least intensively, at the areas of pasture where there is likely to be little in the way of finds or information to be found, but which none the less can supply, for instance, environmental information.

Transects. Because it is simple to lay out and efficient in terms of labour, the transect is a popular means of sampling for archaeologists (Fig. 2.3). In field-walking it involves laying out a narrow strip, often running at right angles across the landscape (e.g. across a valley or a field), which is then surveyed intensively. It is also very common in excavation in the form of a 'trench', for instance sampling or following the line of a linear feature such as a road or bank by laying out a trench at right angles across the feature.

SITE ORGANISATION

The director has to take into consideration a number of factors when deciding where to locate trenches within the site. To underline the fact that there is no ideal way of excavating, I shall take some of the excavation methods from the past and the present and show how these compare with our ideal of open area excavation. The five approaches are:

Qasr es-Segir

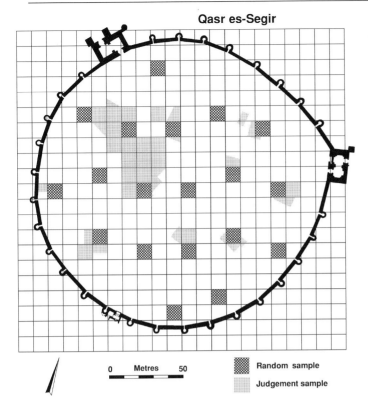

0   **Metres**   50

▨ Random sample

▦ Judgement sample

2.1. Random and purposeful sampling.
One of the few settlements which has
been excavated using a random
sampling technique is the Portuguese
and Arabic trading settlement of Qasr-
es-Seghir in Morocco. The excavator,
Charles Redman, randomly selected
areas to excavate, but opened trenches
sufficiently large to allow a meaningful
interpretation of what was excavated. It
allowed, for instance, the possibility of
looking at biases in the amount of
imported pottery coming from different
parts of the town, rather than, say, just
having a sample from the trading or
upper-class area where it may be over-
represented, or from the poor district
where it would be under-represented.
However, in addition to this random
sampling, he undertook purposeful
sampling of some of the more
informative areas, like the public
buildings in the centre of the site. This
combination is the ideal for maximising
reliable and usable information.

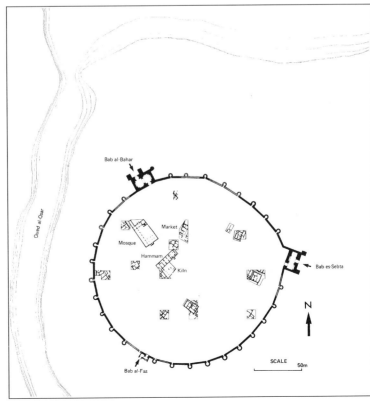

2.2. Systematic sampling. The Roystone Grange project in Derbyshire was aimed at understanding the development of a landscape over a period of five or six thousand years. Part of the project included looking at the density of artefacts, especially Neolithic and Bronze Age flints. To obtain the necessary information small pits ('shovel pits') measuring 1 × 0.5m were dug every 10 metres, and the soil sieved to maximise recovery. This allowed the construction of contours showing the density of finds, as well as locating some areas for more intensive investigation. This is only possible where there is no stratigraphy or structures, for instance in ploughsoil. (Note: the sheep in the foreground show a random distribution!)

Trench excavation. This is the excavation of a number of discrete trenches usually of small dimensions. This technique is especially used for site definition (the digging of trial pits) or as an economical way of following features such as roads, or sampling linear features such as ditches.

Box or grid excavation. This was the method developed by Wheeler at Maiden Castle using baulks between a grid arrangement of square trenches (Figs 1.4, 1.5). The baulks might subsequently be removed to allow a more extensive plan, but this is not physically easy to do stratigraphically. This technique was typical in Britain under the Culture-Historical paradigm, and is still used in some parts of Europe.

Schnitt excavation. This is the system of parallel trenches favoured by German excavators such as Gerhard Bersu and Werner Krämer (Fig. 1.6), and likewise favoured under the Culture-Historical paradigm. It is most useful in contexts where trenches have to be opened by hand, as at the Iron Age cemetery at Owslebury (Fig. 2.4).

Squares excavation. This was typical of sites such as Star Carr (Fig. 1.2), where strict stratigraphical control was needed to relate finds to the environmental sequence, or to show the density of finds on a settlement. It differs from open area excavation in that each

(Opposite) 2.3. The transect. The excavation of the A710 motorway near Clermont-Ferrand in France by Vincent Guichard is an example of purposeful sampling using the transect. The area along the line of the motorway had first been surveyed by fieldwalking and other techniques, but the depth of the soil masked much archaeological information. So two parallel trenches each 6km long were dug, and all recognisable features planned and excavated. Areas of intensive occupation were then chosen for open area excavation. Finds were recorded by using a base-line along the bottom of each trench from which offset measurements could be taken.

square is treated as an independent entity, and only rarely is a large surface of one period open at any one moment in time.

Open Area Excavation. In true open area excavation the total area to be excavated is opened as a single entity (Fig. 1.9). Where there is no stratigraphy (e.g. the site can be cleared to the bedrock), each feature cutting into the bedrock can be excavated separately (Fig. 1.8). Where there is stratigraphy, each layer is stripped off in chronological sequence, and features cut from the surface are cleared out before the preceding phase of deposits is excavated (Fig. 2.5). It is thus possible to see all that survives of each phase at one moment in time, before it is removed to reveal the preceding phase.

The factors which affect decisions about the strategy for excavating a site are of varying importance and, as we have seen in the discussion of paradigms, the priorities may differ from one excavation to another and from one period to another. They include the following (Fig. 2.6):

Site expansion. Often excavators are digging 'blind', in that they do not know what they will unearth. The most important and interesting features may lie on the edge of the area exposed, and so expansion of the excavation may be needed (Fig. 2.7). From the beginning of the excavation the spoil must be located where there is least likely to be anything of interest, or it

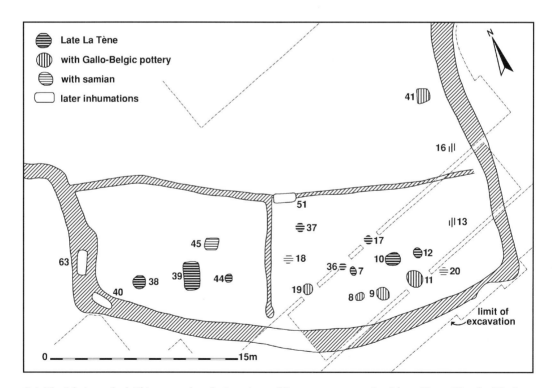

2.4. The Schnitt method. This was used on the Iron Age and Roman cemetery at Owslebury, Hants. Ploughsoil had to be removed by hand, as deep ploughing had cut through the pottery vessels in the graves, and these had to be recovered during the surface clearance. An overall view of the site did not matter, and as resources and labour force were limited the area was excavated over a number of years, one or two trenches being dug in each season.

will have to be moved. With trench excavation it may merely be a matter of extending the trenches to the new areas of interest. The Schnitt, grid and squares methods of excavation are all flexible, and can be shifted in any direction the director wishes by opening up new trenches or squares. The least flexible system is the open area; digging away at the edge of an open area contradicts the aims of the whole method. The other methods all allow archaeologists to reach the earlier phases, which are often the most interesting, at least in a substantial number of the trenches opened; with open area excavations there is a very real danger that too much time will be spent on the later layers and the earliest levels will never be reached.

Spoil disposal. The removal of the spoil from the excavation is one of the most time-consuming aspects of the excavation. The dump will always take up part of the site, unless the decision has been made to cart it away, as may be necessary on some restricted urban sites; there is, however, always the possibility that the hole can be sold to the contractor, who may thus be saved the expense of digging it and carting away the earth (e.g. for an underground car park). Dumps need to be located sufficiently far away that they are not in the way of the excavation, and do not threaten the stability of the site by placing too much weight on the edge of a deep trench; equally they should be sufficiently close so that diggers do not spend too much time emptying buckets or barrows.

On most sites a combination of buckets or baskets and dumping into wheelbarrows is the most efficient way to remove spoil. Though conveyor belts may seem tempting, it is difficult to use them in the actual area being excavated, as they are heavy, noisy, difficult to move, inevitably cover part of the area which needs excavating, and tend to need a lot of looking after. Hoists to take barrows or buckets out of deep trenches are useful, but most excavators stick to barrow runs using plank walkways as the most flexible method.

Movement on and off the excavated area has to be carefully organised to minimise damage to exposed surfaces (Fig. 2.7). The most efficient methods for spoil disposal are trench and *Schnitt*, where spoil can be dumped on the side of the trench; however, it must be dumped sufficiently far away that spoil does not roll back down into the trench, which can be both a danger to the excavators and a source of contamination. Though the grid method of excavation provides good walkways for removing the spoil, it can become dangerous if the trenches are deep or unstable, and also survey points on the baulks tend to get knocked out by careless wheelbarrow drivers. The least efficient method for removal of spoil is open area excavation, not only because of the distance that spoil has to be moved, but also because, if the site is stratified, there are often delicate areas which *cannot* be walked on.

On-site movement. Movement around the site in such a way as not to damage it is obviously best where there are specific walkways on which to walk. Again, stratified open area sites are the least efficient from this point of view, and the team will need careful instruction on where it is possible to walk, and perhaps special planked walkways will need to be installed.

Worker control. When there are untrained workers on site, it is easiest to keep an eye on them and to confine their activities if there are well-defined limits. Again, most of the methods are good for this, except open area excavation. For open area sites where there are discrete features, this problem is easily overcome by giving each excavator his or her own feature to excavate or, in the case of large features, by subdividing them (Fig. 3.4). A ditch can usefully be split into lengths, and each digger given a separate strip. On stratified open area sites, however, there are no such barriers, and much greater discipline is needed, together with a more skilled work force.

2.5. Open area excavation. The photographs show a sequence of views of a stratified urban site at Exeter in Devon during excavation. In the first photograph (Fig. 2.5a) the overlying modern rubble has been removed, and some modern features such as sewer trenches have been removed, giving a preview in their sides of the earlier deposits on the site (and so saving the digging of trial pits). Traces of walls, floors and pits are beginning to show, which are cleaned and planned. In the second photograph (Fig. 2.5b), most of the modern, post-medieval and medieval pits have been removed, leaving a site that looks like Gruyère cheese. The undisturbed Roman deposits show up as little islands, which can now be excavated in sequence (see also Figs 9.7a and 9.7b).

Fig. 2.5b.

	Trench	Grid	Schnitt	Squares	Open Area
Site expansion	G	G	G	G	P
Spoil disposal	G	G	P	P	P
On site movement	G	M	G	M	P
Worker control	G	G	G	G	P
Communication	P	P	M	G	G
Over-all view	P	P	P	P	G
Site planning	P	P	P	P	G
Find location	G	G	M	G	P
Stratigraphical control	G	G	G	G	P
Horizontal control	P	P	P	P	G
Contamination	P	P	P	G	G

2.6. Advantages and disadvantages of different excavation strategies. This table shows the ease with which various tasks can be carried out using various methods of excavation. G = good or easy; M = moderate; P = poor or difficult.

Communication. On site there should be continuous communication among the team, so that information can be shared; it also fosters team cohesion. If there are inexperienced people on site, they should be working with one or two other more experienced people who can give continuous advice; this sort of 'apprenticeship' is probably the best way to learn. The least useful methods from this point of view are the trench, grid and *Schnitt* systems where individuals are isolated from one another.

Over-all view. This is the whole *raison d'être* for the open area method, and it is the only one which scores highly in this respect. The example noted in Chapter 1 of Wheeler's excavation at Stanwick (Fig. 1.5) shows the abject failure of his method, even in the hands of the inventor. The importance of the intersections between the various gullies that defined the timber buildings were destroyed before their importance was appreciated, and we are left with no understanding of the chronological sequence.

Site planning. The mechanics of planning a site are greatly eased if there are no intervening baulks and dumps. Again, open area excavation scores highly. This is discussed in Chapter 6.

Find location. Labels must be placed on finds to show where they have come from. This is easy with the trench- and square-based systems, as there are well-defined limits, so finds can easily be numbered with a trench and layer number; it is less easy with open area. This is discussed in more detail in Chapter 6.

Stratigraphical control. Traditionally archaeologists have followed geologists in seeing the section through the deposits not only as a major tool of interpretation but also for locating objects within their stratigraphical position. The nearer the control section is to the location of the finds, the easier it is to be sure of its stratigraphical position. The square method scores highest in this respect, and open area lowest. Ways around this problem are discussed in Chapter 6.

Horizontal control. The cross-relating of deposits and features from one part of the site to another is much more easily achieved if there are no intervening baulks; open area is by far the best.

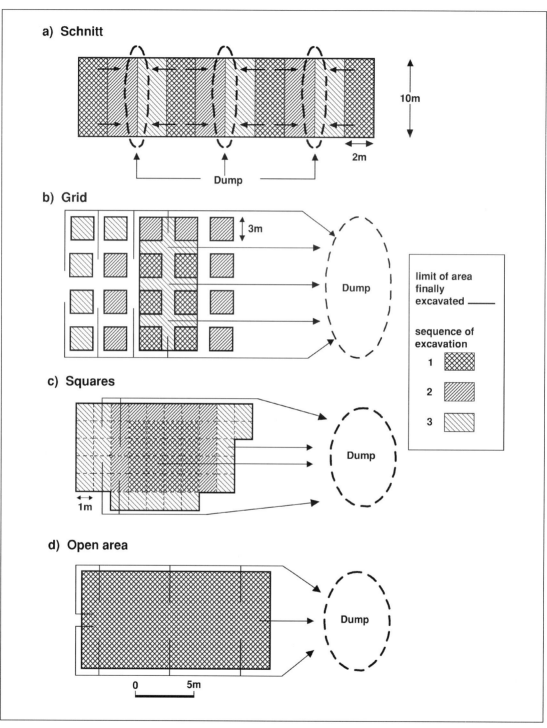

2.7. Site organisation. The illustrations show the four principal ways in which excavations of areas are organised as described in the text. The diagrams show the possible sequence in which the excavation could proceed, with three hypothetical phases. It also shows the routes whereby spoil has to be removed, and the possible location of dumps.

Contamination. Finds can easily fall into excavated areas from sections or dumps, or when later deposits are being removed in an area which has already been partially excavated. This problem is most easily avoided by not having sections, and by removing *all* later deposits before earlier ones are tackled. The squares method and especially open area excavation cut down the level of contamination.

THE RECORDING FRAMEWORK

As soon as data starts to be collected on a site, it is necessary to set up some sort of permanent recording system so that the data can be correlated with information that will be collected later – sometimes many years later. Fixed survey points must be selected, preferably ones which are marked on maps, or can be easily located in the future, such as buildings, roads and other fairly permanent features; it is impossible thirty years later to locate sites tied in with trees or fences.

There are three main ways of establishing the recording framework. The first two rely on a fixed base-line of some sort to which all other information can be tied, the third is based on a series of fixed points to which reference can be made. In the computer world the base-line system is referred to as a raster system, which is used for programmes such as PhotoShop or the sending of faxes (by using a rectilinear system of pixels); the third is a vector, which is used by systems such as AutoCAD, and is based on mathematical formulae. Both are commonly used in the archaeological world and are important when data are being computerised.

Linear system. This is most useful for long linear sites, like pipe trenches or drainage systems (Fig. 2.8). In central France we cut 6km-long trial trenches along the line of a motorway (Fig. 2.3). A base-line was then laid out running along the centre of the trench, but ignoring changes in angle (the line of the trench was easily located on a map). Nails with the recorded distance from our base point were then knocked in at 25 metre intervals. The position of features and even of individual finds could then be noted by their distance along the base-line, and the distance north or south of the base-line obtained by measuring at right angles ('offset' measurements), in theory giving an accuracy to within a few centimetres.

Grid system. This is the most common form of recording on archaeological excavations (Fig. 2.9). A base point is selected, and from this a rectangular grid is laid out, very much in the same way as the National Grid in Britain. (Indeed, some purists would argue that it is better to use the national standard rather than construct an arbitrary grid. The problem with this system is that numbers can get very high, and also the orientation of the grid may be inconvenient for a site laid out skew to it, which can cause problems of orientation on site.) Normally I try to keep my base point in the south-west corner, like the National Grid. Points can then be located by measuring along and up the grid lines. If the grid is 100m square, an eight-figure grid-reference will locate any point to within a centimetre, which is more than accurate enough for most archaeological purposes. The system should be capable of expansion in any direction, so it is best if the area opened is given numbers in the middle of the 100m square. Preferably the numbers for the different axes should be clearly distinguished so as to reduce the possibilities of getting them the wrong way round. (My first check on the computer for finds with grid references is to see which ones seem to come from outside the area we have dug – usually corrected by changing the two numbers round!) Some directors prefer a system using numbers on one axis, and letters on the other to avoid this confusion, but this does not allow the flexibility of recording of a purely numerical system and is less computer compatible (e.g. for printing out finds distributions). If more than one 100m grid is needed, these can be distinguished by using the letters of the alphabet, in the same way that the Ordnance Survey distinguishes its 100km squares. In other countries the grid system may be more complicated, such as the Lambert system in France which tries to avoid the problems of the curvature of the earth by having no fewer than three different grids covering the country. On site, visual guidance should be given to excavators and recorders to locate themselves within the grid, either with a series of pegs placed around the edge of the excavation, or by placing a grid of nails across the site. Individual nails can be numbered with tags for quick reference, or the number of each grid line placed on signs at the edge of the site.

Vector-based systems. Four forms have been used commonly in excavation; the more primitive ones are still useful in situations where sophisticated surveying equipment is unavailable. The first is *triangulation*, in which two tapes are attached to fixed points, and the point to be located is fixed by taking the measurements at the point where the two tapes overlap. This can be transferred on to a plan using compass circles scaled down from the original measurements; the point is located where the two circles intersect. Triangulation is also a useful way of quickly laying out right angles, with $3 \times 4 \times 5$ triangles and $5 \times 12 \times 13$ triangles. The second method is the *plane table*, which is a horizontal board on which paper can be fixed. A sighting piece is placed on the board and aligned from the base point, marked on the paper, to the point to be

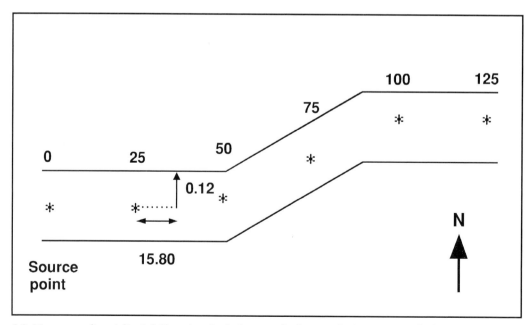

2.8. Linear recording. A line is laid out (e.g. in the bottom of a drainage ditch). Points can be fixed by measuring along the line from a base point, and then by offsets on either side of the base-line. The point noted in the diagram could be recorded as 40.80m, 0.12m N(orth).

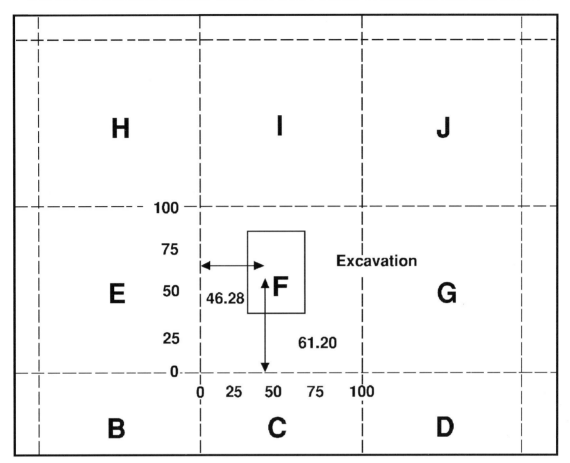

2.9. Grid recording. The excavation area is placed within a 100m grid, preferably with opportunities of expansion in any directions, and where the x and y co-ordinates are unlikely to be confused with one another. Each of the 100m squares can be given a letter of the alphabet. A point can be located to the nearest centimetre by measuring along (from West to East), and up (from South to North). That shown would lie at F4628 6120.

fixed, and the distance measured with a tape. This, scaled down, fixes the point on the paper immediately. A more sophisticated instrument is the theodolite, for measuring both angles and levels. Most commonly, however, archaeologists use electronic forms of the Plane Table and theodolite, most notably the *Electronic Distance Measurer* (EDM), which allows data to be transferred on to a computer and plotted (Fig. 2.10). It needs to be linked in with fixed points, but once this is done, it can record points quickly and accurately in three dimensions. More recently, archaeologists have begun to use GPS (global positioning systems); at present these are rather less accurate, but very useful for surveying where there are few fixed points; such systems will become more common as their accuracy increases and the cost of equipment decreases.

It is also necessary to have a fixed point for fixing the height of features above sea level, linked in with some absolute national standard (in Britain we use the Ordnance Survey Newlyn datum). By sighting on to this fixed point, the site can be levelled and contoured.

This is important not only to allow certain aspects of interpretation (e.g. in which direction water in an ancient channel may have run), but also to relate different archaeological deposits to one another, allowing such calculations as the density of finds per cubic metre. Levelling is usually done with a dumpy level (cheaper than an EDM), and the use of this is a skill most diggers are likely to acquire (Fig. 2.11).

In fact, most archaeologists tend to use a combination of the grid and EDM. A grid is useful to help diggers and recorders locate themselves on site, and also for recording the position of finds in the archive – a grid reference is more meaningful than the information recorded by the EDM. The EDM, however, is useful for laying out the grid initially, and for recording points such as the location of finds; it is much more accurate and faster than grid-based methods which rely on hand measurement. Whatever method is used, there must always be fixed points on the site to which reference can be made; these are often set in concrete, in places where they are unlikely to be disturbed by excavation or passing wheelbarrows.

SITE PREPARATION

Decisions have to be made about how to prepare the site for excavation. Overburden may need to be removed. Is there information in the overburden that will need to be recorded – finds, ephemeral traces of phosphates and so on? Or is it possible to use a mechanical excavator, and if so, what sort? A good driver well directed can save enormous amounts of time and money; a centimetre of soil left on a large site means huge numbers of barrow-loads of soil to be removed; a centimetre too much taken off, and the site may be irreparably damaged.

There are basically four main categories of mechanical excavator; the hire price varies considerably, reflecting the complexity of what each can do. (I shall use British terms, but they have their equivalents in other countries.)

The *JCB* is the most common machine used (Fig. 2.12); it can push forward to remove soil, but also has a back hoe to dig trenches, and can also remove soil over an area without having to run across the exposed surface. It is also fairly mobile. However, its rubber wheels can sink into soft ground, churning up archaeological deposits, and use of the back hoe is relatively slow and does not leave a very smooth surface.

The *Drott*. This has always been my favourite machine for excavating areas on chalk (Fig. 2.13). Machines with caterpillar tracks do not sink in as easily as rubber-tyred ones. Though they compact the soil, this only affects the immediate surface, and it does provide a smooth surface, especially if the machine does its last run across the site backwards with the blade partially open to clean the surface; this does tend to pull out stones, so is not so good where there are stone walls. Drawbacks are that the surface it leaves is difficult to scrape clean and it is slow. It should be used in conjunction with a dumper truck or lorry.

Box Scrapers are the large machines used on motorways to remove large quantities of soil fast – they are good if there is a large area to be cleared, but expensive to hire.

The *HyMac*. Though the JCB is a good trenching machine, it is less flexible than the HyMac which has an extra joint in its arm for getting into awkward corners. Again it is a more specialist machine which is more expensive to hire.

There are, of course, various other types of machine available, especially small ones which can be used for excavating large features under urgent rescue conditions.

2.10. The EDM. The instrument is set up and sighted on to a fixed point by directing a beam on to a prism held by an assistant. The prism is then moved round to the points required for plotting, and the data recorded automatically in digital form. This can then be downloaded on to a computer, and the information plotted using a vector system.

TEAM STRUCTURE

In constructing an excavation team a director has to marry up two sometimes mutually incompatible imperatives: the skills and number of people needed to carry out the programme of work, and the personnel and resources actually available. Across Europe, and indeed on some British excavations, there is still great variation in the sorts of people who are employed on excavations and in how they are deployed. In Britain there has been a long tradition of volunteer involvement on excavations, and although in some areas in the 1970s and 1980s there was conflict between such volunteer groups and the new class of professional archaeologists, in many regions co-operation was seen to be more useful. This view is now dominant, as archaeology has become more answerable to the society which supports it, and archaeology, under various community projects, is seen increasingly as an educational and leisure activity. However, Britain is unusual in not having a system of permits restricting who has the right to carry out archaeological work, though these are required under the Valetta Convention, which the British government has just signed.

In Germany there has never been such public involvement. Excavation is seen as a specialist activity to be carried out by technical staff working under a professional academic, based in a university, local government department, museum or research institute (though the recent trend has been to follow the British tradition and expect students to dig as well as record, and directors tend to be on short-term contracts). Unskilled workers are engaged on major rescue projects, often as short-term employment. In Greece work permits often stipulate that local workmen have to be employed, though

2.11. The Dumpy Level. This is used for measuring heights. First a backsight is taken to the reference point (a known point above sea level set up on site for permanent reference); from this the height of the sighting line on the dumpy level can be calculated (instrument height), by adding it to the height of the fixed point. Then a measurement is taken when the staff is placed on the point to be measured; its height can be calculated by subtracting this measurement from the instrument height.

this can often include labourers with extensive excavation experience and skills. In France there is a centralised state organisation, AFAN, which has a virtual monopoly for rescue excavation; indeed, it is probably the largest archaeological employer in the world. Though it is difficult to get into the organisation, it has a good training system for staff and provides them with field experience and high standards of staff support.

A team can thus, depending on circumstances, include an interesting mix of professional and amateur, of skilled and unskilled, of people with academic training and without, of specialists and people with general skills. It is one of the challenges for a director to knit such disparate groups into a cohesive team, and to set up a chain of control that ensures that the various components of an excavation – digging, recording, finds processing, specialist reporting and publication – function properly, and can be tied together; divisions between the different groups can be disastrous. I have worked on projects where there was just such a division, and where the macho, beer-swigging field workers considered themselves above such 'effeminate' activities as finds washing or computer input; the result was poor quality recording on site which took a lot of work to clean up. Joan Gero has documented such attitudes in the United States in looking at the sorts of grants archaeologists request and obtain; males are out in the field hunting, and women tend to be at home processing the results. Such divisions lead to poor archaeology, as every member of the team should know how others in the group work, what their needs are for carrying out their tasks, and everyone should make sure that the information is recorded in such a way that it can, for instance, be computerised and made available to those who will be writing up the results. One solution is to involve each worker in every aspect of the project, as far

2.12. The JCB. It is most useful for the use of its back hoe, but because it is rubber-tyred, its wheels tend to sink into soft deposits when it is pushing. The back hoe is an excellent tool for digging trenches; for clearing large areas it is slow, but leaves an uncompacted surface.

2.13. *The Drott. The caterpillar tracks in fact do little damage to the site, other than compacting the top centimetre or so of the deposits. By back-scraping it can produce a smooth and relatively clean surface. However, it is slow moving, and for large areas a dumper truck or lorry speeds up the operation.*

as possible. All this also implies the need for quality control at all stages of the system, so that recording systems can be checked as quickly as possible, to ensure that excavation techniques are up to standard, and so on. This will be a constant theme in this book.

In Fig. 2.14 I have shown some of the ways in which teams can be (or have been) organised. The biggest contrast is between the hierarchical system in which there is a clear social division between those who do the digging (labourers), and those who do the recording and directing (academics), and where there is little or no interchange between the two groups. This is still fairly common in central and eastern Europe. I once shocked my Polish hosts by picking up a shovel and helping to remove the topsoil – this was not expected of an academically trained student even under a communist regime! In contrast, in western Europe most students start off as humble excavators, and the archaeological labourers have been replaced by younger people who may already have academic archaeological training. Those directing excavations have usually worked their way up from digger though site supervisor to director. Such excavations can be run on a hierarchical system, but some projects prefer to work in a more egalitarian system where diggers have more responsibility for their own recording and labelling. I discuss the ways in which such structures have developed in the professional context in Chapter 13.

TRAINING

It is one of the adages of competitive tendering that the first things to suffer are pay and training. Good employers, however, know that a skilled, informed and happy team will operate more efficiently, and that training should be built into the operation; indeed, in Britain this is now becoming a formal requirement for organisations registered with the

Institute of Field Archaeologists. This may take the form of formal training, such as short courses before and during the excavation on matters such as Health and Safety. There should be introductory talks which place the site in its perspective, both academically and administratively, covering many of the matters dealt with in this chapter. Subsequently training will depend on the nature of the site, though even with small teams some formal periods must be put aside to ensure that information is flowing around the team.

Ideally there should be no divisions within the team. Though site huts may have specialist functions, for documentation, storage of tools, consumption of food and drink and so on, allowing separate huts for the director, the supervisors and the diggers can create problems in communication, and may produce resentment. I know of one case where the diggers (justifiably!) burnt their hut down in protest at the enforced hierarchy (their hut was the only one without heating!). Informal contacts can help to keep information flowing, both on site and during rest periods. On site, arrangements need to be made for experienced workers to work with inexperienced, and to pass on skills, though some types of training, for instance in specialist surveying equipment, may not be possible in the context of a rescue excavation. There needs to be an agreement between employer and employees about what training will be done, but these are matters which I shall discuss in the final chapter.

QUALITY CONTROL

All well-conducted excavations will build in a series of checks to make sure that the system is working properly. This will start with the process of excavation on the site itself, to ensure that everyone is pulling their weight (especially if they are being paid!), and that the standard of digging is acceptable. This can be done on site, in part by establishing small groups which work together (especially to give training to the inexperienced). Someone should have overall supervision of this – with workmen a foreman will probably be employed; with volunteers or ordinary diggers it will be the site supervisor or director. The process of labelling should be mutually checked by the digger and the person writing out the label, though as I suggest later there should also be a number of checks on the label itself by which mistakes can be rectified later. Site records will need to be checked by the site or project director, or, as they are computerised and archived, by a data manager. Some ways in which quality checks can be built in are suggested in my illustrations of staff structures in Fig. 2.14.

HEALTH AND SAFETY

It is the duty of the director to make sure that all members of the team are aware of the legal requirements for Health and Safety, and that they are carried out. This will include matters such as clothing (the use of heavy boots with steel toe-caps, hard hats, etc.), the control of heavy machinery, the shoring of deep trenches, etc. There must be first-aid kits on site, and staff should have basic training in their use. Everyone should know what to do in an emergency – how to contact doctors, the location of the nearest hospital, and a list of relevant telephone numbers should be posted in the site hut. Ideally, there should be a mobile telephone on site.

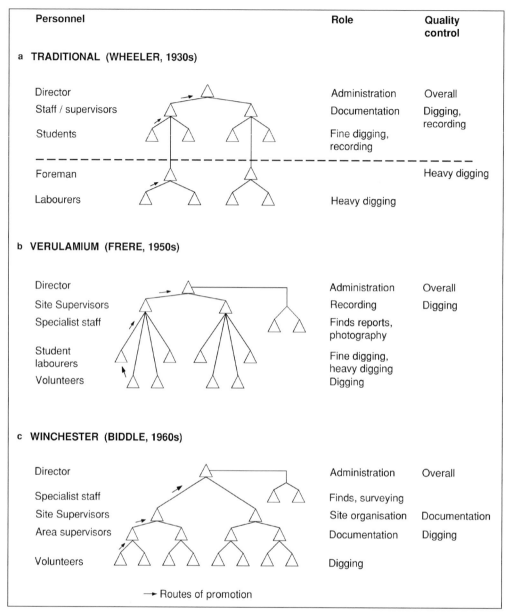

Personnel		Role	Quality control
a TRADITIONAL (WHEELER, 1930s)			
Director		Administration	Overall
Staff / supervisors		Documentation	Digging, recording
Students		Fine digging, recording	
Foreman			Heavy digging
Labourers		Heavy digging	
b VERULAMIUM (FRERE, 1950s)			
Director		Administration	Overall
Site Supervisors		Recording	Digging
Specialist staff		Finds reports, photography	
Student labourers		Fine digging, heavy digging	
Volunteers		Digging	
c WINCHESTER (BIDDLE, 1960s)			
Director		Administration	Overall
Specialist staff		Finds, surveying	
Site Supervisors		Site organisation	Documentation
Area supervisors		Documentation	Digging
Volunteers		Digging	

→ Routes of promotion

2.14. Team structure. These diagrams are intended to show the major relationships within the team, with the lines showing to whom a person is responsible. In diagrams (a) to (d) the arrows demonstrate ways in which individuals may be promoted within the system. Six systems are demonstrated here, but structures often have to be built around the abilities of specific individuals in the team:

(a) Wheeler hierarchical system. Note the 'glass ceiling' for labourers with no academic training. They have their own hierarchy, but are unable to rise any further than foreman within the structure.

(b) The system operating at Verulamium in the 1950s. In this the upper echelons of the structure are recruited from that below, and so directors will have worked their way up from the bottom. The volunteers may well be students working for, or already with, an academic degree. The specialist staff, such as bone experts, are undeveloped, and often would probably not have an archaeological training.

(c) The Winchester system from the 1960s. The class of labourers has disappeared, and there is now a straight hierarchy from volunteer to director, but specialists still tend not to have any archaeological training.

Personnel		Role	Quality control
d PROFESSIONAL UNITS (1980s)			
Director		Administration	Overall
Finds specialists		Specialist reports	
Site supervisors		Field direction, field documentation	Field records
Professional diggers		Digging	

→ Routes of promotion

Personnel		Role	Quality control
e COMPLEX PROJECT			
Project director		Administration	Overall
Site director		Field direction	Fieldwork
Finds co-ordinator		Report writing	Specialist reports
Data co-ordinator		Data computerisation, archive	Field records
Site supervisors		Site control, recording	Digging
Professional diggers		Digging, some recording	
Finds specialists		Specialist reports	

◄──► Additional essential links

Personnel		Role	Quality control
f MORE EGALITARIAN SYSTEM			
Project director		Administration	Overall
Field co-ordinator		Field direction	Digging
Data co-ordinator		Computing, archive	Documentation
Finds co-ordinator		Finds deposition, report commissioning	Specialist reports
Professional diggers		Excavation, field documentation	
Finds specialists		Finds reports	

◄──► Additional essential links

(d) The main system operating in Britain today is a development of that in Winchester in the 1960s. The volunteer has largely been replaced by the young professional with a degree, who will be hoping to be promoted up the hierarchy. The finds experts such as environmentalists are also often recruited from the same group, who, with their excavation experience, are better able to understand the nature of the finds with which they are dealing than are specialists from other disciplines.

(e) A larger project where more data are computerised requires a larger recording staff, but one that is closely integrated with the field team.

(f) In a more egalitarian team, each digger deals with his or her own recording and labelling, but more stringent quality control is needed over the field data. Similarly the finds 'specialists' are more likely to be in direct contact with one another. As they are likely to share an archaeological training in common, they can work as a research group rather than be answerable individually to a finds co-ordinator or director.

THREE

ON SITE

In chapter one we saw how excavation has shifted from trench excavation at the beginning of the nineteenth century, through area excavation with Pitt Rivers and his contemporaries, back to trench excavation with Wheeler and Bersu, back to open area in the 1960s, and something of a shift back to trench excavation in the 1990s. At each stage lessons have been learnt, like the need for stratigraphical control and site discipline which Wheeler emphasised under the Culture-Historical paradigm, or a better understanding of what we are sampling as a result of the large-scale excavations of the 1960s and 1970s. Open area excavation may be the ideal norm, but it brings it own special problems: controlling individual workers; moving about on site; general cleanliness; recording the details of where finds come from. In this chapter I want to consider the various ways in which effective excavation can be achieved.

Every excavation will have its own way of organising itself. When you arrive, the first thing you should expect will be a talk from the director or a supervisor about what is happening on site; where you can and cannot walk; what finds there are and how they should be recorded; how fast the excavation should proceed; and who will be giving you orders. If you have never dug before you should be shown how to use a trowel, but all too often supervisors assume that people already know certain things, like how to use a pick and shovel (few people do!). When your task is allotted to you, hopefully you will be put next to someone who already knows what is going on, so that you can ask for advice without having to continually ask the supervisor, and also you can watch what other, experienced people are doing. But, if things are still not clear, then *ask*.

HEALTH AND SAFETY

The only preliminary precaution that should be universal is an anti-tetanus injection, which is virtually painless. You should have a booster every few years. Directors should tell you of any other requirements, and if you have any ailments, such as epilepsy, you should warn the staff so that they know what to do. Not all excavations will be covered by insurance – though they should be. Volunteers and staff working abroad will normally be expected to organise their own personal health insurance – for British diggers, Form E111 (for countries where there is a reciprocal agreement) is adequate for most things, but not all. Sites must have a first aid kit available, and *everyone* should know where to find it; the site director and supervisors should also know what to do in an emergency and important information, such as where to find the nearest telephone, hospital, etc.

Generally, pace yourself to do what you think you can do, especially in the first few days. It may take several days to adjust to the sun, or lifting weights or getting your hands hardened. If the sun is too hot, get in the shade – directors should understand, but are less indulgent of hangovers.

Safety on site is largely a matter of common sense. Supervisors should keep workers sufficiently far apart that they will not hit one another with a pick, and everyone should stay well away from machinery: all workers should obey such orders. Though in general hand-dug trenches are safer than machine-dug, adequate shoring to support the edges of the trench should be provided, along with safety clothing such as helmets. However, archaeologists do tend to delay shoring for as long as possible, in order to see as much of the section as possible before it is covered – a fault which is disappearing as we become more safety conscious.

OFF-SITE BEHAVIOUR

Though excavating should be fun, all projects rely on the staff working regular hours – sometimes very long hours if there is an emergency. We do not expect workers to appear a couple of hours late, bleary-eyed and unfit for work because they had too much to drink the previous night. Archaeology is only worth doing if it is done well and efficiently. Projects will vary in the amount of control they maintain over off-site activities – if there is a hostel which has to be kept clean and tidy, or standards of behaviour which if not kept will lead to the project being closed down, then supervision may be close. But most of us leave our workers to look after themselves with few questions asked, as long as they behave sensibly. Sensitivity to particular situations is vital. A rural community which starts work at daylight does not expect to be kept awake at night by archaeologists who may start somewhat later, and projects always depend on local support and encouragement. A drugs raid of the excavation's headquarters hardly helps local relationships. Especially when working abroad, matters such as styles of female dress, which in Britain may be regarded as normal, may be considered provocative. Directors should advise on how they expect diggers to behave, but consideration for the local community, one's fellow workers and the project generally should be uppermost.

WHAT TO WEAR

This will naturally depend on the circumstances – recently I was digging in France in the summer, and in the Derbyshire Peak District in the winter – two very different propositions (I wonder sometimes if I have got it the wrong way round!). The director should offer advice beforehand, especially if conditions are exceptional. Normally, clothing should be as light as possible – shorts, etc., in hot weather – but be prepared to cover up, as the reflection of some subsoils such as chalk can be disastrous until you are used to it. Don't expect to be able to go barefoot or in sandals even in hot conditions – stones and site grid nails tear one's feet to pieces and lead to infections, and in most countries it is actually illegal to go on site without steel-capped boots. Derbyshire calls for heavy boots and several layers of pullovers, long johns and good waterproofs. If there is any danger of stones or other items falling on one's head then a protective helmet is essential, and this is legally compulsory in many situations. Legal requirements have been tightened up considerably in recent years after a number of avoidable accidents.

MOVING ABOUT

The first thing you will learn is that there are places you are *not* allowed to tread. Indeed, good excavation should involve moving your feet as little as possible, especially in wet conditions. So do not wander about to see what other people are doing or have found unless you have permission. One problem with open area excavation is that if one is digging in the centre of the site, it is difficult to remove the spoil without trampling over archaeological deposits. There are two ways around this: you can use either a series of planks or raised walkways, especially where the deposits are delicate (for instance where wood is preserved), or designated pathways so that damage will be kept to a minimum. Usually I try to start excavating a site from the centre and work outwards so that cleaned surfaces are not walked on, but a more common method is to start at one end of the trench – preferably that furthest from the dump – and work systematically across the site (Figs 3.1, 3.2). On sites where features are cut into the subsoil, movement on site is easier as blank areas can be defined, but planks may be needed to take wheelbarrows over ditches (Fig. 3.3).

Be sensitive to what other people are doing on site. You may learn new words of abuse if you wander on to an area which has just been cleaned for a photograph or for planning, or where there are features that can be easily damaged. If baulks have been left in, do not tread on the edges, especially in wet weather or if there is soft soil such as sand; the baulks will crumble, destroying evidence and leaving a mess, and I know someone who broke an ankle when a 10cm deep section collapsed beneath him! Nor should you sit on baulks.

SMALLER DIGGING EQUIPMENT

The one item that everyone is expected to provide for themselves is a trowel; indeed, the degree of wear on your trowel can be a matter of prestige. A good builders' pointing trowel, solid cast and drop forged, costs about £15 at the time of writing (2000); mark your trowel distinctively with your name or initials or you may find it has walked (not always inadvertently!). Some bright red paint on the ferrule will also make it show up in mud and murk. The best make in Britain (some would say in the world) is the WHS brand, made by Spear & Jackson of Sheffield; in America the Marshalltown has a similar reputation, though it is a rather different sort of tool. The WHS is solid, for hard scraping and digging, a sort of cutlass; the Marshalltown is more of a rapier which will cut through soil more cleanly. For normal digging, buy one with a 4in (10cm) blade, but on softer soils, or if you are digging a lot and wear trowels out, then a 5in (12.5cm) may be better, but certainly not larger. One problem that can occur is the blade becoming loose in the handle. Some strong glue will usually solve this. But whatever you do, do not buy a cheap trowel, especially one with a riveted blade – they simply do not survive the rigours of excavation.

Though most equipment will be provided by the project, the experienced may prefer their own toolkit. Most common is the kneeling mat, especially if you are digging skeletons on stony ground. A variety of plasterers' and dentists' spatulae can be useful for more delicate work, and wooden spatulae are good for work on bones and other soft materials. One digger used to turn up with a variety of spoons: a long-handled one specially bent for removing soil from post-holes, and two dessert spoons with wooden strips bound to the handles – these were for scraping surfaces (one for each hand), and most effective they were. The choice of tools for scraping surfaces clean will depend on the subsoil – I have used triangular paint-scrapers on chalk, while others swear by swan-

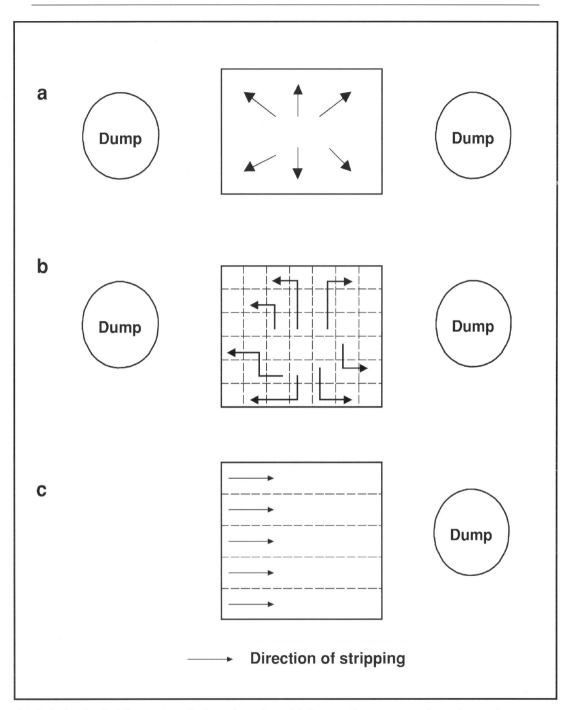

a

b

c

→ **Direction of stripping**

3.1. Stripping the site. Three main methods can be used to minimise trampling over areas where other people are excavating. A: If all the finds are being measured in, the diggers can start from the centre of the site and work out, with no concern about where each person works, other than ensuring that the whole area is covered systematically (see also Fig. 3.2). B: If finds are being collected using a grid, each digger will complete a square before moving on to the next. Again, work can best start from the centre of the site. C: In the 'racing track' method, lanes are laid out across the site, and the diggers start at the end furthest from the dump.

3.2. Excavation at Wigber Low. Clearance of the limestone blocks which form the Bronze Age cairn has started in the centre of the site and is proceeding outwards. As every find is plotted in, it does not matter who is working where on the site, as long as work progresses systematically, without leaving areas unexcavated.

3.3. Excavations at Owslebury. Individual excavators each have their own feature or section of ditch to excavate. The surface of the site, after it has been initially cleaned and planned, can be used as a working surface for wheelbarrows, etc., with no risk of damage to the site. Other members of the team, seemingly wandering around at random, are involved in supervising, labelling and planning.

necked hoes; on softer soils a long-handled onion hoe works well. Finally a variety of paint and hand brushes are useful. The best stiff bristle brush for normal work is the churn brush which is specially designed to get into difficult corners; they should be used with a beating technique, as normal brushing just smears; indeed, it is often best not to use a brush at all if you are looking for difference in soil colour. Small, round soft brushes smear less, and can be good for cleaning up more delicate work.

LARGER DIGGING TOOLS

It may not be socially unacceptable to call a spade a spade, but never call a shovel a spade as they are two totally different implements. A spade is for cutting and removing turf or for digging a garden. The angle of the blade is more or less a continuation of that of the handle. A shovel is for removing loose soil, and the blade is at an angle of about 120° to the handle, so you do not have to bend down so far. The short-handled shovel can have a T- or a Y-shaped end – I find the latter easier to handle. Also the blade should be thickened for heavy work; there are lighter shovels available for shovelling coal, but these are not good for excavation, except for soft soils like sand. The heavier shovel can be turned round, and the back used to cut sections straight. The long-handled shovel (common on the continent and in the west of Britain) requires very different handling skills, but is very good on sand or for tossing soil some distance.

One of Wheeler's famous statements is that the pick is a delicate instrument in the hands of a skilled person – and I wholeheartedly concur. Some diggers seem to think it part of a macho male image that they can swing the pick over their head and bring it crashing down somewhere in the ground. In fact, one should rarely swing it much above shoulder height if one is to control where it goes and how deep, and it can be used as effectively by females as by males. The mattock is a pick with a broad cutting edge, good where rough clearance has to be done, such as removal of turf, roots and undergrowth, or in heavy soils such as clay, but it is also good for cutting pot-sherds and bones in two. I have also occasionally used a fork, notably in a rescue context where holes had to be dug quickly to follow the lines of a wall to recover the plan of a Roman building, but be wary: one famous Iron Age site in France was reputedly dug with a fork – with disastrous consequences!

The use of the pick and shovel is something that takes considerable training and experience. The pick should be used to loosen the soil gently, dragging it back from the working face. Let your lower hand slide along the handle as you let the blade drop as this reduces strain on the back. Do not loosen too much soil at once. If required, the loose soil can now be sorted through with the trowel. The short-handled shovel can be pushed under the soil, using the knee – not the arms and shoulders! Use the working face to shovel the loose soil against. Keep the wheelbarrow or bucket as near as possible – the secret of picking and shovelling is not to work too hard! If you do have to throw the soil, it should be tossed – practise by just letting it jump off the shovel at your feet, then try to send it a bit further, keeping all the soil together in a lump. Hold the shovel at the point where the ferrule and the wood of the handle join, and do not let your hand slide, or the soil will spread all over the place. There is no point in shovelling if more soil is going to land on the site than in the wheelbarrow.

Removing spoil from a site can be a problem, especially from a deep site. My experience of conveyor belts is not over-happy – they are heavy to move around, stones can get caught in the belt, and they tend to break down. A hoist for buckets or wheelbarrows can be more effective. Dumper trucks are useful if a lot of spoil has to be moved a long distance, but they are not good for the excavation surface, are less easy to fill than a wheelbarrow, and are more expensive to hire and run. On most sites the main method will be bucket and wheelbarrow. The major consideration is what is most efficient and least damaging to the site – sometimes volunteers have to be stopped from dragging every bucket load up to the spoil tip instead of using a wheelbarrow, mainly because they are reluctant either to try wheeling a barrow up a plank, or to ask others to do it for them. In fact, the wheelbarrow should be easy to manipulate, as long as it has a pneumatic tyre and there are wheeling planks. If you feel you cannot manage a full barrow, load the spoil towards the front, over the wheel. While going up a plank, make sure you are central, by keeping your eye on the plank in front of the barrow. Keep your arms stiff and lean forward as you go up a slope. To empty, don't stop, just give a quick flick of the hands, and catch the handles when the barrow is upright – it's easy when you know how! Buckets are easily broken; they cost money, so don't drop large stones in them and *never* sit on upturned plastic buckets; however light you think you are, they easily split. However, wheelbarrows, tipped so that their handles are on the ground, make comfortable seats for armchair archaeologists. You can measure a site's efficiency by how well inflated the wheelbarrow tyres are and how much the axles squeak!

LAYING OUT THE SITE

For ease of planning and recording, most sites are laid out with a grid of pegs and nails, and this can also be important for the control of the excavation. Firstly some fixed points must be decided on, and wooden or metal pegs hammered in; if the excavation is likely to be lengthy these may be set in concrete, accurately surveyed in. Sometimes it is most convenient to lay pegs out at one- or two-metre intervals around the area to be excavated (Fig. 3.4). From these temporary points can be established within the area of excavation itself by running a tape across the area and dropping a plumb-bob at the relevant points. There is no ideal way. At Exeter we used long metal bars which were hammered in at 2m intervals (Fig. 6.5), but it was difficult to get them vertical, especially if one hit a stone. Nowadays I tend to use large nails, banged in at 1m or 2m intervals, but on a deeply stratified site they have to be replaced continually. Also Sod's Law states that there will *always* be a stone at the point where the nail should go in! The tops of all pegs and nails should be painted to make them more visible (I have spent many happy hours hunting for lost nails on site or in cornfields). Red is the best colour – it is very visible, and disguises the blood of anyone unwise enough to trip over the peg, but the nails should be banged in flush with the surface to protect toes. Alternatively they can be banged through tin lids or coloured cloth. Some excavators like to use string to lay out their grids, either laying it on the ground or stretching it across the site from the edges of the excavation. Personally I don't like to use string: it expands and contracts, and is soon inaccurate and sagging. People inevitably trip over it and, if it is suspended above the site, it not only hinders moving around site, but is a positive danger, garrotting people as they duck under it. In caves or standing buildings plumb-bobs can be suspended from the roof, but this takes time to set up, and such a grid is difficult to lay out accurately. The use of site grids will be discussed more under recording, in Chapter 6.

3.4. Excavations at Aulnat. Digging to find objects is best done by working at a face as in this photograph, using the pick or the point of the trowel to loosen the soil, and the blade of the trowel to sort through and pull it away from the digging face. Objects and changes in soil colour should be quickly visible. Not too much soil should be loosened at one go, and care should be taken not to scatter it on to surrounding areas, or to tread on it. In dusty conditions the hand brush (churn brushes are best) can be used to sweep up dust and keep the area clean. The site has been laid out with wooden pegs at 2m intervals around the site, and nails are banged in the area under excavation. Each excavator has been given a square in which to dig and is removing a 5cm spit of soil, under the watchful eye of the supervisor.

CONTROL OF THE EXCAVATION

Wheeler resolved the control of personnel by assigning small groups or individuals to a single trench or square defined by baulks. This option is not available on open area excavation. If it is a site where all the features have been dug into the subsoil, the solution is relatively simple: each individual is given his or her own feature to excavate, be it post-hole, pit or whatever. Larger features can be subdivided. At Owslebury we divided ditches into lengths of about 3 metres, and excavated a trench 1m wide in each to check the stratigraphy before excavating the rest (Figs 1.8, 3.3). All the excavators thus had their own length of ditch to excavate, and control was relatively easy.

On open sites with complex stratigraphy the situation is more difficult. In part it depends on the system for recording finds (see below). Where all finds are measured in, it is enough for the excavators to start in the middle of the site and work out, stripping off one stratigraphical level (Fig. 3.1). They can be instructed merely to link up with the people on either side so that nothing is left undug. Another method has been to lay out 'racing tracks' with string across the site: the diggers start at one end and work systematically in a row to the other end. This system was used at Cadbury Congresbury by Peter Fowler and Philip Rahtz. Unfortunately excavators all work at different speeds, and there is a tendency for the bit under the string to be forgotten, or left to the slowest, making them yet slower.

The normal method is to allow the archaeology to define areas to dig; for instance, a layer or context will be defined in area, and then excavated by the number of diggers who can be fitted in without crowding. For reasons discussed below, I do not like this system, and on my excavations I use a grid system of 1m squares defined by the grid nails. Each digger is assigned to a square, and moved on to the next as they finish. Most people have no problems keeping within their area, and it reduces the amount of string floating around on site. The supervisor is then free to move around, ensuring that people are not going too deep, cutting into underlying levels, or not going deep enough, and also making sure that each area is left clean and tidy (Fig. 3.4).

DIGGING AND CLEANING

You should be told on arrival the speed at which you are expected to dig. Choices always have to be made on excavations, influenced by the budget, the labour force and the time available. It may be that total recovery of the finds is required, or simply a reasonable sample such as is found in normal trowelling, or from picking and shovelling. On some Dutch sites it is the plan that is paramount, so large areas are stripped off mechanically, planned and then stripped again, thereby allowing the archaeologists to understand total settlement or landscape layouts, sometimes over several square kilometres, but producing minimal finds.

I make a distinction between digging and cleaning. When digging (Fig. 3.4), you stand on the surface to which you are working, and have a working face at which you dig, be it with a trowel or a pick. The soil is dragged towards you, and finds should 'jump out' as you dig. The quicker you see them, or notice any change in soil colour, the less damage you are likely to do – so never dig blind, by picking too far back behind your working face, having too deep a face or digging into already loose soil. If you keep the edge of the area you are digging square, you will be able to judge depth more easily, and by loosening a small amount at a time, you will also be able to follow more easily the level or surface you are working to.

Cleaning, in contrast, means leaving the surface as clean as possible, and so not treading on it – you are working backwards, systematically, in one direction (Fig. 3.5). On sites where finds are left in position, all digging may be done in this way. Generally it is best to rely on the trowel to clean the surface – if you use a brush, it should be used in a beating fashion to flick the soil grains out, as ordinary sweeping just smears the distinctions, especially in damp conditions. Much the best method is to use an industrial vacuum cleaner; these are widely used on the continent but strangely little in Britain, and they make an enormous difference both in the time needed to clean a surface and in the standard achieved. They are also useful for sucking up dirt from difficult places such as post-holes or burials (along with finger bones!). They do, however, need a power source, such as a generator, but the investment is worth every penny.

SITE CLEANLINESS

Dirt left lying around on site will get trodden in and thus will contaminate the site. While digging, loose spoil should be kept down to a minimum, especially if it looks

3.5. Use of the trowel for cleaning. If you are cleaning, or leaving finds in position, scrape toward yourself and avoid standing on the surface you have just cleaned or excavated. Do not try to go too deep (1–2cm maximum), or you will be masking what you are digging with your spoil. The trowel should be angled to prevent dirt jumping back over it, though for tough clay the angle may be changed to cut through the deposit. Try not to leave streaks of dust or a corrugated effect. Angles between sections and the excavation surface should be sharpened up with the point of the trowel, as should stones and other features. If the soil is hard, extra pressure can be applied by using both hands on the trowel. Do not use the brush after scraping as it smears the surface. Cleaning with an industrial vacuum cleaner produces the best results.

likely that work will have to be abandoned because of the weather. You should never tread on soil you have just loosened. When you finish digging, all loose soil should be scraped or brushed up – the area should always be left cleaner than you found it, and dirt should not be allowed to spread on to neighbouring areas. As you dig, the edges of your area should be kept square, with sharp angles between the vertical and horizontal surfaces and around protruding objects such as stones. Inevitably rain, frost and natural weathering will cause dirt to accumulate, but this can be periodically cleaned up, perhaps for the visit of some bigwig or a local society. It is good for morale to work on a clean site, but it is not always possible if there is only a small team on a large site. Here the principle should be to keep clean the areas that are actually being excavated.

On most prehistoric sites smoking is banned because of the danger of contaminating C14 samples, and there is a recorded case of a specialist spending a whole day analysing a strange prehistoric tissue, only to find it was the remains of a cigarette filter. Though it may seem fun to 'plant' finds on the gullible, this can backfire. Major finds have turned up on dumps because someone thought they were being had – so don't do it!

BUILDING A DUMP

Another part of Sod's Law states that the dump will *always* be placed over some vital part of the site, and will have to be moved. Otherwise, archaeologists seem to take little interest in their dumps (other than to look for important finds missed in the digging). But dumps need to be carefully planned, so that removal of the spoil from the site can be achieved as efficiently as possible. Often there is little choice where the dump has to go; sometimes on urban sites it has to be carted away, which is an expensive option. It is best if someone is appointed to be in charge of dumps, to ensure that no one tips spoil in the main access routes, and that the balance between building upwards and outwards is maintained to allow minimum effort in emptying barrows. Some suggestions are made on Fig. 3.6.

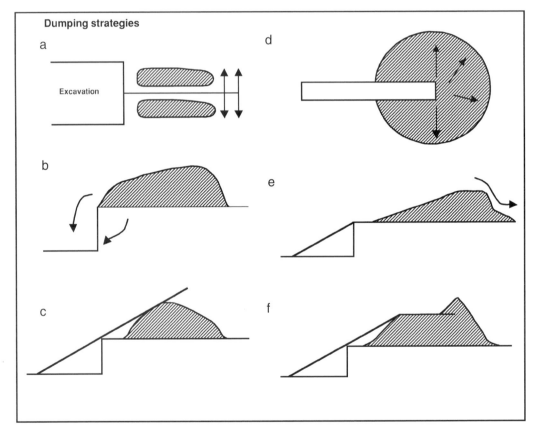

3.6. How to build a dump. If no one is in charge, soil will be dumped at random or in such a way that the dump spreads out over a large area (a). Nor should the dump be too close to the edge of the excavation (b); dumped material will roll into the trench causing contamination, and the weight of the dump on the edge of the excavation may cause it to collapse. What is needed is a ramp, preferably with wheeling planks, to take one up to a plateau. The soil is dumped over the edge of the plateau but make sure the ends of the plank are secure or disaster will ensue (c)! If it starts building up, it should be shovelled level (f), until finally the plateau becomes too large. Then soil is allowed to build up, prior to extending the ramp and building a higher plateau. In this way dumps will take up a smaller area and it will take less time to empty a barrow.

FOUR

FINDING THINGS

The purists of archaeology often tell us that not finding things is significant in itself, and that negative evidence can be as important as positive. This is indeed true (though it can be a con trick by directors such as myself to encourage workers who are not having much luck!), but the reverse statement is also true: the more we find, the more we can say about the ancient societies we are digging up. However, a find in itself is fairly meaningless – it is up to the archaeologist to give it a context, to date it, to say how it was made, what it was used for, who used it, and what it can tell us about the people who used it. This is one of the essential differences between archaeologists and treasure hunters. It is up to excavators, therefore, to provide as much contextual evidence as possible, and this concerns what we can say not only about the object itself but also about the context of discovery as well. For example, was a find a unique object on this site, or were there others which may have been missed because the diggers did not recognise them? To what extent can we make direct comparison between what we find in a ditch, say, which was filling up during the year and collected one kind of rubbish, and a storage pit which may have been filled in at one specific season of the year with a very different sort of rubbish? This process by which objects are buried and survive is called 'taphonomy' in the jargon.

It is thus vital for every digger to know what sort of finds to expect and to be able to recognise them, but they should also be able to realise when something exceptional turns up, and to react to it appropriately. They should know what the collection policy of the site is – are all oyster shells or bits of Roman brick to be collected; if not, who decides what to throw away and at what stage? Evidence must not be destroyed, for instance by breaking animal bones, or lost, for example by some people saving a certain category of finds and others not, so that the spread of those objects through time and space on the site cannot subsequently be reconstructed. Orientation on matters like this should be explained in the literature sent to participants before they arrive on the site, and then reinforced by site talks on arrival. Inexperienced workers should have a chance to be involved in finds processing at as early a date as possible so they can see what sorts of finds are coming up.

In this chapter I shall consider the various categories of finds, what they can tell us, and how to deal with them, though I do not intend to cover questions of conservation (I would recommend every project to have a manual on site such as that produced by the organisation Rescue, *First Aid for Finds*). But all finds have certain things in common. When something is found, you should dig all round it to get its dimensions – levering a piece of pot or bone out of the ground before it is totally cleared is likely to break it. It may have an interesting relationship with other finds; for instance, bones, animal or human, may prove to be in articulation, and may need cleaning up for photography (Fig. 4.1); or a pot may be broken in position, or be part of an offering in a grave. Never remove anything from the soil until you are sure it will not be necessary to record it in position, and that it will not break as you take it out – a large iron object may need to be lifted, for instance, in polyurethane foam. In the field, attempt as little cleaning as possible – soil can be removed at the washing stage, and some corrosion products may contain traces of textiles, and can only be dealt with in the laboratory. Certainly you must never scrape bits of pottery or bone with your trowel – at most wipe the dirt off with your fingers.

But the general rule about anything you do not understand is to ask, and the golden rule is *if in doubt, don't chuck it out.*

POTTERY

Pottery is in many ways the easiest material to deal with, because everyone can recognise it; it is generally stable; if it gets broken, it can be stuck together without too much loss of information; and it can often be dated even when out of stratigraphical context. On most historical and many prehistoric sites it is the main source for dating layers and the site. It can also tell us about the trade connections of the site, whether it was producing a surplus to trade at a local, regional or international level. It tells us about the level of industrial organisation of that society, what in Marxist terminology is referred to as the 'mode of production' (was it made in the home, or by specialists using advanced technology?). It can also tell us about the social status of the inhabitants, and their access to resources such as fine pottery. It may tell us about the activities on various parts of the site, for instance the contrast between domestic and industrial activity, or perhaps which building was the farmhouse and which the dairy. All these approaches require quantification of the data, so it is essential not to collect just the large pieces of pottery or the decorated fragments, or the sample will be biased.

Diggers may assign the wrong level of importance to groups of finds. For instance, if one is dealing with 'primary rubbish', that is material picked up and thrown away into a rubbish pit, then this is likely to include pots that can be restored, and so be good for display. But little broken scraps missed in the clearing up of a broken pot and trodden into a floor may be of even greater importance, first of all in dating a context such as a house where rubbish tends not to accumulate, and secondly in telling us the context in which certain types of pots were used and broken, what the pots were being used for, and which people on the settlement were using them. Thus all finds of pottery should be treated with equal respect, however unimpressive they may be.

BRICK AND TILE, AND OTHER CERAMICS

Material such as brick and tile represents a problem in that it can sometimes appear in quantities too large to deal with easily. On some sites, for instance, a Roman town site or a post-medieval settlement, it may simply be discarded as processing and storage cost too much. On the other hand, in fieldwalking such finds may be indicative of a Roman villa, though other sorts of site also used tile. On some sites fragments may be counted, weighed and then discarded, so that ratios of different types and their distribution on site and

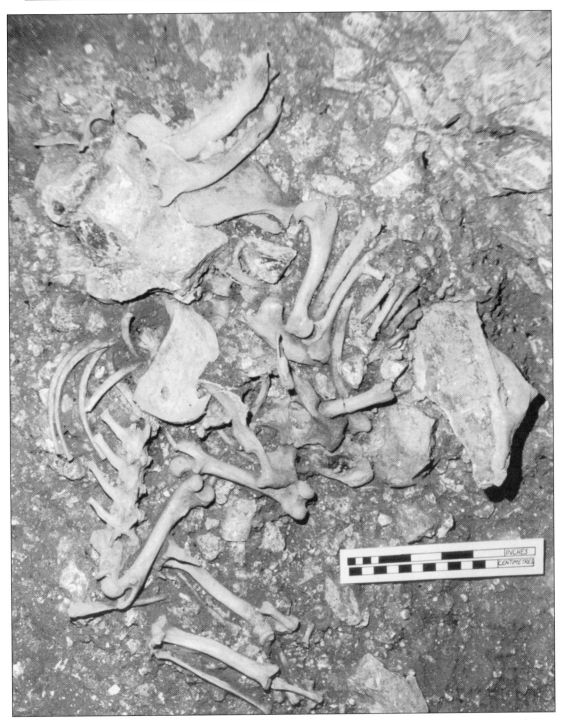

(Above and following page) *4.1. Animal bones from Owslebury.* Two examples of animal bones which were noted in time and left in position for recording. The first case (Fig. 4.1a) is the skeleton of a dog which had been cut into pieces, and buried while still in articulation. The jaws were found, but not the skull. Knife cuts on the joints suggest the animal was skinned or had the sinews removed. The second case is also a dog (Fig. 4.1b), which had been lying on the surface long enough to become partly disarticulated, but was finally buried with some bits of the vertebrae still articulated.

Fig. 4.1b.

through time can be studied. Samples may be kept for further study, for example to identify from the fabric where it was made. One interesting use is by Loïc Langouet at Rennes; working on the assumption that tiles were normally fired horizontally, he dates them using archaeomagnetism (and so dates the phases of building activity without excavating), but a substantial sample is needed for each site.

Other items of burnt clay may be found, like the baked hearths and firedogs on Iron Age sites in France, or the clay figurines found at all periods throughout the world. But fragments such as those from pipe clay figurines of Roman date may not be readily identifiable when found (they are white and look a bit like chalk). Clay was used to construct houses, to make moulds for casting metal objects and as briquetage for making and trading salt. All should be saved, and only discarded at a later stage if quantities prove too great to deal with – but that is a decision for the director.

FLINT AND STONE

The oldest surviving materials used by man include flint, chert, quartz and obsidian. The recognition of struck flint is not always easy, especially on sites where flint occurs naturally, but it often looks more fresh and shows signs of working, such as the 'bulb of percussion' where it was struck off the parent nodule. It occurs widely on all prehistoric sites, and will commonly turn up on sites of later periods, sometimes deliberately collected – like arrowheads in Iron Age burials or handaxes from Roman temple sites. Smaller flints such as microliths can only be recovered systematically by sieving, but the colour and patina of struck flint often makes it easily visible.

On sites where hard rock occurs naturally, or where it has been imported in quantity, for instance on urban sites, there should be a plan for looking at rocks systematically to see if they have been worked. A major Roman inscription from Winchester was only noticed when the stone turned over as it was deposited on the dump! Querns (stones for grinding corn) and mortars are easily missed, and may be identifiable only from one ground or pecked surface or because the stone is foreign to the site. In the last few years there has been an increased interest in studying quarrying and movement of stone, either for itself or simply for use as ballast in ships. Foreign rocks will normally be sorted out for specialist identification, whereas local rocks can only be selectively sampled.

Items such as ground stone axes or whetstones are usually fairly identifiable when whole, but chips of axes on prehistoric sites need a trained eye and are proving more common than early excavations might lead us to expect. Schist, shale, jet and related stones that were carved to make ornaments, statues or items of furniture tend to be distinctive, as are gemstones, but for their small size. Shale should be reported immediately as it must be kept damp or it will split.

GLASS

Iron Age, Roman and post-medieval glass is usually strong and stable (though inclined to flake) and readily recognisable as glass, though it can be easy to miss small items like beads. Early medieval phosphate glasses, however, tend to decay, with a tendency to turn brown and peel, if not to turn crystalline. Ask for advice if you find any.

METAL OBJECTS

Of ancient metals, only gold will normally survive untarnished. Silver may, but is more usually covered with a black oxide; under bad conditions this will turn to a purple colour and be very porous. Bronze is variable but usually turns green, and in advanced cases of decay will be bright green and powdery. If it is a large or fragile object, it may need to be specially lifted. Small items like coins may not be easy to notice. However, they do often cause a black stain around them or may stain neighbouring objects green, so look out for this. On one site I found more coins than the rest of the diggers put together, mainly, I suspect, because I was looking for the stain rather than the coin – the only way to find the minute late third- and fourth-century minimissimi, except by extensive sieving. Lead and pewter may look well preserved, though often have a whitish colour; however, the metal is often very crystalline and easily broken.

Iron will only survive well in very dry or very wet conditions. Often it will have corroded right through, and will be simply an amorphous lump of brownish-yellowish oxide. If it is a large object, it will need special treatment before lifting. Smaller items such as nails usually survive quite well, but site conditions vary. Look out too for the waste products of metal production – the various pieces of slag may look like iron when they appear, but often they are more porous and have a glassy texture. Slag from blacksmithing is sometimes small and has to be picked out with a magnet; if an area of iron working is suspected, there should be some sort of sampling process in use so that the minute debris can be picked out. Where smelting has taken place, you can also expect fragments of the ore to appear – this usually looks like a piece of foreign stone.

BONES

On alkaline sites bones may be as common, sometimes more common, than pottery and flint, but they have never been treated with the same concern by archaeologists, and all too often collections of bones presented to bone experts are not worth bothering with since they have been so badly collected and damaged. I am an advocate of throwing away most bones, which is a condemnation of most excavators rather than a belief that bones are unimportant. There should always be someone on site who can do basic identification – I personally believe all professional archaeologists should be able to deal with the basics, if only to know whether they are dealing with the skeleton of a dog or a baby – and it is essential to try to interest all the excavators in such a way that they will deal with bones carefully. One false move with the trowel and a sheep's humerus becomes sheep/goat, or a bone that could have provided useful measurements to allow the sex to be identified becomes a useless pile of scraps.

No attempt should be made to lift a bone until it has been completely cleared round and its limits defined. If it is in articulation it should be left in and cleaned up for recording (Fig. 4.1) – all groups of articulated bones should be kept together and the bone expert informed. In the case of complete skeletons, human or animal, it is customary to clean them up *in situ*, and photograph and/or draw them. This is described in greater detail in Chapter 11. Even groups of bones partially or not in articulation may be of interest to provide information on the processes of deposition, and prehistorians especially are interested in 'special deposits' associated with feasting and other ceremonial and ritual activities.

Bones are in fact more important than pottery on many sites – until relatively recently the majority of the population was engaged in farming, and meat procurement whether by farming or hunting was one of the major activities for most people. Bones can tell us about diet; about the economy – hunting or farming, and the relative importance of the various species and how they were exploited; about the environment; and perhaps about the social status of a site: for example, the sites of the ruling classes in the medieval period produce a lot of deer bones, while peasant and town sites do not. They may tell us about cultural differences, such as certain species not being eaten. They may also indicate not only the different functions of different sites (a kill site as against a campsite in the Palaeolithic) but also seasonal activities or different activities on different parts of the same site. There are also, however, bones of smaller animals, such as fish or rodents. Mesolithic shell midden sites were notorious for not producing fish remains until systematic sieving was introduced; the majority of fish bones had decayed, but the ear bones (otoliths) survive well (though they are only a few millimetres long) and can be identified to species. These may need special sampling procedures to recover adequate information. In brief, bones are important and fragile, and should be treated with care.

SHELLS

There will certainly be a site policy on shells, if they are present. On a Mesolithic shell midden there is no possibility of keeping every limpet. On Roman sites there is a tendency not to keep oysters – though we did at Owslebury, as a quantifiable part of the diet, and this approach is now more usual as it becomes possible to identify sources of shells and say more about their exploitation and the trade in marine products. Normally other sea or freshwater shells should be kept. Shells were often traded – *Dentalium* in Neolithic Europe, and cowries, *Pecten* and cockles in the Iron Age. They were sometimes used as pendants – in parts of Germany during the Iron Age mussel shells filled with red ochre were worn by young girls who had reached puberty. Snail shells of land species were also used both as ornaments and as food – especially the edible and garden snails. My usual policy is to tell diggers to keep the snails, which means they find the large ones which could have been used in this way, but smaller varieties will only be found in sampling.

ORGANIC MATERIALS

Generally, organic materials will only survive under exceptional conditions of damp, of cold or of dryness – anywhere where bacterial activity is prevented. Sites where items such as wood, leather or textiles survive are unusual, and if you are working on such as site you can expect to have special instructions (Fig. 4.2). Such items do, however, occasionally survive in contact with metal objects, for instance textiles on a bronze object from a grave, so special attention and care should be taken when dealing with such potential information. Charcoal is the one organic material likely to be found on most sites. Again, there is likely to be a sampling policy to recover wood and seeds, but care should be taken not to fragment larger pieces which may be needed for identification, C14 testing or dendrochronology.

4.2. The Somerset Levels. The unusual preservation conditions here impose special digging conditions. It was not possible to walk on the site, so all digging had to be done lying on planks, and with fingers as the trowel would damage the wood. When exposed to air, timbers will start to decay and crack unless kept wet.

FIVE

CONTEXTS

The term 'context' is one piece of jargon which every excavator must pick up immediately, as it is one of the basic concepts with which all archaeological excavators deal, and indeed it is now taking on an international life, for instance in France as the US number (unité stratigraphique). It lies at the basis of the recording techniques which are employed in archaeological excavations in Britain in the form of 'Single Context Recording'; though I shall be describing other techniques, it is this methodology with which students should most familiarise themselves. 'Context' is, however, a term that has been gradually extending its meaning since it was first coined, and, as I shall explain in this chapter, some of us would like to see its scope extended even further, in response to the needs of computer databases.

The term has its origins in the 1970s in the work of Ed Harris, a member of the Winchester team working on the publication of the extensive excavations carried out there in the 1960s. Harris had the task of trying to correlate the stratigraphical data recorded on the most complicated of the sites excavated, the Lower Brook Street site, which had a complex sequence of domestic and ecclesiastical buildings, starting with the Roman period and continuing until the late medieval period. Not only did one house succeeded another, but also each one went through extensive repairs and rebuilding with new hearths, new floors, etc. Another problem was linking together the different buildings, deciding which phase was contemporary with which. The written record of the site had been done in the traditional way advocated by Wheeler and Kenyon: a written description in a notebook, with reference to which layer overlay or was overlain by another layer.

Harris quickly realised that some of the data he required had not in fact been adequately recorded – even if the major relationships had been recorded in the site book, and the extensive-detailed plans showed many others, it was sometimes the less obvious relationships that were the key, and these may not have been thought important at the time. He went on to suggest a *pro-forma* way of recording (the so-called 'context sheet'), and then looked at ways in which to systematise the recording of relationships, and presenting it visually – the so-called 'Harris matrix'. His book, *Principles of Archaeological Stratigraphy*, now in its second edition, is a basic introduction which all excavators should study.

Under the Wheeler system each recognisable archaeological layer was given a number. Usually there was a sequence of layers in each trench, so the different numbers would then be distinguished by adding the trench number. Trench IX layer 10 would probably be completely different from Trench X layer 10. Other sequences of numbers would be recorded. Certain finds like coins were sorted out for special treatment, by measuring in their position, and these objects were given 'small find numbers'. Burials, walls, buildings, soil samples, photographs, slides, bags of pottery, phases – each would have its own numerical system, leading to a proliferation of lists. To distinguish them, some of the common ones were coded; layer numbers were always placed in a circle, small finds or bag numbers for finds in triangles, and trench numbers were given Roman numerals; unstratified material was just a + in a circle. In this chapter we shall see not only how this complex numbering system has been simplified down (I recommend a single numerical system to cover everything), but also how other sorts of archaeological features such as cuts and interfaces have been added to the information recorded.

STRATIGRAPHY

This is a term borrowed from geology and refers to the superimposition of 'layers' (strata) of soil or other sorts of deposit one on top of the other and which archaeologists strip off in sequence starting with the latest. The basic theory says that the one on top will be later in date than the one underneath although there can be exceptions, like the filling of the heating ducts under a Roman floor, but these are usually obvious in the field. The objects found in the layers can date the deposits and these in turn can date undated objects found with them. Thus the animal bones are dated by the pottery; coins date the pottery; and historical records date the coins. A sequence can be built up for the site and relationships established, for instance between walls and floors, so that walls can be dated even though they are unlikely to produce finds themselves. Groups of deposits can then be put together to define periods and phases, for example all the walls, buildings, rubbish pits and other deposits associated with a house, and the finds used and discarded by the occupants, can be treated as a group.

Some pieces of stratigraphy are simple – there is no mistaking a mosaic floor as you come down to it – but other soil formations are less easy: there may be subtle changes in the soil colour, its texture, the quantity of stone or the appearance of flecks of charcoal or mortar. The recognition of these changes is one of the skills that come with experience, but even so there may be situations where there is no clear stratigraphy. Deposits may gradually grade from one to the other, like the stone rubble filling in the centre of a ditch which may be forming at the same time as stoneless soil on the edge of the ditch. If it is a soil in which there has been a lot of worm or microbial activity, or where the process of formation went on over a long time, thick deposits may build up with no obvious distinctions in them. Under these circumstances it may be necessary to dig in arbitrary spits – this I have been doing on the black soils of central France, which have taken in some cases several thousand years to form, with Neolithic finds at the bottom and Roman at the top. In this case we stripped the soil off in 5 or 10cm spits, and these were then treated as layers. But if stratigraphy is visible, the layers should be excavated separately. As excavation proceeds, layers are recorded, stripped off and the underlying deposit recorded, until the undisturbed bedrock ('natural') is reached. The simple sequence may, however, be more complicated as it is often disturbed by the digging of pits, ditches or footings for houses, and these have to be identified and excavated first, or they will contaminate the underlying deposits.

Thus we can see the primary meaning of the 'context'. It is a discrete stratigraphical deposit that can be distinguished, more or less, from other layers; it will have a horizontal dimension which can be planned, and a vertical dimension which will show up in section. It is usually recognised in terms of its homogeneity in contrast to the deposits which surround it. Thus one floor could be made of mortar, overlain by a dark level containing ash from a fire, in turn overlaid by a tile floor; each of these deposits is distinctive and is treated as a separate entity. Each is also a container of finds and other information (a wall, a floor, a pit, etc.), and as such it is the building block for all archaeological recording and interpretation. However, we already have one extension in the potential use of the context number, and that is an artificial division of a stratigraphical context – either an artificial subdivision according to depth (a 'spit'), or an artificial division horizontally (e.g. the finds from one square metre being kept apart from those from the adjacent squares).

CUTS AND SURFACES

Deposits represent events on a site. However, they are not the only sorts of event; material can be removed as well as deposited. So, if we wish to write the history of a site, these 'negative' events also need to be recorded; indeed, the deposition of a thick deposit of soil can be the product of a few days if not hours of activity, whereas a negative process such as the erosion of a street surface could take a century or more. Harris has identified these sorts of breaks as 'interfaces' and they can be of various kinds. The most obvious example is digging a hole; the boundary between the filling of a pit and the soil into which it is cutting is an interface, and there may be many years' difference between the deposits on either side of the interface; indeed, if the pit cuts into the natural bedrock, the difference can be measured in millions of years. Harris argues that such interfaces should also be given context numbers to give us a complete sequence of events.

This in fact takes us one stage further, as the pit itself will contain deposits. In terms of logic, the number of the interface or cut can be said to *be* the pit, and the material inside it is 'contained' within the cut. What would have been given a separate pit number under the old Wheeler system in fact merely becomes a type of context number.

The logic can be taken further. On Fig. 5.1a, I have imagined a road which, as was common in antiquity, gradually formed a hollow as its surface was worn away. When it went out of use it was filled with deposits, and so it can be treated as a cut, just like any other pit or ditch. If the erosion had not been so great, there might have been only ruts or pot-holes on the surface, which became filled with whatever covered the rest of the road surface, and so they do not contain their own specific filling (Fig. 5.1b); none the less they are also cuts. However, if the surface of the road was really solid, perhaps of cobbles or stone flagging, the wear may have been only a millimetre or two, or perhaps only a polish (Fig. 5.1c). The surface may have been in use for many years but no cut is visible, even though there has been some loss of the deposit. So, logically, such a surface is a cut and may be very important in the chronological sequence of the site, and should have its own number. We need not take the argument much further to show that every clear interface or boundary between layers should have a context number, though very few excavators have yet taken this on board in their recording schemes. A clear example of this would be a mortar floor. One that was in use for only a short period of time would be thick and prominent in section; one that had seen long use would be thin, indeed might be completely worn away in places. Numbering the phases of erosion can bring out such differences. The same is even more relevant for upstanding features like walls; the construction of a wall may lie early in the sequence, but the interface will survive as long as the wall is upstanding, which can be hundreds of years (Fig. 5.4). This can best be

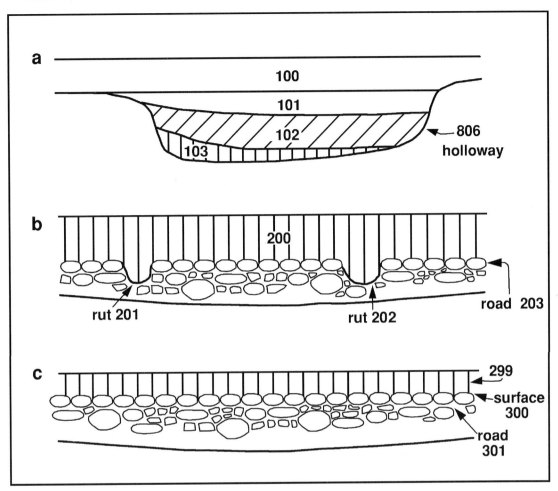

5.1. Hollow ways and road surfaces. If use causes the surface of a trackway to be eroded away, a hollow may form, especially where the track runs up a slope. If this becomes filled with deposits, we can obviously treat it in the same way as a ditch – that is, it is given a cut number and the subsequent filling will 'fill' it (a). Similarly we can do the same for ruts and potholes that might form in the surface of a road surface, but in this case I have shown the fill of the ruts as simply that which covers the road surface, so there is no separate 'fill' for these features (b). However, most excavator would still be inclined to give them feature numbers, especially as they would appear both in plan and section, and indicate a long period of use. In the third case (c), the surface of the road is only marked by wear, which takes the form more of a polish than any measurable erosion. Archaeologists would now tend to give such interfaces a number as well, as they can be important in chronological terms.

understood if we think of wall surfaces; they can be added to vertically, by adding a layer of plaster, paint or wallpaper, in a form of vertical stratigraphy; if the floor surface is raised and the wall repainted, the surface which the floor (and its predecessors) butted against will be different from those lying on the new floor which will butt against the newly painted surface (the paint itself is a layer). Painted surfaces that are no longer exposed can thus be dated by the layers butting up against them (the painting must be earlier), an important argument in, for instance, dating Palaeolithic cave paintings, while those on exposed rock could be of any date up to the modern period. A painted surface can have cuts in it, in the form of inserted window embrasures or graffiti scratched on it.

TYPES OF CONTEXT

We have now defined a number of types of context which can be identified in the field, and we have reduced the range of sequences used by archaeologists to one simple series which encompasses pits, graves, post-holes, ditches, etc. (all of which can be labelled as cuts); street surfaces, wall surfaces, layer boundaries (all of which are interfaces); layers, pit fills, walls (all of which are deposits); arbitrary divisions such as spits; and unstratified material without a detailed context. We can thus potentially create a tick-list to show what sort of deposit we are dealing with:

Stratigraphical layer. This will include everything which has a positive existence and which has been defined using stratigraphical criteria. It will include layers of soil, floors, walls, fillings of pits, etc. It can contain finds.

Artificial layer. This is also a positive deposit, but one which has been defined consciously and arbitrarily by the archaeologist, for instance a spit. It is given arbitrary dimensions by the excavator, either horizontally (e.g. a 1m square) or in terms of depth (e.g. a 5cm spit). It too can contain finds.

No context. This is for material which has lost its context – finds picked up on the dump, or finds that have lost their labels. Some information can be recorded, e.g. the day on which it was picked up, and its possible origin (e.g. the type of soil it was mixed with on the dump). By definition it contains finds.

Cut. This can be used to number pits, ditches, burials, foundation trenches, etc. It cannot contain finds, as it has no substance; only the contexts which fill the cut can have finds.

Horizontal interface. This is a boundary between deposits (layers). It cannot contain finds.

Vertical interface. A boundary between an upstanding feature and deposits which have developed against it, e.g. a wall surface. It does not have finds.

RELATIONSHIPS

Stratigraphical units can have a series of relationships, most of which are of a binary nature. These are:

No relationship. Usually this is not recorded, as there are too many non-relationships, but it can sometimes be important to record, to show that one looked for the relationship in the field but it could not be established.

Above/below. A layer is above, or below, another deposit.

Cut/cut by. A context can cut, or be cut by, another context.

Butts/butted by. A wall may be butted by a series of floor levels. Though the floor is later than the wall, there is no cut, nor does one overlie the other; there is, however, an interface.

Fills/is filled by. Deposits will fill a pit, ditch, grave or other dug feature; the cut will usually be filled by deposits (graffiti cut into a wall surface are one exception).

Equals. The deposit is the same as another deposit. The two could originally have been one, but have been separated by the digging of a linear feature such as a ditch, or the archaeologist could decide to subdivide the deposit for various reasons. When I am making arbitrary divisions I use this a great deal, as I just describe one square or spit in detail ('the type square'), and then make all the others 'equal' the type square.

Certain of the relationships are unique to specific types of deposit. A layer (which is a positive feature) cannot cut another feature; only 'cuts' can cut. Equally 'cuts' cannot cut 'cuts', they can only cut positive deposits such as layers. This is a concept which even experienced excavators sometimes have difficulty in grasping. If a pit is dug, and then a post-hole cut into the bottom of it, we can only demonstrate the relationship if the post-hole cuts through deposits which have accumulated in the pit; if no deposits have formed, logically we cannot demonstrate the relationship. Though we may argue in terms of logic that the post-hole must be later, the relationship is similar to post-holes that form a structure; we can argue that they are contemporary as they form a pattern, or occur in the same part of the stratigraphical sequence, but as they do not cut one another the relationship is not physically demonstrated.

THE HARRIS MATRIX

The most important point to make about the Harris Matrix is that it represents a form of logic which helps us in the analysis of the sequence of deposits which we are digging up, and so in the interpretation of the site. This in turn has imposed the use of forms for collecting data ('context sheets') which have greatly improved the collection of data. There are also now computer programmes which help with this process of analysis. However, the logical analysis which leads on to phasing of the site also needs visual presentation, both to help the analyst and also to present the results comprehensibly to a wider audience. Drawn sections and plans can help, but usually, as in the example Harris chose to illustrate the method, one section or one plan will only tell part of the story, and it is important to collate *all* the information into a single visual presentation. So he went on to develop a way of presenting the data visually, using what is now known (in shorthand) as the 'matrix' or the 'Harris Matrix' (though in fact it is the whole structure which is really the matrix, not just the visual presentation element).

The matrix is usually presented visually as a sort of flow diagram, showing which layers lie on top of which, which are equal to one another, and those which have no relationship. Each of the numbers is put into a rectangular box, and these are then joined by lines to other boxes to signify the relationships. The different sorts of relationships can be demonstrated by vertical and horizontal lines; the conventions which I personally use are shown in Fig. 5.2. Usually the earliest deposits are put at the bottom of the diagram (as in a real stratigraphical section – Fig. 5.3, see p. 71). The bewildering confusion of lines needs to be gradually decreased until only the essential ones are kept – a 'cut' may cut a lot of layers, but only the latest layer that it cuts in the sequence is in fact relevant. Various other ways of presenting these data have subsequently been devised, for instance increasing the size of the boxes according to the length of time a context (e.g. a wall) may have been functioning, and examples of these are shown on Fig. 5.4 (see p. 72). The system has been a great help in thinking more logically about sequences on site, and should be carried out in the field to ensure that important relationships which might otherwise be missed are in fact looked for and recorded. Harris has produced printed

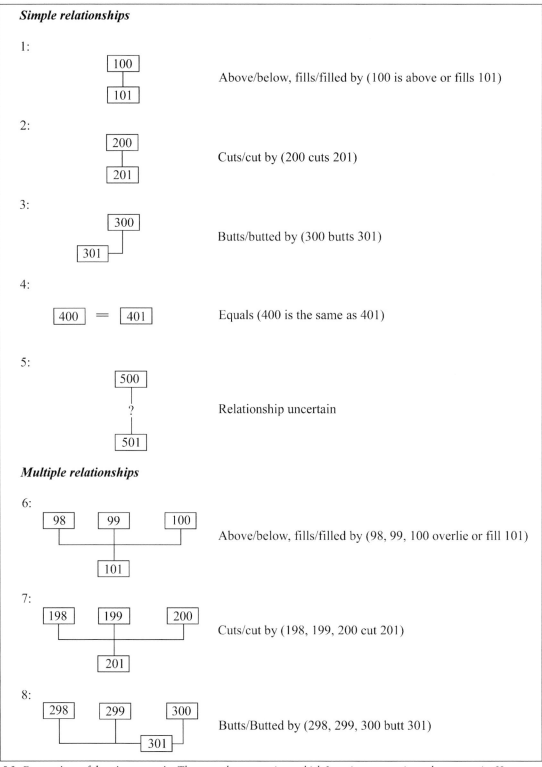

Simple relationships

1:

100

101

Above/below, fills/filled by (100 is above or fills 101)

2:

200

201

Cuts/cut by (200 cuts 201)

3:

300

301

Butts/butted by (300 butts 301)

4:

400 == 401

Equals (400 is the same as 401)

5:

500

?

501

Relationship uncertain

Multiple relationships

6:

98   99   100

101

Above/below, fills/filled by (98, 99, 100 overlie or fill 101)

7:

198   199   200

201

Cuts/cut by (198, 199, 200 cut 201)

8:

298   299   300

301

Butts/Butted by (298, 299, 300 butt 301)

5.2. Conventions of drawing a matrix. These are the conventions which I use in constructing a drawn matrix. However, if you are involved in drawing these matrices, check with your site director which conventions are in use on the site.

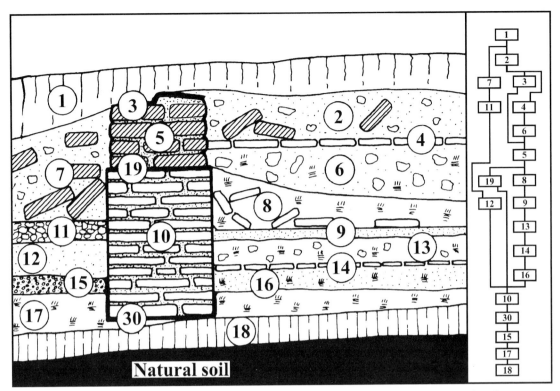

5.3. The site matrix. Every deposit should be given a number. In addition cuts, for instance for pits or foundation trenches for walls, are also given numbers, as logically a deposit which is accumulating cannot cut another deposit. On the context sheet for a cut, it is then possible to list all the layers contained within that cut, useful information both in writing the final report, and in informing specialists about the context of finds, and showing which ones go together as a group. A matrix can then be built up showing the logical relationship between deposits, and these sequences built up into an over-all site sequence. On site as many relationships as possible should be recorded. Some will later prove irrelevant for the construction of the matrix, but it is better to have too many than not enough. The matrices should be constructed on site while digging is in progress so that important relationships are not overlooked. The method is described in full by Ed Harris in Principles of Archaeological Stratigraphy. *This example is taken from his book.*

forms of little boxes with which to do this, but most excavators tend to use large quantities of old envelopes while working them out!

However, contexts and sequences have to be thought through logically. In Figs 5.5, 5.6 and 5.7 (see pp. 73–4) I give some examples of conundrums and brainteasers!

FURTHER DEVELOPMENTS

Potential further simplification of the various number systems used by archaeologists is possible using the concept of the context number, and you may encounter excavators who have already moved on to these wider definitions of a 'context'.

Phasing. In the analysis of the site, context numbers can be used for the interpretation and phasing of a site. Thus, a room of a building can be given a context number, and all the

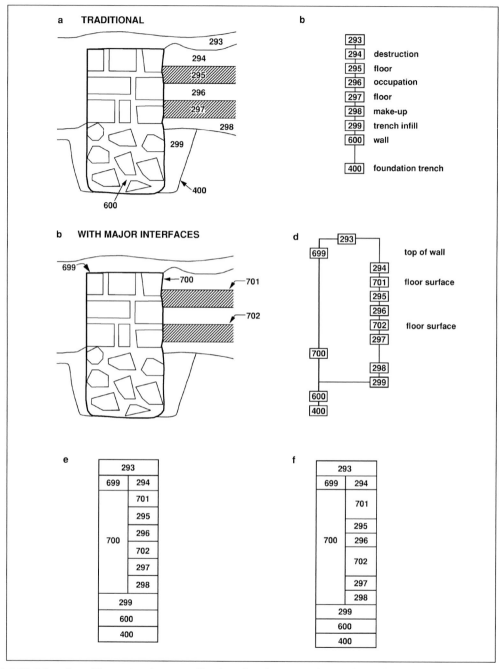

5.4. Wall interfaces. *The section shows a wall with its foundation trench, and the floors constructed while the wall was still in use. The traditional form of the matrix (a, b) simply showing the sequence of deposition does not give this relationship; the wall and any finds in it belong early in the sequence, and it is not the wall but the interface between the wall and the deposits butting against it that is long-lived (c, d). I offer two other ways of depicting this sequence. In the first (e) the size of the box varies according to the number of relationships, so the digging of the foundation trench is small in comparison to that of the wall interface which is long-lived and has many relationships. The other version (f) attempts to vary the size of the box according to real time, giving greater emphasis to the floor surfaces, though even this is relative, not absolute; the filling in of the foundation trench or the laying of a floor may represent a few hours, the floor surfaces could be decades, if not centuries.*

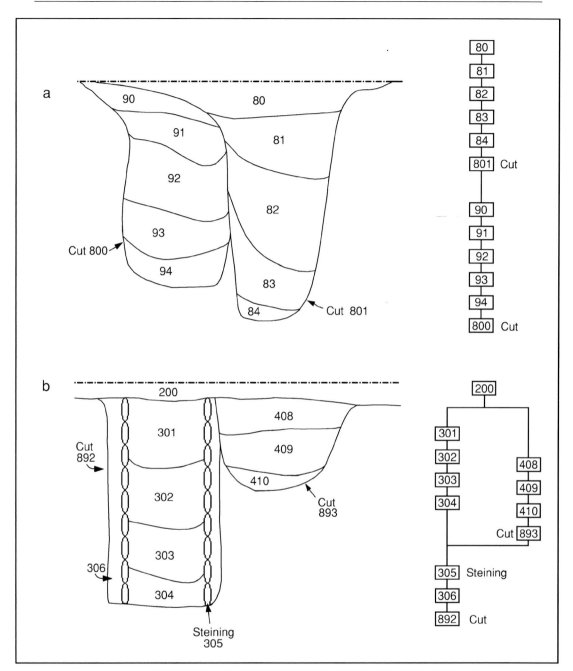

5.5. Pit cuts. *Archaeologists often talk about one pit cutting another. This, however, is not logical in terms of the Harris matrix. What is really happening is that the second pit is cutting the **fill** of the earlier pit (a). In fact, if the pit took a long time to fill up, there could be a long period between the cutting of the pit and the infill. The second case (b) shows the logic more clearly. Though the later pit cuts part of the filling of the well, it is only cutting the construction phase; the actual fill of the well could be later than the pit, but the stratigraphical relationship between the fills of the well and the pit cannot actually be demonstrated.*

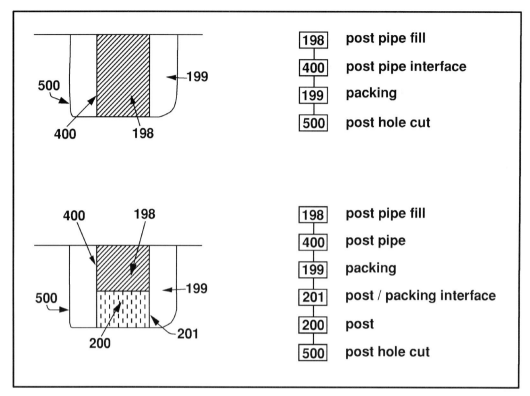

Fig. 5.6.

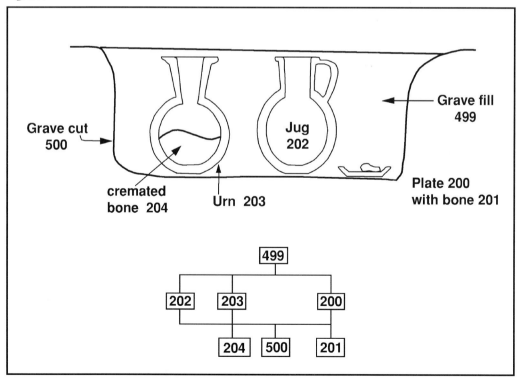

Fig. 5.7.

walls and floors which make it up can be said to 'fill' that context number, in much the same way as contexts can fill a pit. In turn the rooms 'fill' a building, so the building can be given a context number with all the walls, rooms and floors which 'fill' it. Any groups of contexts can be gathered in this way; indeed, if there are alternative interpretations, the context numbers could appear as 'filling' both contexts, for instance if there are two different possible configurations of post-holes (see Fig. 9.2).

Written records. Notes on the site may also be needed, and again the record can be numbered and any mention of deposits can be documented by the concept of 'fills'.

Drawings and photographic records. It can also be used to archive site records. Section drawings and plans can be given context numbers, and these are 'filled' by the contexts which appear on them. The same can be done for photographs and slides; in other words, the whole record of the site and its documents can be brought within one system.

The advantage of this system is that it becomes much easier to search for all of the information on a given context, from its description and the record of it, using computerised databases. On recent sites I have worked on, we have tried to systematise this by giving certain types of number to different categories of context. Thus, plans and sections can all have 8000 numbers, cuts all have 4000 numbers. One can also make distinctions between different types of cut – post-holes are in the 3000s, pits in the 4000s – so that one can tell immediately on a plan or on a label which sort of feature one is dealing with.

DIVIDING THE CONTEXT

Sometimes we need to record more specific information within a context, and so I personally have developed a system of numerical numbering which I call 'bag numbers', as a subdivision of the context. This will be discussed a bit more in the following chapters.

(Opposite, top) *5.6. Post-holes. The normal way of recording a post-hole with packing is shown in the upper version of the matrix. In this the cut for placing the post in the ground is one cut, and the post-pipe is another. However, this is not logical in terms of the sequence, which is: digging the post-hole; placing the post in (so forming the edge of the post-pipe); infill of the packing; rotting of the post; infill of the post-pipe. The situation becomes clearer if we assume that some of the original post is left in. The sequence we then have is: cut for post-hole; post with interface for the post; packing, which then gives reality to the interface between the post and the packing; decay of the post-hole, producing another interface; infill of the void left by decay of the post. In other words, the edge of the post-pipe is in fact an interface for two different phases, one for the post and one for its decay, and there could be a hundred or more years between the two events.*

(Opposite) *5.7. A burial with grave-goods. Dealing with the grave-goods and skeleton in a grave is quite straightforward, as they are all parts of the infill of the grave, and so 'fill' the cut for it. But how do we deal with the contents of the pots, for instance the cremated bones? Though it is part of the infill of the grave, it is not necessarily contemporary with it, as the urn could have sat on the mantelpiece for twenty years. Was the offering of meat on the plate placed there before or after it was put in the grave? How do we deal with this? I offer one solution, which demonstrates that we do not in fact know the chronological relationship between the digging of the grave and the contents of the pots, and makes the point that anything with the cremated bones in the urn is not necessarily contemporary with the burial in the grave.*

Simply, I have a separate field in the database which can be used for the bag number, and these subdivisions are entered in numerical order (whatever the reasons for subdivision), and the information entered on the context sheet. The circumstances in which I use it are as follows:

Special finds. Items that are too fragile to remain with the other finds, or that are special, such as coins (these items are often referred to as 'small finds'), can be removed and given a bag number. Additional specific information such as their three-dimensional position can also be recorded.

Samples. Samples of soil, charcoal and other material can also be given a bag number.

Different excavators. I like to distinguish between the finds of different diggers, so if two people are digging the same context they can be distinguished by using different bags of finds.

Different dates. For security, every day after work the site should be cleared of all finds bags. Rather than people hunting out their bags the following morning, it is easier to give them a new bag, with a new date and a new bag number.

Finds sorting. During finds processing various finds or groups of finds may be sorted out and indeed finally bagged separately. These can include special groups of pottery (e.g. samian ware) or animal bones which will be sent to the relevant experts. These too can be given bag numbers, though this requires close communication between the site and the finds processors, to know how many bag numbers have already been assigned and to ensure that information is entered on to both the context sheets and databases. The advent of on-site computerised recording will help to speed up this process.

COMPUTERS AND DATABASES

A point to which I shall be continually returning is the necessity of following the recording system exactly and in such a way that it is compatible with the computer. On a number of occasions I have had to deal with messes caused by people in the field not understanding how computer systems and databases work, and changing the recording system in some minor way – but sufficiently to make it incompatible with the input on to the computer, thus making subsequent sorting impossible. Having to go through a database changing context numbers 'because someone thought that context numbers could be duplicated as long as they were distinguished by different square numbers' destroys the whole basic logic of using the computer. Fields on a database are defined according to the data that go into them, so for the context number there will normally be a five- or six-digit number or, for the initials of the excavator, the computer will be expecting three letters. Thus, if two contexts are accidentally mixed, or excavated together, a new context number needs to be generated to deal with this mixture; the computer will not be able to accept an entry such as 1289/1295 as a context number, or AFT/BGJ as the initials of the excavator.

How much further context numbers and their subdivisions can go is a matter of discussion. I have already noted how 'small finds' can be incorporated into the system by using 'bag numbers', but as an alternative these too could be given context numbers, as could individual pot-sherds and other finds. They can then be said to 'fill' the context in which they were found, and I note a case in Fig. 5.7 where this might help to resolve a recording conundrum. This, however, is not a case of the technology driving the recording paradigm. The problem had already been created by the change of paradigm which has led to the need for more detailed recording of much larger data sets than our predecessors would have required; the computer and the adjustments we make in our ways of recording are merely a response to the problems initially caused by the new paradigm. This sort of detailed, logical recording was foreign to nineteenth-century antiquarians, or even to excavators such as Wheeler and Bersu, and it is new theoretical developments that have caused the change.

SIX

MAKING THE RECORD

The record of a site basically consists of three elements: the written description; the drawn/photographic record; and the finds. These three elements have to be linked together. Thus, if there is a written description of a deposit, this should relate to deposits which are shown on plans and sections. These in turn should relate directly to the finds that were made in this deposit. This sounds easy in theory, but is never quite so easy in practice – indeed I have been responsible for trying to publish a site in Winchester in which the three elements clearly did not mesh – the description of layers did not tally much with the drawn sections, and the mixture of finds suggested that the site was not dug stratigraphically anyway. But this is easily done – if the excavator digs slightly too deep, or not quite deep enough when taking a layer out, then the correspondence will not be exact.

There are two basic types of recording system which I shall label 'finds-driven recording', and 'context-driven recording'. Though they share much in common, such as the use of contexts, open area excavation, etc., none the less the choice of system has implications about the way material is recorded and labelled, as well as how the labour force is organised on site. I will firstly describe these two differing systems, and then deal with the other features of recording that they have in common, but also noting where they differ (e.g. in the nature of the labelling of finds, and the way the labour force is organised on site).

FINDS-DRIVEN SYSTEMS

As the name implies, this recording system is driven by the recording of finds; each find is individually measured in, and so the material coming off the site will consist of bags, each containing a find with a unique number. This is the ideal way of recording, as introduced by Pitt Rivers, but for many reasons such as time and expense it is rarely feasible in practice. Often digging more with less precision will give us more information than digging less with too great and unnecessary precision.

This is a system which I used on a burial site at Wigber Low (Fig. 5.2). This method really only became possible with the advent of computer technology which allowed the computer to do the plotting of the finds, once the data had been put on the computer and checked for mistakes. At Wigber Low it allowed us to identify scattered cremation, a type of burial rite suspected but never demonstrated before, and it also allowed us to identify excarnation (defleshing the body by exposing it, as practised by modern Pathans) of bodies on the site (see Chapter 11). In the excavations at West Heslerton the excavator Dominic Powesland plotted in every find, and was able to identify the position of palisade trenches, otherwise largely invisible, from the concentrations of finds. At the Palaeolithic cave site at Creswell Crags the amount of stratigraphical deposits that have survived the activities of early excavators is now strictly limited, and most must be kept for future generations. But there is a need to understand the way in which deposits have formed, so one square metre was excavated, over a period of a year or more, and the position and angle of rest of every single bone (mainly rodents such as mice, and insectivores such as shrews and bats) was plotted using three-dimensional computer graphics.

The way in which I have organised this method of recording in the past is to use pierced plastic plant labels, numbered from 0 to 999. I use numbers generated using punched numbers on coloured sticky tape such as Dymo-Tape; this gives me the opportunity of using more than a thousand labels at one time by varying the colour of the tape, but generally I have found a thousand an adequate number. These are pinned together with safety pins in sequences of groups of ten, and then bagged in batches of a hundred. Each digger is given a batch of ten labels and nails, so that when a find is made, the tag can be pinned in position. Each excavator is then responsible for filling out a finds label, which includes the number of the find. The digger will be told the context number, and what the true number is – i.e. is it number 345, 1345, 2345, etc. The label and find are then put in a bag, ready to be taken off site. The plastic plant labels are then measured in (either by using off-set measurements from a grid, or using an EDM); they are then removed, cleaned and pinned together for reuse. The labels are used more or less in numerical order, so that when 999 is reached, the team can start again at 0, but recognising that 1000 has to be added to the label number. If finds are coming out quickly and a second group of labels has been made, this would be the time to change the colour of the labels to avoid confusion on site.

This system means that individuals are responsible for their own labelling. As commonly one layer is being stripped at one time, everyone should know the context; as soon as features have been defined, a digger will be assigned a feature and a new context number. Two sets of data are being collected, which will need to be married together off-site; first the information on the label (see Fig. 6.3); and secondly, the information about the location of the find. It is also useful to identify the digger (by putting the initials on the label), so that the location of any digger on any day can be fixed in case some mistake is found at the plotting stage. Mistakes can usually be quickly identified. First, if the wrong number is written down (e.g. 1345 instead of 2345) this will show up from the date on the label; secondly if the wrong context number is written down, this will generally be recognised by noting that the location of the find is wrong when it is plotted. The implication for digging is that one does not have to regiment the excavation team, for instance, to be digging in a specific square or area on the site; individuals can happily move from one area of the site to another, as their finds will still be located by the fact they are measured in.

However, this method is very time-consuming and expensive, and though the computer can potentially deal with hundreds of thousands of finds, the cost of individually bagging, measuring in and processing every single find is usually prohibitive in terms of time and money. Also, life is too short, and this sort of information may not even be particularly relevant. For instance, if a site has been heavily turned over by worms, the finds tend to sink to a common surface, so only two dimensions may be relevant.

CONTEXT-DRIVEN SYSTEMS

These are the norm on most British excavations. As previously mentioned, measuring in every find, while the ideal, is not feasible at sites where large quantities of finds are turning up, and where resources such as time and money are in short supply. The solution is to group finds together in a box or bag, and these are then treated as a group. The question is, though, what should be the unit of collection? Under the traditional Wheeler/Kenyon system, the collection unit was the trench/layer, and this can still be useful if trenches are being used. However, for open area excavation the bounds of the site are clearly too large, so some form of subdivision is needed. Two related systems have been devised:

Single Context Recording. This is the standard on most excavations in Britain, and is that described in the influential handbook produced by the Museum of London Archaeological Service (MoLAS), and versions of it have been widely adopted not only in Britain but also in other parts of Europe; it is also that described by Ed Harris in his book *Principles of Archaeological Stratigraphy*. The unit of record is the context (the feature or layer as I have described it in the previous chapter) as a discrete stratigraphical unit. Each context is recorded (see below) and when excavated the finds from it are placed together in a bag bearing that number.

Split Context Recording. This is a system which I have adopted in central France, when faced with a wide expanse of black soil in which few discrete stratigraphical units can be identified. We were thus forced to divide up the area into 1m squares, and these became the collecting unit. We were also forced to dig in spits – not an ideal solution. However, we extended the principle of digging in metre squares even to situations where we could identify stratigraphical units (though they were excavated stratigraphically). There were three reasons for this: first, it is always easier to use one uniform system on a site, as this causes less confusion for the team; secondly, it allows us to look at the density of finds across the site, as it is easier to deal with simple geometric shapes such as squares rather than the irregular shapes stratigraphical units normally assume (this is becoming less important as computerised planning programmes such as AutoCAD become more powerful); and thirdly, as demonstrated in Fig. 6.1, it cuts down the potential for contamination, while giving greater flexibility in interpretation. It does, however, generate large quantities of context numbers, and so introduces potential for confusion; ways around these problems are discussed below.

However, with both these systems it is very important that individual diggers are working in specific, defined parts of the site. Each digger must stick to the specified stratigraphical unit, and in Split Context Recording also to the specified square, otherwise finds from different contexts will become confused. In both these systems *it is the context number which gives each group of finds its unique number, and duplication of any number destroys the system.*

CONTEXT SHEETS

The written record should link in with the visual recording, not merely confirming information on drawings, such as the physical relationship of deposits, but also giving supplementary data, for example about the texture and colour of the soil, indeed anything that might prove useful at a later date. Traditionally this information was recorded in a 'site notebook' but as excavations have become more complicated, perhaps with several thousand contexts from a single site, so it has become too easy to miss out a vital piece of

*6.1. Contamination and precision. In this hypothetical case, I have assumed that there is a stratigraphical unit (e.g. a floor level) which has been defined; it has been cut by a later pit which, because of the similarity between the layers, has not been identified. When the layer is excavated, according to the principles of Single Context Recording, **all** the finds labelled with the context number will contain a mixture of finds from the pit and the floor. With Split Context Recording using 1 metre squares, it will be possible to assign most of the finds with certainty to either the pit (402) or the floor, and only **some** of the bags of finds will be mixed (397, 401, 403, 406, 407). In addition, it is possible to compare the finds which come from one part of the floor with those from another. Split context recording is also useful where the subsequent history of a deposit may be different from one area to another. Thus a layer may be covered by an earthen bank in one place, but be left exposed for another hundred years in adjacent areas. This will show up in drawings of the site matrix, but the finds sealed under the bank need to be distinguished from those that are not.*

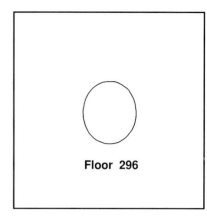

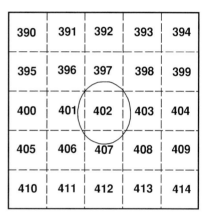

information in the recording, and harder to find the specific data required. During the 1970s there was a gradual move to using a *pro-forma*, with boxes to fill in, to remind people that they should be recording all the data listed in the previous chapter as well as ensuring, for instance, that they check for the presence of items such as charcoal or tile fragments. These *pro-formas* are called 'context sheets', and are still the norm on most excavations (Fig. 6.2). They also require information about where on the site a context is, using a grid reference, and a detailed plan of the context.

When using grid systems it is vital to make sure everyone knows where they are in the grid, and also to make sure that the co-ordinates are written down correctly, as discussed in Chapter 2. But there is the additional problem of making sure that the right context number is written down for the right square. One way of avoiding mistakes in Split Context Recording is to systematise the assigning of context numbers – a line of squares can, say, be labelled from 200 to 220, and the next layer down 300 to 320, so that 200 will be above 300, 201 above 301, and so on. One problem with such grid systems is that people in ancient times, even orderly people like the Romans, were incapable of laying out their sites with any consideration for the site grid. So pits will inevitably appear partly in one grid square and partly in another. However, even if I have a post-hole in the corner of four different grid squares, I keep the finds separate, as it can still be useful to see the whole overall density of finds per grid square over the site. This subdivision of small deposits into several context numbers is not a problem with normal Single Context Recording.

LABELLING FINDS

No find must leave the site without a label. This is one of my absolute rules. Where each find is being measured in, it is usually easiest to make everyone write their own labels, but on large sites with many contexts someone is usually employed to record the context information and to write the labels. This allows for greater efficiency and consistency in recording. On my excavations we start with new finds bags every day, and several times during the day the recorder will come round labelling; finished bags can then be removed from the excavation area. At the end of the day the site is cleared. However, if for some reason – such as heavy rain – it is impossible to get everything labelled, bags are left in their squares for labelling the following day. Individual diggers may be tempted to take their bag off site, thinking that they will remember it, only to find they are assigned to something else the following day. By the time they get back the finds have gone *unlabelled* into the processing system, never to be recognised again – a great waste of everyone's time and a total loss of archaeological information.

I have scientifically proved my own inability to write numbers down correctly – a sort of numerical dyslexia – and I suspect similar failings in others. For this reason I always put additional information into all of my recording so that mistakes can be identified and corrected. If a bag of finds comes in with only a number, one can only tell if it is wrong if, for instance, it is a group of medieval pottery in what should be a Roman layer, but there is no means of knowing what went wrong, let alone correcting it. By recording non-essential information like who dug it up and when, there is always the opportunity of asking the person involved; other information may make it clear what the mistake was. Some site labels are illustrated on Fig. 6.3.

Usually sites are given a shortened code which can then be written as a form of shorthand on the finds, but the labels should have the name of the site in full. Those of us who have worked in museums or departments to which people from all over the country send finds for identification will often have encountered site codes on bags that have become separated from the information about its origin – and often one just has to throw it away. In the old Wheeler days all the labels had to be laboriously written out in full in longhand, but in these days of cheap printing and photocopying there is no excuse for leaving such information off labels. In many European countries this problem has partly been resolved by numbering sites according to the administrative part of the country they have come from – in Germany the *Kreis*, in France the *Département*. For example sites from around Frankfurt are labelled F followed by a number, and those from the Puy-de-Dôme are 63 – the same as car matriculations.

I usually mass-produce *pro forma* labels on a photocopier, though there are problems with paper labels owing to their friable nature. I always put in two labels with groups of finds so that if one becomes damaged, the other will, I hope, survive. Also, if two or three labels are found in the same bag and they do not all say the same thing, you will know that something has gone wrong. The reasons for these precautions will become more obvious when we discuss finds processing. Another problem is that paper, being organic, will rot if it gets damp. Any paper label that may have to stay with finds or samples in a bag for some time must be double-bagged; either place one bag in another bag, and put the label in between the two bags, or put the labels into a small self-sealing bag, and then put this in with the finds or sample. Whatever, the label must not come into contact with the damp material. Alternatively, and better, especially if one is working on a wet site, plastic labels should be used, though these are much more expensive. The labels should be written in some ink that will not fade – preferably Indian ink – but under most conditions a biro will do. It is common practice to write the information on the plastic finds bag rather than using labels. I personally do not approve of this, partly as it takes us back to

CONTEXT RECORDING SHEET

MUSEUM OF LONDON

Grid Square(s) 110-115/210	Area/Section B	Context type DEPOSIT	Site Code XYZ 89	Context 137

DEPOSIT

1. Compaction
2. Colour
3. Composition / Particle size (over 10%)
4. Inclusions (under 10%) occa/mod / freq
5. Thickness & extent
6. Other comments
7. Method & conditions

(1) VARIES FROM LOOSE TO COMPACT
(2) DARK GREYISH BROWN
(3) SAND (40%), SILT (60%)
(4) FREQUENT LARGE FRAGMENTS OF POTTERY AND TILE; FREQUENT MEDIUM AND SMALL FRAGMENTS OF BONE; OCCASIONAL MEDIUM AND SMALL FRAGMENTS OF LEATHER, SMALL FRAGMENTS OF METAL, AND WHOLE OYSTER SHELLS (ALL INCLUSIONS WELL SORTED).
(5) THICKEST TO NORTH (25 MM), SLOPING DOWN TO THE SOUTH/EAST (10 MM), THE LOWER BOUNDARY TO THE NEXT HORIZON IS IRREGULAR.
(6) OCCASIONAL LENSES OF ORGANIC MATERIAL
(7) WEATHER DRY; EXCAVATED WITH MATTOCK.

PTO

CUT

1. Shape in plan
2. Corners
3. Dimensions/Depth
4. Break of slope- top
5. Sides
6. Break of slope- base
7. Base
8. Orientation
9. Inclination of axis
10. Truncated (if known)
11. Fill nos
12. Other comments
Draw profile overleaf

Stratigraphic matrix

121	135								

This context is 137

154	155	148							

Your interpretation : Internal   External   Structural   Other (specify)

PUMPED DEPOSIT

Your discussion :

LARGE QUANTITY OF POTTERY AND BONE AND OTHER MATERIALS, AND WELL-SORTED CHARACTER, SUGGEST THIS IS A DELIBERATE DUMP OF REFUSE.
MIGHT BE ASSOCIATED WITH [95] (STRUCTURE)?

Context same as :   PTO

Plan nos : P 137 (X 2)	Site book refs :	Initials & date NRA 24/8/89
Other drawings : S/E	Matrix location :	Checked by & date SF 2.9.89
Photographs : ☐ Card nos :		

Levels on reverse

Tick when reduced and transferred to plans : ☑

Highest :		Lowest :	

Finds (tick)

None	Pot	Bone	Glass	Metal	CBM	Other BM	Wood	Lea-ther
☐	☑	☑	☐	☑	☑	☐	☐	☑

Environmental samples (23) BULK FOR
Sample nos & type : SIEVING (FISH BONES)

Other finds (specify) :
Finds sample (BM) nos :

Finds Sieving : on site ☐   off site ☐   Metal detecting : in situ ☐   on site ☑   off site ☐

Checked interpretation :

PTO

Provisional period	Group	Initials & date

6.2. Site context sheets. The site context sheet is an aide-mémoire for information that should be recorded. Optimistic forms contain all the information which should be recorded, but most of us use shorter versions, knowing that in the pressure of on-site work, it is better to get the basics properly recorded than have half of the boxes not filled in – and perhaps lose vital information. The examples given are those produced by the Museum of London Archaeological Services (a) and the ones we use in central France (b).Though there is a common parentage, the actual boxes reflect different ways in which we recorded information owing to problems and methods specific to our sites. On the examples from France, for instance, we have introduced a system of bag numbers for subdivisions of the finds, allowing us to include more details such as a three-dimensional location.

GERZAT-PATURAL 1990		AREA M	DATE 14/07/1990	CONTEXT No. 14823
SOUTHWEST Co-ordinate			**Spit level**	**= Type Square**
48 E / 63 N			5	14820

CONTEXT TYPE									
Layer		Cut		Spit	✓	Unstratified		Other	

RELATIONSHIPS	
Cuts	
Cut by	8063
Equal to	14820
Fills	
Filled by	
Above	14923
Below	14733

DESCRIPTION	
Colour	BLACK
Texture	CLAYEY
Geology	CHERNOZEME

COMMENT POSSIBLE CONTAMINATION FROM DITCH 8063

INTERPRETATION (wall, pit, etc.)

FINDS	Date	Initials	Method	Description	Co-ordinates		Level	Back-sight
Bag 1	14/07/1990	JMW	PT	GLASS BEAD	4820 E 6331 N		1·06	1·22
Bag 2	14/07/1990	JMW	PT		48 E 63 N			
Bag 3	14/07/1990	JMW	PT	BRONZE COIN	4832 E 6328 N		1·09	1·22
Bag 4	14/07/1990	JMW	PT	SOIL SAMPLE	48 E 63 N			
Bag 5	16/07/1990	JBY	PT		48 E 63 N			
Bag 6	/ /1990				E N			
Bag 7	/ /1990				E N			
Bag 8	/ /1990				E N			
Bag 9	/ /1990				E N			
Bag 10	/ /1990				E N			

RECORDING (plan, section, photgraph)				
Type	Number	Date	Initials	Comment
		/ /1990		
		/ /1990		
		/ /1990		
		/ /1990		
		/ /1990		
			Recorded by	BCD

Fig. 6.2b.

the Wheeler days of writing everything out in longhand (unless bags are pre-printed), and partly because it hinders re-bagging without re-writing all the information. The more often information is re-written, the more likely it is to become garbled, as human brains seem to have some sort of in-built scrambling device.

It is vital to write legibly. You may be able to read your handwriting, but others several years later may not. Continentals tend to write the number 1 with a tail, which can be easily confused with a British seven, so I insist that everyone 'crosses' the number 7.

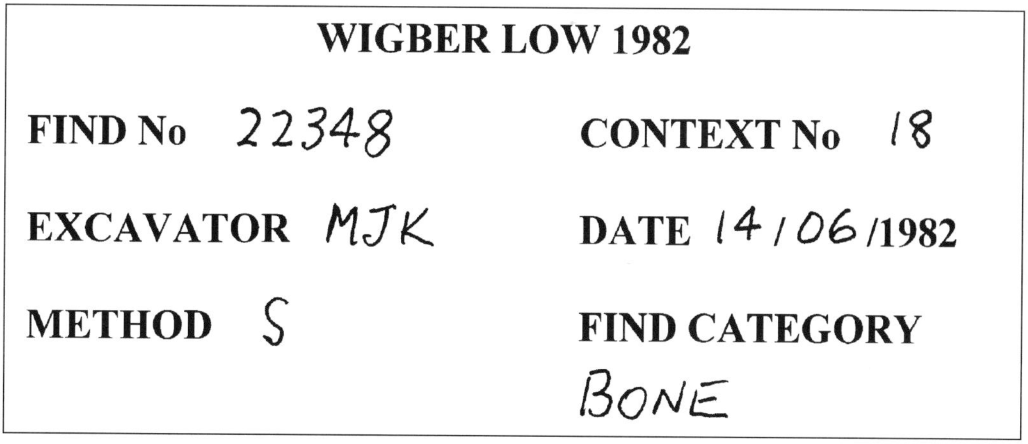

WIGBER LOW 1982

FIND No 22348   **CONTEXT No** 18

EXCAVATOR MJK   **DATE** 14 / 06 /1982

METHOD S   **FIND CATEGORY**

BONE

6.3. Examples of labels. Labels should be specifically designed to give more information than needed so that there will always be a check if, for instance, the wrong context number has been written down. This extra information takes only a few seconds to write down, and can save hours at a later stage. It does also offer potential additional analysis, such as the bias in recovery of individual diggers – some people pick up every little scrap, others have coarser recovery. There will also be differences in recovery from different methods of excavation – picking, trowelling, sieving – and so this should be recorded as well. The first (a) is one which was used for a finds-driven system, the second (b) for one that is context-driven.

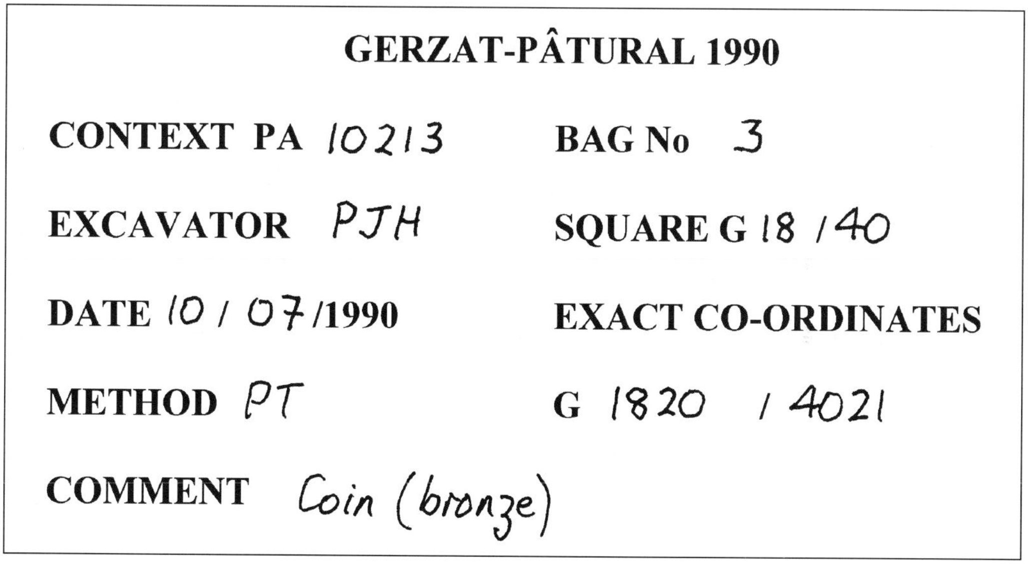

GERZAT-PÂTURAL 1990

CONTEXT PA 10213   **BAG No** 3

EXCAVATOR PJH   **SQUARE G** 18 / 40

DATE 10 / 07 /1990   **EXACT CO-ORDINATES**

METHOD PT   G 1820   / 4021

COMMENT Coin (bronze)

Fig. 6.3b.

Finally, it is up to every digger to check the labels produced by the site recorder for his or her square. Check that the square is right, that the context number corresponds with that on the site label, and that both labels say the same. We all make mistakes!

SPECIAL FINDS

In Context-driven Recording small, fragile or valuable finds may need to be picked out, as they may get damaged or lost if they go through the normal system. Special finds may need extra attention: they may need to be entered on the database so that they can be picked out quickly (especially items like coins or brooches), and we may also want to record their position on the site three-dimensionally. Also, as I have mentioned, I start a new bag every day, so in contexts left unfinished the previous day, or where two different people were digging in the same square, the finds are kept separate. In other cases we have needed to subdivide a context more finely: on one occasion we encountered concentrations of pottery which may have been either deliberately dumped or burnt or broken *in situ* on a funeral pyre, so each square was divided up into 20cm blocks.

To deal with this type of situation, I have developed a concept of 'bag numbers', which give a subdivision for each context number, and allow any different or additional information to be included. This is entered on the context sheet, giving a field record, and the additional information added to the finds labels. Additional fields on our computerised database allow us to enter information identifying the material ('Bronze', 'Glass') and the type of object ('Coin', 'Bracelet'), which provides an instant system by sorting on these two fields for quickly recovering lists of special category finds such as silver coins or glass bracelets. Any special finds that had been missed in the field but turned up at the finds processing can also easily be added, though of course we would not have all the information like the three-dimensional location. The advantage is that all our information is included on a single database without the proliferation of other lists, thus avoiding the duplication of information to be entered.

BAULKS AND SECTIONS

Baulks are blocks of earth that are left in position to record the stratigraphical sequence, and the sequence as preserved is called a section. On many excavations there is often a conflict between the need to understand the vertical sequence and the horizontal plan. Open area excavation aims primarily to produce a series of plans. But there are certain things that can only be understood properly in section, such as soil formation processes. Where relationships, say between walls and other deposits, are not clear in plan, some reference material needs to be left *in situ* to allow reconsideration at a later date. Under these conditions baulks may be left.

There are three kinds of baulk/section:

The *permanent baulk*. As we have seen in Chapter 1, this dominated the excavation methods from the 1930s to the 1950s in Britain (Figs 1.4b, 1.5a). It has the advantage of being always available for reference, but it can mask important information, as in the case of Stanwick. Being static, it may be that the section is not in the right place to answer a particular question. The sides of the excavation area, however, will usually provide a permanent record.

The *cumulative section*. For this a line is chosen for the section at the outset, laid out with string, but the baulk is not left *in situ* permanently. For each phase the section is drawn, adding to what has already been done, then the baulk is removed and the area planned. The baulk is then laid out again on the same line, while the next period is excavated. This is the method advocated by Phil Barker, and used by Martin Biddle in Winchester, notably on the Lower Brook Street site. It has the advantage of allowing a complete plan to be seen and giving complete sections through the site, but there can be a problem if part of the baulk gets eroded or accidentally destroyed, and one is left with a gap in the drawing. It also shares the disadvantage of the permanent baulk in that it may not always be in the right place to answer questions.

Small *temporary baulks*. My preferred solution, these can be set up to answer specific questions, such as the relationship of a wall to the adjacent deposits (Fig. 6.5). It has the advantage that it can be placed where the information is most likely to survive. Once its job is done and it has been recorded, it is removed. The sections for the next phase may be laid out in totally different places. Temporary sections may also be laid out across the fillings of pits and other features to demonstrate the process of infilling.

The production of large-scale section drawings is very much a part of the archaeologist's mental picture of archaeology, and is a throw-back to the Wheeler obsession with sections; indeed, ultimately it derives from geology. My own personal view is that often these large sections show no more than that the fourteenth century came after the thirteenth century – something we already knew!

In addition to the sections, the topography of the site at any one time will be recorded by taking levels across the site. This should be done for each layer. This allows the reconstruction of hypothetical sections anywhere across the site, as well as the calculation of the volume of soil taken out and the relative number of finds to that volume. Levels can be taken at every metre or half metre as the nature of the deposits dictates.

DRAWING PLANS AND SECTIONS

Under the Wheeler system, planning mainly involved showing the interpretation of the whole (or a substantial part) of the site (Fig. 1.6b), with detailed plans appearing in the site notebook. While the production of large-scale plans on sites is still normal, they tend to show less interpretation than in the Wheeler style (Fig. 1.9), so overlays may be needed. Also, they do not show the details of individual stratigraphical units which Single Context Recording requires. It is now normal for a grid to be printed on the back of context sheets, on which the outline of the context can be plotted, with a number of levelled points. This information can then be computerised using AutoCAD, making it easy to see the relationship between different contexts, both vertically and horizontally, so that observations in the field can be checked. These detailed plans and levelling are an essential component of Single Context Recording (discussed in detail by Ed Harris).

The drawing of both horizontal plans and vertical sections employs the same basic technique of taking offset measurements (Figs 6.4, 6.5a). In the case of the plan, measurements at right angles can be taken off one of the grid lines to draw something fairly simple like the outline of a pit. Where the deposit is more complicated, it is usual to employ a portable grid or 'drawing frame', preferably with extending legs so that it can be set up horizontally. Any features can then be sketched in by eye, though there can be problems with parallax if for some reason the frame cannot be placed flush with what is being drawn. In these cases, it is best to use a plumb bob to get a few points fixed first.

A more sophisticated instrument is the pantograph, which allows the drawing of features such as stones to be done very much more quickly, but they are somewhat more expensive than a grid! A number of experiments have been conducted using electronic pantographs (at Siena) and video to take vertical views which can then be edited (Mont Beuvray), but neither method has been widely adopted. More flexible is the use of the digital camera to take vertical pictures which can then be processed on the computer (see below).

As part of the record, 'profiles' showing the outline of a feature are drawn, or more usually 'sections' which show the characteristics of the deposits (soils, stones, etc.). They are usually drawn by setting up a horizontal string, using a level or a line level, and then a tape is laid out along the line of the string (Fig. 6.5a). Measurements can then be taken by measuring up and down from the string at known points. Incidentally, never wrap tapes around nails – always use a bulldog clip or a clothes peg to clip it in position as this is much less damaging, and tapes are expensive. For more elaborate sections, it may be worthwhile setting up a drawing frame. If I have a small section or profile to draw, for instance a post-hole, I usually use a long wooden rule, which can be set up horizontally by clipping it to a nail and placing a spirit level on it, and adjusting until it is level – datum line and horizontal measuring scale are thus set up at the same time. I usually pick out prominent features such as the outline of the feature or lumps of stone to measure in, and then I sketch in the rest by eye.

It is important that these plans and section can be linked with the context sheets and the finds. This is normally done by pinning labels with the context number into the relevant deposit so that it can then be noted on the drawing. On complex sites these context labels may have boxes to tick to show that they have been planned and the section drawn. The labels should be written in ink which will not fade as they have to survive the vagaries of the weather, perhaps for several months.

STYLES OF DRAWING

There are basically three different styles of drawing (Fig. 6.6, see pp. 91–5). First, there is the purely interpretative drawing, in which firm lines are used for the boundaries of features and layers. Secondly, there is the schematic drawing, as advocated by Wheeler, in which some form of symbolic representation is used for different soil types, and some major stones and other objects may be included, but minor characteristics are suppressed or schematised. Thirdly, there is the pictorial style which tries to give some sort of photographic representation of the deposit. It is this latter style that has now become most widely adopted, especially on medieval sites where firm boundaries between deposits are not always apparent. But, as Wheeler points out, this style can lead to woolly thinking, and an interpretative overlay is always useful. Thus subtle changes in soil colour can be shown, which may only become meaningful as excavation progresses; for instance, the fill of a pit may be inadvertently recorded by its colour before it has been identified and defined. For chalk sites I have developed a black and white pen technique in the pictorial style which allows me to fade layers one into the

6.4. Planning. The normal method of planning is to use a planning frame gridded with strings at 10 or 20cm intervals. Using these as guides, features, stones and soil colours can be sketched in quickly and accurately. All site plans should have the following information: name of the site in full; number of the drawing for the site archive; position of grid points with an absolute minimum of two grid points numbered, preferably more; north sign; name in full of the artist; date of drawing; scale of drawing; and all relevant context numbers. And just a note on the conventions used: will someone in ten years' time know that the circle you have drawn is a post-hole and not a stone?

other, and in one case I was able subsequently to identify a feature in the drawing which I had not recognised at the time. None the less, by deciding where to break lines, how thickly to draw them, and how straight, I still impose interpretation on the drawing.

In Germany there has been a long tradition of producing coloured site plans and sections, partly to show the subtleties of layers, partly as a code to show different types of material; this use of colour was introduced extensively in urban excavation in Britain in the 1960s, for example in Winchester. In Exeter we developed a coding system with standard symbols or colours for different types of stone and tile, etc. Most major excavation units have developed their own styles; planning tends to be a specialist activity,

6.5. A parish boundary at Exeter. The wall in the photograph marks the line of a medieval parish boundary in Exeter. In several places its relationship with the adjacent deposits whose finds might date it has been destroyed by later pits and walls. Open area excavation makes it obvious where the evidence survives, so temporary baulks are set up to show the relationship. Note too the use of yellow bars to mark the grid.

backed up by manuals on the norms for the use of symbols and coding. On complex sites attempts at realistic colour representation are now common, and can, if necessary, be reproduced as colour fiche or on a CD in the final report or site archive, but it is more normal to redraw and simplify in black and white for publication.

It is best if drawing is done on some transparent medium. Tracing paper expands and contracts with dampness and temperature, as does paper, and most sites use some form of drawing film, which offers both stability of size, a good surface on which to draw, and transparency so that plans can be overlaid one on top of the other. I usually use 2mm thickness, with a double matt surface so I can draw on either side. My preference is film with a millimetre grid printed on it, but alternatively plain film can be overlaid on graph paper, bearing in mind that the graph paper may expand and contract slightly.

PHOTOGRAPHY AND VIDEO

On most excavations photography is an adjunct of the recording system rather than an integral part of it. It allows for general views of what the excavation looked like, its progress, and detailed views of particular aspects of the site. It provides coloured slides for lectures, and black and white photographs to illustrate the excavation report, and a more objective record. It can also give an idea of the general standard of excavation –

6.6. *Section drawing. The techniques for drawing a section are much the same as those for drawing a plan, in that some form of grid is set up and offset measurements taken (a). Usually the base-line just consists of a levelled horizontal string with a tape to give the scale. Measurements can then be taken at right angles from the string, measuring up and down. These are then plotted on graph paper. Various styles of drawing have been developed. The simple outline drawing (b) where the strata are merely shown as lines is useful as a guide to interpretation, but does not usually represent an adequate record of the evidence – divisions between strata are not always as black and white as depicted here. The layers do not make sense in terms of what we know about pit fillings, but we cannot reinterpret on the basis of this drawing. The technique devised by Wheeler (c) in which standard symbols are used to represent layers is little better. Gerhard Bersu at Little Woodbury developed a more 'pictorial' or 'photographic' style, originally recorded in colour in the field, but as black and white for publication. Here reinterpretation is possible. However, the various pictorial styles which are in use nowadays can become very woolly and unclear. The draughtsman must be aware of what is being depicted and the interpretation. Most sites have their own forms of representation – use of colour for stone identification, etc. The style shown here (e) was one developed at Owslebury. Flints are filled in black, chalk left white. Soil can then be shown by vertical lines, varying the thickness of the lines, the distance between them, and how broken they are, to show intensity of brown colour, and straight or wobbly lines to show looseness (e.g. straight is clay). Other symbols were devised to show brick, bone, clay, burning, etc., and the sections annotated. Only the outline of the features is shown in hard lines, but clear divisions in layers are shown by breaking the line consistently at the boundary between layers. Where there is no clear division, the layers are allowed to fade into one another. All section drawings should have the following information written on them: name of the site in full; number of the drawing for the site archive; location of the section (with grid references if there is a grid); name in full of the artist; date of drawing; scale of drawing; position of datum line, and orientation (north–south, etc.); height of datum above sea level or site datum; and all the relevant context numbers. I also include any additional notes thought worthwhile, e.g. about interpretation, and I usually try to include a matrix of the deposits.*

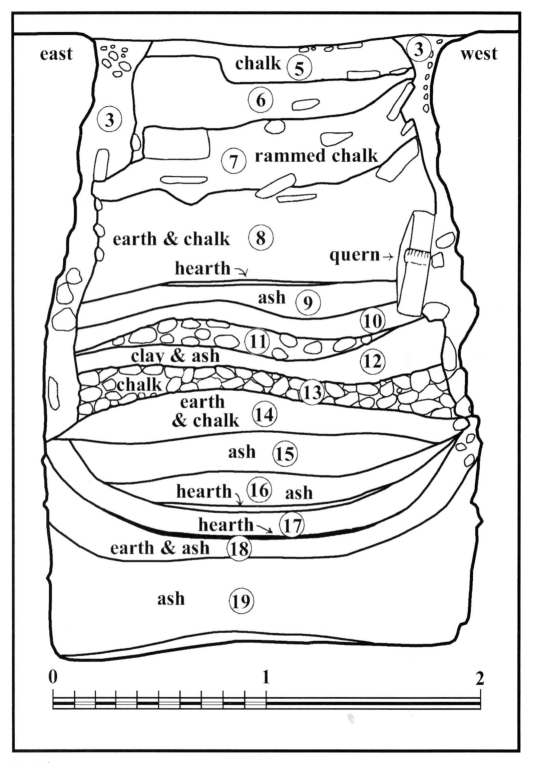

Fig. 6.6b.

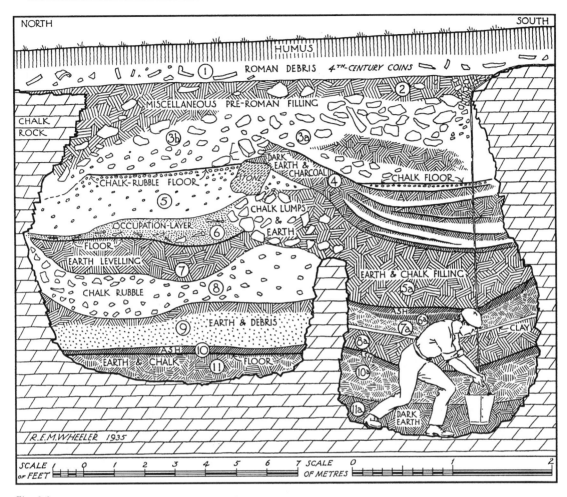

NORTH   SOUTH

HUMUS

ROMAN DEBRIS   *4TH-CENTURY COINS*

①   ②

CHALK ROCK

MISCELLANEOUS PRE-ROMAN FILLING

③b   ③a

CHALK-RUBBLE FLOOR

DARK EARTH & CHARCOAL

STONE

④   CHALK FLOOR

⑤

CHALK LUMPS & EARTH

OCCUPATION-LAYER ⑥

FLOOR

EARTH LEVELLING

⑦

CHALK RUBBLE ⑧

EARTH & CHALK FILLING

⑤a

EARTH & DEBRIS ⑨

ASH

⑦a   ⑥a

CLAY

⑧a

ASH

EARTH & CHALK ⑩   FLOOR

⑪   ⑩a

⑪a

DARK EARTH

R.E.M.WHEELER 1935

SCALE of FEET   0   1   2   3   4   5   6   7   SCALE OF METRES   0   1   2

Fig. 6.6c.

ideally showing clean trenches, well-cut sections and properly labelled features. I personally like to concentrate on detailed photographs of features, both as a simple record to supplement drawings, and to show any aspects of the site which I do not understand. I also like views of work in progress, as these can remind one at a later date of the processes and decisions that went on. The overall formal view of the excavation can be useful, but usually it is not detailed enough to show information other than of the most general kind, and it can take an inordinate amount of time to prepare the site – perhaps several days – merely to clean it for a photograph, and repeated scraping can be damaging to the site. Many archaeologists would suggest that a site should be kept clean enough for photographs at any time, though, as I argue below, some preparatory work is usually needed. General views of sites are best taken from a height. Many sites have access to some sort of photographic tower or perhaps fire engines or elevators for repairing streetlights; even tethered balloons have been used to give aerial views.

Attempts to take vertical photographs of the site to replace plans have met with some success, but there can be problems of distortion if the camera is not high enough, and

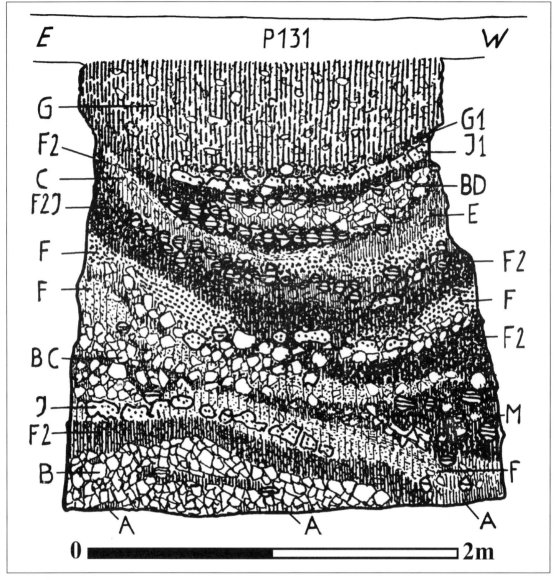

Fig. 6.6d.

proper photogrammetry can be expensive. Photography has never taken over from drawing for a couple of reasons. First, the results are not instant, and a lot can go wrong between taking the photograph and getting prints, though the advent of digital cameras is overcoming this. Unless there is instant access to a darkroom, work may have to stop until it is certain the record has come out. Secondly, photographs give an overall view – they record everything. All drawings are selective and interpretative, and it is possible to include on them identifications of the stones and other items, context numbers and comments. Digital cameras allow overlapping vertical photographs to be taken simply using a hand-supported rod, and the photographs can be blended together using the computer, and the final images manipulated to remove distortion; contrast or the direction

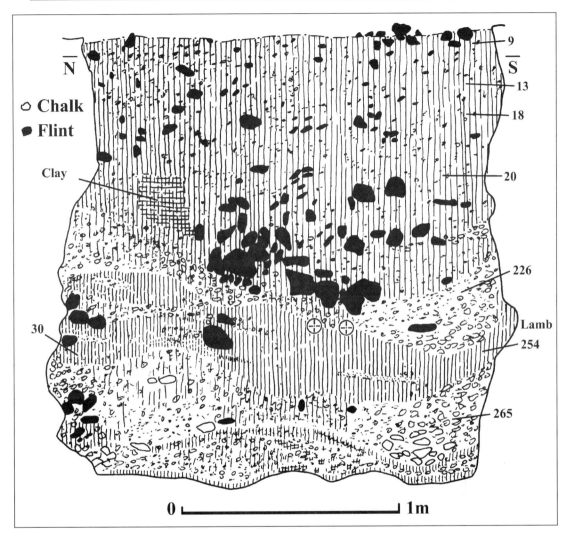

Fig. 6.6e.

of lighting can be varied. It also allows instant printout of photographs on a printer, and we are likely to see a big increase in their use in the next few years; indeed, in Italy there are now specialists who travel from site to site producing very effective visual images to supplement the drawn plans.

Cleaning a site for a photograph is something of an archaeological fetish, not only because judgement will be passed on the quality of an excavation from what the photographs show (what abominations may occur on site between one photograph and another is nobody's business), but a poorly prepared photograph will very often not show the information required. Edges must be extra sharp to make them show up, and picked out with the point of a trowel, colours must be brought up as well as possible, perhaps by spraying with water, and stones and other features must be made to stand out from their background. Though dust and other rubbish must be removed, try not to use a brush, as it smears the deposits, and again a vacuum cleaner is ideal if it is available.

Cleaning should logically start at the highest point, so that dirt does not fall on already cleaned areas, and try to organise the cleaning so that you do not have to step on something already scraped. Cheating does take place at times with 'differential' cleaning; for example, to make a post-hole stand out, you clean the area around it better than the post-hole itself; in other words, the camera can be made to lie. Indeed, a picture of a row of emptied post-holes or stake-holes does not mean they necessarily existed! To give an idea of scale, painted rulers or ranging poles are arranged, either parallel with the frame of the photograph, or with the subject being photographed, and sometimes human figures are introduced, which can bring out the sexist attitudes of certain male directors. Extraneous items such as buckets and trowels should be moved out of the way as they distract from the subject.

The advent of cheap video has still not made a major impact on site recording – film was previously too expensive for extensive work, but video film is now both cheap and reusable. General shots of work in progress and of the excavation at various stages can be useful as a general site record, and at a later stage, if it is good enough, it can be used in public presentation of the site. Some excavators use video as part of the main record, to record sections and other features in detail, and even general comments each day on the site and the interpretation. Good use of video is, however, a skill. Beginners tend to jump from shot to shot, or to pan too quickly; it is better to concentrate on one item for some time. I also take close-ups of people's faces as they work which can be used to fill in gaps in the film ('cutaways'). There is a slight doubt about the durability of video film as a medium for long-term storage of information, but this may be solved by the advent of videodisk and CD technology.

CLEANING AND WEATHERING

The sort of cleaning that has been described for photography is also often essential preparation for planning – features are rarely instantly visible. A complex site, like the timber buildings from Yeavering mentioned in a later chapter, may need several cleans before it is good enough to see all the details.

Archaeologists are worse than farmers in their complaints about the weather! What we usually need is good dry weather with the occasional day of light rain, preferably when the site has just been cleaned – but not heavy rain as that can cause puddles and erosion gullies. Rain will bring up the contrasts of colours and textures, and make the features more visible. On some sites, such as gravel, it may even be necessary to note the position of features by outlining them with a trowel before they dry out again and disappear. At Yeavering, for example, Brian Hope-Taylor got up at first light one morning after overnight rain to take all the major photographs of one area in which little had been visible up to that time; the differences quickly disappeared again as the sun dried out the site.

Sites should be observed in as many different weather and lighting conditions as possible. On some sites features may only start to appear after weathering, perhaps even a slight frost to break down the soils and bring out contrasts between heavier and lighter soils (Fig. 6.7). Lighting may also be important – a rising or setting sun can emphasise colour differences. Drying conditions can also be very important – small features like post-holes may be more water-retentive and will only show up after the rest of the site has dried out.

6.7. Weathering at Aulnat. This site was exceptionally difficult to dig, as the features were filled with black soil which cut into black soil. When the soil was wet, everything was a uniform black; when dry, a uniform grey. However, pits and other major features did show up as the site dried out, and approximate edges of features could be defined. The effects of frost and rain on the surface eventually broke down the filling of the pits so that they showed up as slightly grey patches – the photograph shown here was taken after this process had happened, and just as the sun was going down, which picked up the features as slightly greyer areas. Even so, I had one feature, measuring 1 × 3m, which I could see as it cut the natural sand and which was visible in terms of its finds, but which proved impossible to define accurately at a higher level. Stratigraphy is not easy!

There are mixed feelings about the advantages of covering sites – polythene covers may allow work to continue in all weather conditions, and may be essential if there are delicate features such as burnt timbers in position, or a sand feature like the Sutton Hoo boat which could be destroyed by heavy rain – indeed, most sites can be eroded by a torrential rainstorm. But covers also keep out the light, and make planning, even digging, difficult. Small covers that do not cover the whole site concentrate water, and can do more damage; movable covers on wheels are a luxury few excavations can afford. Artificial lighting also tends to disguise soil colouring, and directional light produces too much shadow contrast for normal digging. Though various people have experimented with sprinkler systems, I have still to encounter one that can properly simulate light rain. Garden sprays, however, are almost part of a planner's essential equipment on dry sites. But as I said, archaeologists are never satisfied.

Seven

Finds Processing

When the finds leave the excavation site, especially if they have any distance to go to the finds processing shed, they should be properly sealed up so that nothing can fall out, or drop into another box or bag. They should also have been properly labelled. Directors of excavations now face a dilemma – whether the finds should be washed and marked straight away, which is the ideal, so that any problems can be identified and dealt with quickly, or whether enough finds should be allowed to accumulate to keep everyone employed if there is a wet day or two. Sod's Law usually comes into play here – as soon as the backlog of finds processing is completed, it starts to rain. The vital thing, however, is that material should be processed fairly rapidly, and certainly before labels rot or memories become too faded about where specific finds may have come from. Large excavations with large numbers of finds will have a permanent team working on finds processing. Some people love it, others loathe it – but it does give everyone an opportunity to see most of the finds, which is impossible on site; indeed, some of the best finds can be made during pot washing, once the dirt has been removed. But anyone working on site should know about what happens to the material coming off the site, and most diggers can expect to do some finds processing, and most excavations have a rota. A good finds assistant or director will tell you about what you are working on – the types of pottery, the identification of bones, etc. – which increases interest, and so, hopefully, the quality of your work.

The amount of finds processing done 'on site' will vary; at one extreme the dirty finds will disappear from site back to the site base, never to be seen again by the excavators; at the other, some of the specialists working on the detailed finds reports will be working on site. It is normal to deal with the basic washing and marking as part of the excavation, and some of the sorting of the finds, so that finds can be passed on to the experts. Commonly, too, the basic site record and listing of finds are computerised as well. Everything must be made ready for, if not move seamlessly into, analysis and publication.

Finds Washing

On most excavations most finds will need washing (Fig. 7.1), but there may be a policy for certain categories not to be washed. Generally these will be obvious (though I did have someone who attempted to wash a soil sample!). Basically anything that is likely to be harmed by washing is left unwashed. This category includes all metal objects, charcoal and other carbonised material, shale, and fragile pieces of bone or pottery, but you should be warned by the person in charge of washing what to look out for. On some excavations specialists may have asked for certain categories not to be washed, such as flints needed for micro-wear analysis (studying the ancient wear caused by using a flint), or teeth for wear analysis.

7.1. Pot washing. *Remember the basics: never leave any finds unlabelled; weight the labels down; avoid every possibility that finds will get mixed – one bag of finds to a box; make sure that there are no holes in the paper; if you pick up a find from a box which is drying, remember which box it comes from; don't wash metal, charcoal or anything that may get damaged; work as efficiently as possible, keeping movements down to a minimum; change the water regularly.*

I usually prefer to work with two bowls of water, one for washing and the other for rinsing, but certainly the water should be changed regularly, as dirty water will leave a thin film of dirt on the finds. Warm water does no harm, and is welcome to cold hands on cold days, but don't put detergents or anything else in the water unless you are told to – sometimes finds need treatment with a gentle acid to remove incrustations. My preference is to wash with a toothbrush, as the bristles can get into all the small nooks and crannies, but it is useful to have a small scrubbing brush or nail brush for larger finds, and paint brushes for some of the more delicate items. Others prefer to wash with a sponge, as the hard bristles of brushes can remove the surface of soft pottery.

Select a box which is large enough to contain the finds from the bag you are washing, and make sure it is empty – something may have got left behind from a previous group of finds. Make yourself as comfortable as possible, and arrange everything so that you keep your movements down to the minimum, i.e. the dirty finds box and the clean finds box should both be within easy reach. First spread out the finds to be washed and pick out anything that should not be washed, and put it in the washed tray where it will not get wet.

There are three golden rules. First, *never put more than one group of finds in a box*. If finds are being moved around, it only needs one slip and they will be irretrievably mixed; someone tripping over the box can have the same effect. I usually reckon to have a good collection of small and large boxes, such as cheese boxes for small groups of finds and fruit boxes for large groups, the latter with paper in them – but make sure there are no holes in the paper that finds can fall through! Secondly, *never leave finds unlabelled.* If the bag has come in from the site with two labels, one must be left with the unwashed finds, while the other should be the first thing placed in the tray for the washed finds. If you get called away in the middle of washing, or go off for a tea break and get run over by a big red bus, it will be clear to your replacement which washed finds go with which unwashed finds. Thirdly, *weight the labels down.* If the finds are going somewhere, e.g. into the open air, to dry, the wind may well blow the labels out of the box. Use one of the finds to weight the label, but if there is nothing suitable, get a stone – but make sure it is something like a brick that won't get mistaken for a find! These precautions should quickly become automatic when starting a new group of finds.

Some finds such as bone and pottery can take a hard scrub, but be careful not to break bits off the bone, and make sure you are not removing the surface or painted decoration from the pot sherd. If you are, stop at once. There is a tendency to wash the surfaces of the pots well, but not the broken edges. In fact, it should be the other way round, as at the sticking-together stage it is the broken surfaces which need to be cleanest. Never tip the finds into a bowl of water to soak. This can be disastrous for fragile finds, and small finds may get lost in the sludge at the bottom of the bowl. After you have washed all the large pieces, you may be left with a pile of dirt in the finds bag which may contain small finds like teeth; this can be dealt with by tipping it into a plastic food strainer, swirling it round with a paint brush, and picking out the finds. Usually this is enough to get them clean. Do not spend an inordinate amount of time scrubbing every little item – they only need to be clean enough for identification. Finally, environmentally and financially conscious directors will ask you to wash dirty finds bags so that they can be recycled on site, but make sure you discard any with holes in; the cleaned finds should be bagged in clean bags.

FINDS MARKING

Finds are marked so that objects from different context numbers can be mixed up together, but will still be put back into the correct context. This may happen at the pot-sticking stage, when fragments of the same vessel may come from several different contexts, or perhaps the bone specialist may want all the left humeri of sheep out at one time to allow a visual comparison. It is therefore vital that the items should be marked legibly! Marking is normally required for museums as well, so that individual pieces can be identified in a century's time. The British Museum had a policy of not marking objects on loan. Inevitably objects became separated from their labels, and in most cases all one could say about the unmarked object was that it belonged to someone else and not the British Museum – but to whom?

Normally marking is done with a mapping pen and Indian ink. Mont Beuvray has been experimenting with automatic marking by adapting a machine used for marking eggs! The briefer the code, the quicker marking is – thus there should be a site code (normally an abbreviation of the name of the site, see Chapter 6), and the context number, or the number of the find. It is vital to mark as quickly and efficiently as possible, or you will get bored! It is like working on an assembly line, so keep movement down to a minimum. Sit at a table, with the unmarked finds to your right, and the marked to your left (vice-versa for the left-handed), and do the marking in between them. I have had numerous arguments with volunteers who think it is just as efficient to sit on the ground, and balance what they are marking on their knee – it is not; you only do about 25 per cent of what can be done at a table.

Obviously items too small to be marked are not done, nor are metal objects or materials that are too soft, like charcoal. For bone, I do not bother with small broken fragments, but I do mark anything that is reasonably identifiable. For pottery, you should work on the principle that the pot may need to be restored and put on exhibition, so the mark should not be too visible. The best places are on the base, under an overhanging rim, on the inside of a jar or cup, or on the outside of a bowl or plate. Do not mark over decoration or painted surfaces if this can be avoided, nor on the broken edge as this will become invisible if the pot is stuck together.

FINDS BAGGING

The finds need to be allowed to dry out well before bagging, or the moisture will cause labels to rot, especially if polythene bags are being used. I prefer polythene as one can see at a glance what the contents are. Self-seal bags are best for small finds, but make sure they are properly closed after putting the find and label in! I also try to use bags which are much larger than the group of finds, so that the top of the bag can be folded over; if there are too many finds, especially animal bones, the bag will be punctured and torn. Don't tie the tops of bags – either fold them over, or use tags to close them; whatever, make sure that finds can't fall out easily.

There are two basic principles in temporary storage of finds. One is to make it easy to locate any particular find or group of finds, and the second is to keep subsequent sorting down to a minimum. So individually numbered finds may be sorted into consecutive numbers for initial cataloguing, and then subsequently into their find category (bone, pot, etc.) to be sent off later to the relevant specialist for identification. Groups of finds may be stored in their context number sequence, though sometimes they may be re-sorted into their stratigraphical sequence, so that all the contents of one layer or of a pit are in the same box; this will aid study. But usually some temporary system has to be adopted, as finds tend to come through the system in a somewhat haphazard order.

On most excavations some initial sorting takes place at bagging, usually into category of find, so that, for instance, all the animal bones are stored together, ready to be sent off to the bone specialist. This may need some basic training. Bone, pottery, tile and glass may be fairly obvious, but more detailed sorting of certain categories of finds may be needed; for instance, samian pottery and wine amphorae may be going to different specialists and will need to be sorted out. The difference between brick and amphora may not always be clear to the untrained eye (or even to the trained). For coins, there will be some form of indexing system, nowadays usually computerised, and preferably linked in with the site record so that one can have an instant list of all the coins and their stratigraphical position for writing the report.

Nowadays, with the greater move towards quantification, some basic counting may also take place at this stage, for instance the weight of the different categories – pot, bone, amphora – and perhaps counting of the number of fragments. I also try to include notes on items of special interest – certain types of readily identifiable pottery, presence of worked or cut bone, sawn horn cores, and so on. This does mean that the finds processing side of an

7.2. Computerisation. Wherever you work on an excavation, you are more and more likely to have to deal with inputting of data on micros. Excavations generate huge databases in the form of descriptions and relationships of contexts, and identification and analysis of finds – machines with hard disks are essential. The quicker this data is put on to the computer the better. But always, when inputting, remember to save the data regularly (every 15–20 minutes); make a back up file or disk (every hour, or half day depending on the type of micro), and get a hard copy (print out) once a day. Keep a copy of the back-up disk in another building so that if a disaster like a fire or theft occurs, you do not lose all your data. Computers are wonderful devices, especially at losing data!

excavation is taking more and more time in comparison with the time spent excavating, but the information available at the end of the excavation allows much more sophisticated instant comment, and much greater ease of manipulation of the data at later stages.

FINDS ANALYSIS

Every excavation project has to go through the basics in the field, but with long-term projects the only hope of keeping abreast of the data as it is coming in is to start work on the analysis as soon as possible – traditionally archaeologists claim that it takes about three to four times as long to do the post-excavation work as the excavation itself. So you may find that some of the specialists will be working alongside the excavation, and may require help. Such work may include the preparation of the site archive for publication – drawings, computerisation of the data (Fig. 7.2), identification of animal bones, and processing of specialist samples, or work on the pottery, sorting, sticking, identification and drawing. This lies beyond the scope of this book, but there are lots of both general and specialist books dealing with these matters, and the general trend in the last twenty years in both professional and amateur archaeology is for individuals to have one or two specialist interests and skills that they can offer a project – drawing of plans and sections or finds, or detailed knowledge about computing, geophysics, or specific types of pottery, etc.

EIGHT

STONE BUILDINGS

In the previous chapters we have considered a number of generalities which most excavations share in common. I now want to move on to some of the problems encountered with specific types of site, such as stone and timber buildings, burials, and so on. Stone buildings in some ways may seem the easiest sorts of structure to deal with, and to a certain extent this is true, as long as the walls are well preserved or are of substantial construction. They are less easy when it comes to the excavation of robbed structures. Equally, it is a sobering exercise to deal with both the underground archaeology and the standing remains of a building, and ask the question, if the foundations only had survived of this building, how much of its history might I have been able to detect?

Good survival of substantial remains can also be a hindrance to archaeological research, with an over-emphasis on the structures themselves, rather than on what they mean. Thus, research on Roman villas tended to degenerate into a study of the plans and architectural history – a worthy study in its own right – but this led to excavators ignoring the agricultural structures, the question of how the building functioned, the economic evidence of animal bones and seeds, and indeed other sorts of Roman rural sites which did not possess substantial buildings. As a result, Roman archaeology was that much the poorer. Because Roman buildings seemed easy to excavate, it also led to a conservatism in techniques, and in Britain the Wheeler grid method lingered on longest in Roman archaeology, persisting until the late 1960s and early 1970s.

The basic questions that one should be asking of a building include: when was it built; what periods of expansion and contraction can be recognised; and when did it go out of use; but you should also ask how it functioned; what were the various rooms used for; what sort of people lived in it; and what was the source of the materials and money for it to be constructed? To answer the last group of questions it is necessary to look at the material and economic evidence; this will not be discussed in this chapter, but these questions should always be in the back of the excavator's mind.

RELATIVE CHRONOLOGY

The structure of the building itself often provides the basic sequence of construction, from the materials and techniques used, to the physical relationship of the various walls. It is only when you start to look at walls in detail that you begin to realise the multiplicity of techniques that can be used, starting with the fundamental contrast between mortared and drystone walls. Archaeologists mainly have to deal with foundations, and these may be of stone, even if the rest of the building may have been carried up in clay and timber, or in cob or pisé (dried clay bricks). In certain cases, as in medieval Exeter, clay may be used as the bonding material. So an analysis of the mortars or clays may give an initial division of the walls into possible phases. Sometimes the contrast between the colours of various mortars may be obvious: greys, yellows or cream-coloured. Sometimes the important factor may be the inclusions – the grains of the sand mixed with the mortar, their colour, size and petrology, or the addition of fragmented brick or other materials. In all cases samples of mortar from each wall should be kept, both for reference and if necessary for chemical and physical analysis. In Winchester certain coloured mortars seem to be typical of certain periods on different sites across the town, suggesting that there were standard mortar recipes at different periods.

The process of construction should not be confused with periods. Most people naturally assume that building starts with the laying of the foundations, and proceeds upwards course by course. This need not necessarily be so. At the Burn Ground long barrow Grimes was able to work out the sequence of construction of the drystone revetment wall because it was started at one point, and then the slabs were piled against this. Thus the stones were not horizontal as in modern Cotswold drystone walls, but sloped at an angle. The town wall of Roman Silchester was built in sections, using very different mortars and construction techniques, and it appears that each section was built to its full height before the next was constructed (Fig. 8.1). The foundations of some Saxon churches are built separately, and the construction may have been carried out in sections, as at the tower house at Montarrenti (Fig. 8.2). Limited excavation of such buildings might lead one to believe there were several phases of building rather than just one.

There are three basic ways in which foundations of walls are built (Fig. 8.3): first, trench-built, in which a trench is dug and filled with concrete, masonry, rubble, chalk or some such solid material, and the wall is built above ground on this foundation; secondly, free-built, in which the wall is constructed within the foundation, leaving a gap on either side (foundation trench) which then has to be filled up with soil; and thirdly a combination of the two. These methods can give a clue to the different periods of construction. The best evidence for phasing, however, comes from the physical relationships of the walls themselves. It is common to find more recent walls simply butted up against a pre-existing wall, and the relationship is obvious (Fig. 8.4). But to make a firmer joint, a groove may be cut into the first wall, and the second wall slotted into it. Again, this is usually relatively easy to recognise, but it is tricky if both walls have subsequently been robbed (see below).

ABSOLUTE CHRONOLOGY

Walls themselves very rarely produce direct evidence of their date, although the odd coin can turn up in the mortar. In any case, mortared walls are often left intact by archaeologists, perhaps because they are too solid to demolish, but sometimes so that they may be conserved for public display. Documentary evidence may be available, but even so it is always important to establish the relationship of a building to the surrounding strata, if only for the wall to provide a fixed point for dating the pottery. But usually it is the other way round, and the wall is dated by the associated finds. This was one of the main failings of the Silchester excavations in the 1890s, and in *Archaeology from the Earth* Wheeler demonstrated graphically how the tradition of following walls could destroy all

8.1. Silchester town wall. This is an example of the use of the trench for excavation. The aims were very limited: to see the amount of destruction caused by roots of trees in advance of conservation, and also to confirm the sequence of the construction of the town defences, and provide more evidence for their dating. As elsewhere, it was found that there was an earthen bank, which had been cut back for the insertion of the Roman wall in front. As chronology was important, the position of every find was plotted in, and projected on to the section. Incidentally, the trench happened to hit the junction of two sections of wall, built by two different gangs of workmen. The mortars and the ways of constructing the string courses (levels of horizontal slabs which increase the lateral stability of a wall) are all slightly different, especially the method of construction of the offset where the wall was narrowed. The left-hand side of the wall was constructed first.

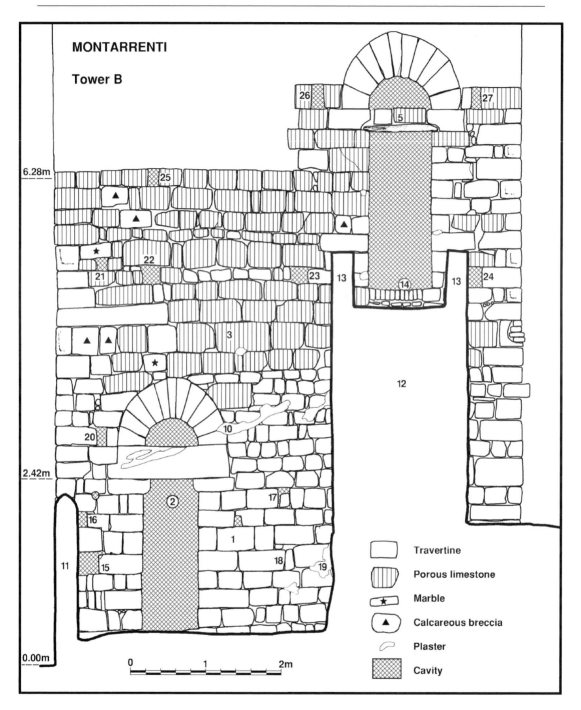

8.2. Tower house B at Montarrenti near Siena in Tuscany. This house was built in the later twelfth century. The analysis by Roberto Parenti is an early example of context numbers applied to a standing building; it shows part of the west wall. One of the archaeological problems was to relate its foundation trench with the archaeological levels adjacent, and it was found that only for about the length of a metre did this relationship survive – it might easily have been destroyed by trench excavation before its full importance was realised. The wall has been drawn stone by stone, except where the stones are masked by surviving plaster. Because of the inaccessibility of this high building, the drawing was prepared from photogrammetric photographs, which then had to be 'corrected' for the effects of

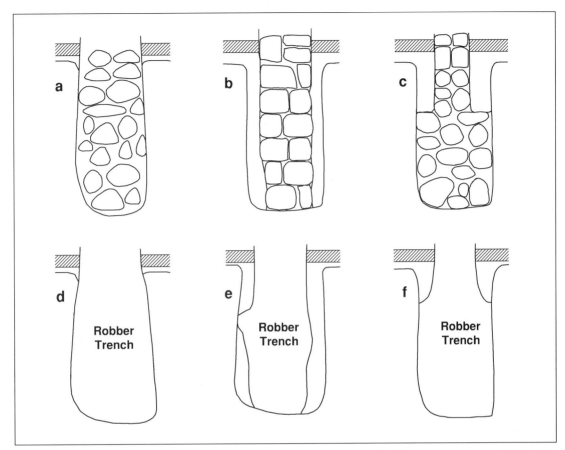

8.3. Wall foundations. *These illustrations demonstrate the three basic methods of wall construction: (a) trench built; (b) free built; and (c) mixed. It also shows the relationships of layers to the foundation trenches. In the lower illustrations (d, e, f) it is assumed that the stone has been robbed out. With the trench built, the relationship of the floor to the wall is not necessarily clear. In the latter two cases something of the foundation trench may survive, giving a peculiar effect of two cuts following almost the same line.*

perspective using a computer programme. There are many peculiarities of construction which archaeologists dealing with only the foundations might not have recognised. One is that in the lowest part larger blocks were used first, and then smaller ones, apparently before a new supply of stone was brought in from a different quarry. Some of the holes in the wall were intended to take wooden balconies and other external structures, but most mark the position of scaffolding holes from the period of construction; in terrace walls, such holes may indicate the presence of drains to prevent water building up behind the wall, which can cause the wall to collapse. When built, this was a high-prestige building, but later in its history it became a multi-storey tenement, with the room heights being reduced to fit more people in. This change of status of the building, and indeed of the site, would not have been detectable if only the foundations had survived, but something might have been surmised of the change of status with evidence of the movement of the élite classes into the nearby town (Siena), the construction of rich buildings there and the downgrading of the quality of the material culture at Montarrenti. It is an example of how even a single building can only be interpreted within a regional context.

8.4. Butt joints. *The first photograph (a) shows an example of Roman walls of various periods from the Roman fort at Dover. The different styles of stone construction emphasise that this is a multi-period site, and the relationships of some of the walls show clearly as butt joints, and much phasing can be done simply from the photograph. The drawings show a longitudinal view of one wall butted against another (b, c), and idealised plans (d, e). Commonly later additions are not major load-bearing walls, and so have shallower foundations. Whatever the form of butt, whether a simple butt (b) or a more complex joint (c), the foundation trenches of the two periods are unlikely to join completely at the lowest level, leaving a tongue or spur of soil between the two.*

Fig. 8.4g.

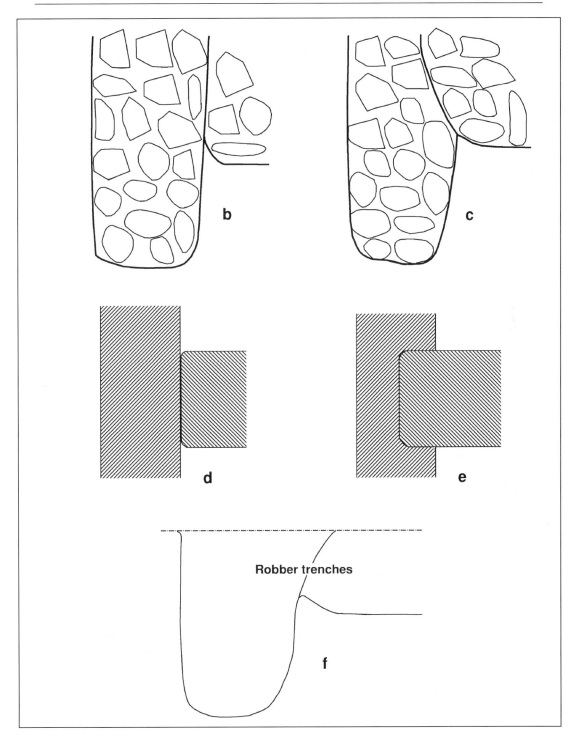

Drawing (f) shows how the evidence of a butt joint may still be identifiable even after robbing. Also, secondary walls are likely to be removed before primary ones during the demolition. The second photograph is of a multi-period terrace wall (g) butting against a pre-existing parish boundary wall (to the left) at Exeter, and shows this phenomenon clearly. At the same time it illustrates how complex walls can be, with various rebuilds and patchings from the medieval period up to the twentieth century. This is not easy to unravel.

the dating evidence. This is not a problem that has disappeared – the remains of churches and other ancient buildings may need protection from the damp, and one way of doing this is to dig a trench around the outside – effectively isolating the building from its archaeology.

A key aim is to establish the relationship between the archaeological layers and the foundation trench. Layers preceding the wall will be cut by it; layers later than it will seal it. This is usually fairly easy to see with a free-built wall, even if it has been robbed, but foundation trenches are not always readily visible, and in some cases subsequent subsidence may cause floors to crack along the junction with the contemporary wall, giving the impression that the wall has cut the floor. Other clues may be given by the presence of mortar spreads, which may be connected with either the construction or the demolition of the wall. In any case, it is vital to distinguish between objects from layers pre-dating and post-dating the construction or destruction.

ROBBER TRENCHES

This is a term used by archaeologists to describe the removal of the foundations of a wall at a later date to recover the stone for building. It is a common phenomenon, especially on urban sites, and many Roman sites were robbed of stone to build churches and castles in the late Saxon and Norman periods – the robbing of Roman Verulamium to build the cathedral of St Albans is documented both from historical sources and from the presence of large quantities of Roman tile in the cathedral's fabric. Sometimes the wall is completely removed – what Wheeler termed a 'ghost' wall – and here the internal phasing and dating of the walls of the building become more difficult.

Clues to different phases of construction may be given by the impression of the foundations in the bottom of the robber trench. For example, in the Saxon Old Minster at Winchester the location of individual blocks was quite clear, outlined by the upstanding pieces of mortar. Where there has been a butt joint, hints may be obtained from the relative depth of the walls, and especially from the presence of a tongue of undisturbed soil between the two walls (Fig. 8.4f). However, one must be careful to distinguish this from the situation where two contemporary walls have been robbed, one of which was deeper because it had a greater load-bearing importance. The sequence of robbing of the walls may also give a clue to the sequence in which the new walls were put up, as has been suggested for the demolition of the Old Minster at Winchester – some of it had to be left standing until part of the Norman cathedral was ready for use. Robbing may also tell one something of the conditions under which the wall was robbed: at Exeter one Roman wall had been totally robbed out in the thirteenth century, except for one small tongue, which presumably marked a medieval property boundary (Fig. 8.5). It seems that the owners had worked up to their fence on both sides and had then stopped, so that the piece of wall actually under the boundary had survived intact.

THE FUNCTION

Stone and timber buildings share much in common with regard to function, so in this section we shall be considering both. First, we have to set aside our own cultural

8.5. Robbed walls at Exeter. This photograph shows that robbing can be a complex phenomenon. This is a room of a Roman building which had a hypocaust (under-floor heating on pillars). Due to considerable erosion in the medieval town, the Roman floor level would have been at about the level of the modern road. On the concrete floor the position of the pillars of the hypocaust could still be identified because the channels were marked by charcoal and soot deposits from the circulating smoke and hot air. The walls around this room are of different constructions and depths, and so are probably of different periods. When the right-hand one was robbed out, the robbers realised there was stone underlying the concrete floor of the hypocaust, and burrowed to obtain as much stone as possible. The result is a mess!

preconceptions about what sorts of activities go on in a house. For instance, some Sudanese cattle raisers, who live in round houses not dissimilar to those found in the British Iron Age, keep the cattle in the house, and they themselves sleep in an upper storey built in the rafters. The medieval longhouse, with cattle at one end and the domestic quarters at the other, is a more familiar version which still survives in the western parts of Britain and in northern Germany, though the cattle are usually banished nowadays to a separate barn. The division between workshops and domestic houses was also generally not so marked as in our own society. A single building, even the same room, can be used for both industry and habitation.

So the archaeologist must look for traces of the activities that went on in the building. Sometimes this is relatively easy, especially if the building is well preserved and floor levels survive. Thus ovens and hearths may be found, and evidence of whether they were domestic or industrial may be gathered in the burnt residues – slag will suggest industry, carbonised food remains domestic; the presence of large heating vats and water conduits may indicate fulling; and so on. Careful sampling may be needed, for instance in a blacksmith's workshop, to work out what activity was carried out where in the room.

The prestige rooms in a Roman villa may also be easy to recognise, either from the presence of mosaic floors and heating systems, or from the good view they afford of the countryside. But models of the likely activities we should expect in a house can be built up both from modern analogy and from the surviving contemporary literature, and this can be compared with the physical evidence. Thus we might expect waiting-rooms in large town houses where a rich man's clients and supporters waited for an audience. But even in some obvious cases there may be more to learn. Burnt patches on mosaic pavements have in the past been interpreted as later occupation by 'squatters', but they may in fact be where braziers were placed on cold days. From the presence of a drain in the corner of one of the best rooms at Chedworth Roman villa, Sir Ian Richmond suggested that the room needed frequent washing out, and therefore concluded that the eating habits of the owners may have been messy, which in turn suggested they ate lying on couches in the Roman fashion rather than sitting at a table in Gallic fashion!

Most rooms, however, are more nondescript, and we may have to consider the evidence of what sort rubbish has been left behind. Here we must be careful, because anyone who has observed an abandoned house will know how it can accumulate rubbish that has nothing to do with its former function. Also, houses can change function from domestic to industrial, as has been noted in Roman town houses. Often it has been claimed that *Grubenhäuser*, the sunken houses found on Iron Age sites in central Europe and on early Saxon sites in Britain, were used for industrial purposes, but often this is based on evidence from rubbish thrown in after the building was abandoned, rather than being directly connected with the period when it was in use. Thus it is vital to consider only the material that is lying directly on the floor or, better, has been trodden into the floor. In the latter case we may only be concerned with extremely small fragments of pottery and other rubbish – the large fragments will have been swept up and thrown away. Thus the size of find may be directly relevant – the smaller it is, the more important! In the case of surviving floor levels, every object in or on the floor should be plotted in.

Wear patterns on the floor should always be studied, not just in timber or robbed stone buildings where even the location of the doors may be unknown. Lack of wear of soft materials like mortar or chalk may betray protected areas where pieces of furniture stood, while heavy wear may indicate where some special activity took place. It should also warn us not to confuse the thickness of floors with their chronological importance. A thin floor may be one that had seen a lot of use, with continual sweeping and cleaning out, while a thick deposit may have had only a short lifespan. The thickness of the floor adjacent to a wall (where wear is likely to have been less) is the important clue to look at. Archaeologists also refer to 'occupation deposits' on floor surfaces (usually a black soil). One wonders, in fact, what these deposits actually are. Did the inhabitants really live in squalor with dirt accumulating on the floor, or are these the remains of rushes mixed with ashes from the fire, or does it represent a period when the room was not in use? There may also be traces of wooden floorboards or timber joists – the large quantities of coins recovered from some Roman buildings at Wanborough suggested to John Wacher that their survival may have been due to them falling through the cracks in the floorboards rather than that the inhabitants were unusually rich. Churning of the floor surface may suggest the stalling of animals – as in the possible stables attached to Iron Age round houses at Hod Hill. Further evidence may be obtained from chemical analysis as the stalling of animals should leave high concentrations of phosphates. Clearly these sorts of problems can only be tackled with open area excavation, and often by minute observation – a wear pattern may only leave a difference of millimetres in a floor surface, and skill with the trowel is needed not to scrape away the evidence.

NINE

WOODEN BUILDINGS

The excavation of timber buildings really deserves a book to itself, and it is a field which has progressed greatly in the last couple of decades. Timber was the main building material throughout prehistory, and in Britain it is only in recent times that stone, brick and mortar really succeeded it. It was with the excavation of the Roman forts on the Rhineland in the early twentieth century that the potential for discovering timber buildings *where the wood had not been preserved* was first realised by Carl Schuchhardt; on nineteenth-century excavations where there was complex stratigraphy, as at Silchester, the recognition of timber buildings was far beyond the skills and techniques of the archaeologists. Excavation of buildings where post-holes and slots were dug into the ground was relatively simple; it was only with the advent of open area excavation in the mid-1960s that more ephemeral traces started to be identified, even though these ephemeral traces might be of large and sophisticated buildings.

Timber structures fall into two general categories: buildings in which timber posts are set upright in the soil, either in individual post-holes or in continuous slots; and buildings in which the uprights are slotted into a horizontal timber – a sill- or sleeper-beam – which itself may be sunk into the ground in a slot, or may rest on the ground or on a stone footing, or may be raised above the ground on timber posts or stones (for instance, the staddle stones of eighteenth- and nineteenth-century granaries in Britain). In both cases the gaps between the uprights may be filled in a variety of ways – with wattle and daub, timber cladding, brick, etc.

In theory, buildings do not really need to be sunk into the ground. As long as they are laterally stable so that they do not collapse like a pack of cards, it is often the weight of the roof that holds the building down – a tiled or thatched roof can weigh several tonnes. So in some cases the digging of post-holes may be primarily a constructional device, to hold the structure in place while it is being built.

POST-HOLES

Even prehistoric people were capable of driving timbers 2 metres or more into the ground, especially if the ground was soft, as the excavations of the Bronze Age site at Flag Fen have clearly demonstrated. Well before the Roman conquest, both in Britain and on the continent, sophisticated bridges were being constructed across rivers on timber piles, as at La Tène, and Les Cornaux in Switzerland. Smaller-sized posts and stakes were normally driven in, but on most subsoils the normal way to set up a post was to dig a hole, stand up the post, and ram in earth and stones around it to hold it upright. Thus archaeologists differentiate between the packing around the post, and the pipe – the outline of the post itself. Finds from the two must be carefully distinguished, as a post can survive a century or more, especially if it is large, of solid oak, has perhaps been charred to prevent it from rotting, and then has been allowed to rot in position (see Fig. 5.6). So there could be a recognisable age difference between material from the packing and from the pipe.

When a post is no longer needed, it may be dug out – usually this is done by digging around the base of the post, and then rocking it in various directions until it is loose enough to pull out of the ground. This should leave distinctive signs in the form of a funnel-shaped top to the post pipe, and a disturbed lower fill. On the other hand it may simply be left standing until it falls down, or is broken or sawn off. The post will then gradually rot and be replaced by soil and silt, leaving the shape of the pipe virtually intact. Alternatively, it may become sealed over, in which case the timber will not be replaced by soil as it rots, and there will be just a void. I worked on one site where this had happened to a series of large posts, found mostly by the unwary suddenly losing a leg down them as the overlying soil gave way!

The generally accepted way of excavating post-holes is by sectioning (Fig. 9.1a), or, if the underlying deposit is the natural subsoil and soft (e.g. sand), by boxing; that is, a small trench is dug, with the post-hole in one of the sections (Fig. 9.1b). Alternatively, it can be quadranted to give sections in both directions, though this is only possible with boxing or with large post-holes. As the post-hole is dug, plans can be made every 5 or 10cm, the sections drawn at the end, and then the other half of the post-hole dug. I have, however, recently gone over to excavating post-holes in plan, taking the whole feature down in 5 or 10cm spits, and planning. This is especially useful where there are complex situations of several post-holes intersecting – in some cases at Montarrenti there were as many as six or seven, and in no way could meaningful sections have been laid out, especially as some post-holes were masked by later ones (Fig. 9.1c). This method is also much quicker than sectioning, though of course care has to be taken that the finds from each phase are kept separate. At the end profiles of the emptied post-holes were drawn in several directions, which allows the reconstruction of sections if required.

Stake-holes present greater problems as it is necessary to prove that they are stake-holes – I have seen sites where supposed stake-holes are simply emptied out, photographed and planned, without any proof that they were in fact stake-holes. Stains can be caused by other factors, such as a piece of bronze, a root hole, solution in chalk or burrowing animals. On one site we found a lot of holes, but they were all flat-bottomed rather than pointed, and were in fact vole holes. In these cases I usually do a box section, though in bed-rock careful excavation, even sectioning, with a penknife is necessary.

Though I am a specialist in the Iron Age, I have never yet found an Iron Age round house, nor have I ever invented one. In some cases patterns of post-holes are completely obvious and make logical sense; sometimes, however sophisticated the analysis, no sense emerges or there are alternative reconstructions, as at Little Woodbury (Fig. 9.2). Faced with a maze of post-holes, there is a tendency for hopeful guess-work to take over. The example shown below of the post-holes from Thorny Down is an object lesson – the post-holes can be chosen to fit what one thinks is likely, but in this case the records are simply not adequate for anyone to be sure – even the depths of post-holes were not recorded (Fig. 9.3).

One of the most brilliant examples of sorting out post-holes from a confused mess is Brian Hope-Taylor's complex of small rectangular buildings at Yeavering (Fig. 9.6a). All

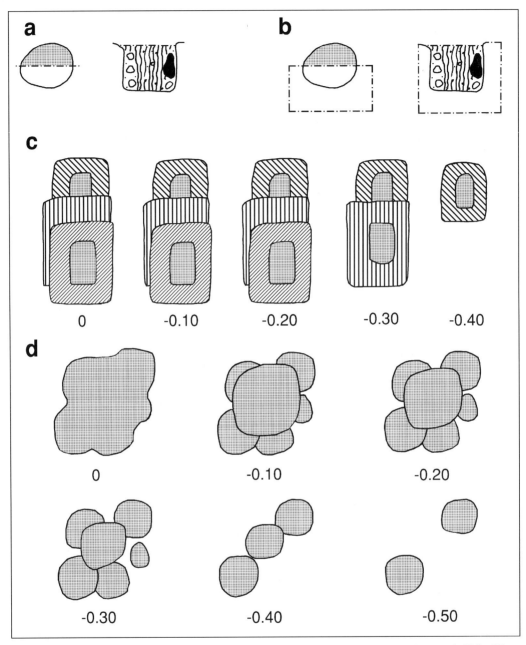

9.1. Excavation of post-holes. In Britain the normal way to excavate a post-hole is by taking out half the fill and drawing the section (a). Plans may be made at regular depths of the two halves as they are removed. On soft soils such as sand or loess, a 'box' section may be made, removing the natural subsoil. This is quicker and gives a better view of the section (b). The disadvantages are that it is not so photogenic if a photograph is required of the building, and also it cannot be used where the post-hole cuts through earlier stratified deposits. At the medieval village of Montarrenti in Tuscany, some of the post-holes were exceptionally clear as clay had been brought from outside the settlement to pack them, and most of these posts had subsequently been left in position to rot. Not uncommonly several post-holes intersected. This could not be a case of buildings just being rebuilt – each post had to have time to rot, and the pipe to fill before it was cut by the next one, so there was some time-lag, implying a continually changing layout. With complex post-holes like this, the only realistic excavation method is to dig in spits (c, d), carefully keeping the finds from each coloured soil separate. At each

9.2. Little Woodbury. *Bersu's excavation in the mid-1930s was in some ways years ahead of its time, though he dug in trenches, not in true open area. His discovery of large circular buildings completely changed our view of Iron Age society – until then it was widely believed that people lived in holes in the ground. There are in fact two houses, one superimposed above the other (a). With this sort of construction it is difficult to repair a house, and once certain posts start to rot, it is easiest to pull the old house down and build another. However, there is still controversy about the reconstruction of these houses – does the square structure form part of the houses, as Bersu believed (b), or is it unrelated, as suggested by Chris Musson (c)? No houses which have been excavated subsequently have produced a similar set of post-holes. Bersu considered it was not possible to roof a house of this size without the central construction – another house at Little Woodbury he considered unfinished because it lacked the central posts. In fact, experimental work at Butser has shown that it is perfectly possible to roof it. The key problem is the relationship to what Bersu interpreted as 'drains' contemporary with the houses. The plan seems to show one of the 'drains' cutting one of the post-holes and the original field notes are ambiguous. The 'drains' can be interpreted as part of an enclosure, perhaps the drainage trench for a later building with an entrance, but which is ploughed out elsewhere (d). The plan shows the posts of the four-post structure cutting the 'drain' which would mean it was yet later. Also the posts have been replaced more often than those of the main house, which would be difficult to do if they were integral to the construction. The records are not quite good enough to be sure, but this clearly demonstrates the necessity of recording carefully all relationships.*

level the surface is planned, and it can often clearly be seen which post-hole is cutting which. Some post-holes may be completely masked by later ones, and only appear at an advanced stage of digging. Using this method, it is also possible to identify posts that have been removed, as the post-pipe will gradually reduce in size, forming a cone shape.

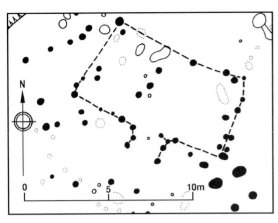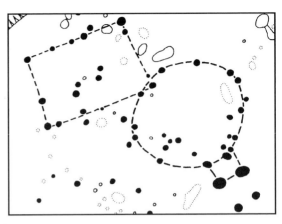

9.3. Thorny Down. The original excavation report suggested that this group of post-holes could be reconstructed as evidence for a rectangular building. At the time of the excavation it was thought that Middle/Late Bronze houses were generally rectangular. Subsequently it has been found that round houses with square porches are the norm, and in fact this makes better sense in terms of the published plan. But as Chris Musson has pointed out, this selection of post-holes is just as arbitrary and biased – if the data are not properly recorded in the field, reconstructions degenerate into pure guesswork.

the post-holes were drawn, and the fillings carefully recorded, for the presence of charcoal, burning and different coloured soils. In fact each building had its own characteristic fills. Hope-Taylor advocated playing with tiddlywinks to sort out the different phases! On the plan each post-hole was covered by a counter denoting the colour of its fill, and in this way the phases emerged. It is also possible using a plan to predict where a post-hole ought to be, and to check that it has not been missed.

On Iron Age hill-forts in Britain small square structures are so common that experiments have been carried out to see if they can be picked out in an otherwise confused plan using a computer programme. However, caution is needed. At Crickley Hill Phil Dixon excavated what looked superficially like a row of three four-posters near the entrance. Careful study of the limestone surface produced wear patterns and drip lines that suggested they were in fact the central aisle of a large rectangular house. But should we expect patterns always to emerge? Pairs of posts for washing lines, drying racks, looms and so on do appear, but many structures only require a single post – wigwams and totem poles, haystack poles, gibbets, or something to tie the goat to. Personally, I seem to find a lot of goats!

So far we have been talking about domestic-sized post-holes, but there are also examples of huge post-holes which were used to construct ceremonial circles and buildings in the late Neolithic and palaces in the Saxon or medieval periods. Often the posts were so large that a ramp was needed, down which the post would be pulled, bottom first, and then it would be hauled upright. This raises the question of how high posts may have stood above the ground surface. As a rule of thumb, an unsupported post should have about a third of its length buried in the soil if it is to remain stable. But, as stated above, once incorporated into a structure this rule need no longer apply, so very shallow post-holes could support quite tall posts. In fact, in

9.4. Le Pâtural, central France. The subsoil of this site was soft, so any post-holes that had to carry much weight would sink into the underlying clay, causing the building to become unstable or to collapse. To overcome this, large flat stones, in some cases rotary querns, were used to spread the weight of the post.

experimental work at Butser, Peter Reynolds has noted that when one of the Iron Age round houses was demolished, the bottoms of some of the post-holes had already rotted and become filled with soil, so in places the structure was just resting on the ground.

We should also consider here buildings with raised floors – some of these will just show up as post structures. The most common interpretation of the four-post structures found in hill-forts is that they are granaries, raised above ground to prevent rodents and other vermin getting in. Roman granaries are more readily identifiable, especially on military sites, with rows of closely set posts. Such raised buildings can best be identified on unploughed sites, where the absence of floors and the presence of drip lines, or evidence of access by stairways, can be demonstrated. This also applies to posts set on post-pads – horizontal slabs of stone which spread the weight of the timber posts which stood on them. Post-pads are quite a common feature in buildings in medieval Hull, but clearly the use of slabs in this way can only be recognised if it is seen as a pattern in an open area excavation. Slabs are also sometimes used in the same way at the bottom of post-holes, where these have been dug into soft ground, as on some of the larger post-holes at Le Pâtural in France (Fig. 9.4).

TRENCHES

Trench-built structures are common features on sites of all periods. However, trenches can be dug for various reasons. For a building it might be either to take a series of uprights or a horizontal sill beam, or simply as a drain around the building to take away water from the roof. But such slots have on occasion also been claimed as the bedding trench for a hedge, for instance around Roman burials. The onus is therefore on the archaeologist to demonstrate the interpretation.

Usually not much information can be gained from the excavation of trenches which contained sill-beams. Often the beam was removed subsequently, and even if it was not, the collapse of the upper part of the filling as the beam rots is likely to remove all traces of the uprights that slotted into it. Only when a building was burnt, like the early Roman buildings at Verulamium, or if the wood is somehow preserved, as at the fort of the Valkenburg in the Netherlands (Fig. 9.5) or on some of the prehistoric Swiss 'lake' villages, is anything much likely to survive. But more commonly sill-beams were kept away from the damp by placing them on low walls, which may be either masonry or dry-stone.

Generally, preservation is likely to be best on more acid soils, or on fine soils where the soil compacts around the timbers, preserving the fine detail. So sands and loess soils are good, but chalk less so, especially if it has been subjected to extensive worm activity. On sand, the wood will often show up as a dark stain – the survival of the outline and details of construction of the boat in the Sutton Hoo burial is a classic example. In ring ditches, one may not only be looking for evidence of upright stakes; in some cases the hurdling may have been partly buried when the slot was filled in.

One advantage of trenches and wall slots is that they do allow archaeologists to experiment. Thus different sections can be looked at in plan, in cross-section or, as advocated by Hope-Taylor at Yeavering (Fig. 9.6, see pp. 124–7), in longitudinal sections down the centre of a trench. However, several excavators have noted that when dealing with fairly slight structures, such as stakes in a ring slot, the soil conditions can vary from one section to another, so that the evidence may only be visible in one part of the trench, and in another may have been destroyed or masked by subsequent soil changes, such as worm activity. The soil through which the slot is cut can also vary; for instance, on chalk it may also run through patches of clay with flints, and visibility of fine structures may be affected by this change of bedrock.

SURFACE CONSTRUCTIONS

Sill beams are quite commonly just laid on the ground. Evidence for such buildings is only likely to survive on sites which have not been ploughed and where deposits have been accumulating rather than eroding. This method of construction seems to be typical of some late Roman towns in Britain; for instance at Wroxeter rafts of rubble were laid down to serve as the foundations (Fig. 1.8). Under these circumstances, the existence of walls has to be conjectured from circumstantial evidence. In the case of Wroxeter regular patterns of different types of rubble, coupled with patterns of wear of the surface of the rubble, could identify regular paths and floors. Sometimes one is faced with deposits which just come to an end – simple enough if it is clearly a floor level, but less obvious if it is a layer of occupation (Fig. 9.7). At Beachy Head, Richard Bradley used the distribution of pot-

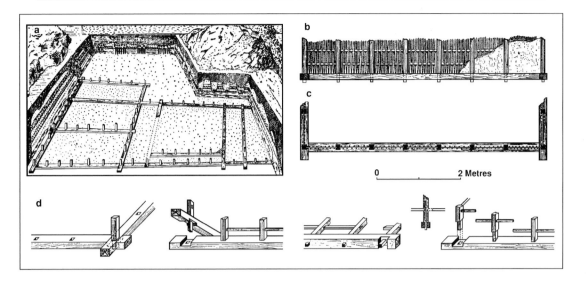

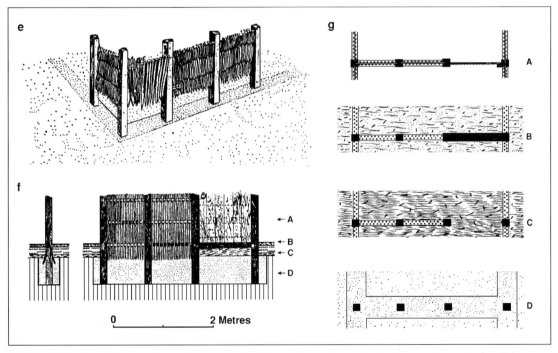

9.5. The Valkenburg. On most Roman forts timber buildings only survive as slots in the ground, usually for sill-beams. As mentioned above, sill-beams in slots are particularly difficult to excavate and interpret. The Valkenburg in the Netherlands is unusual in that the timbers have survived, showing the great range of construction techniques which were in use in the early Roman period.

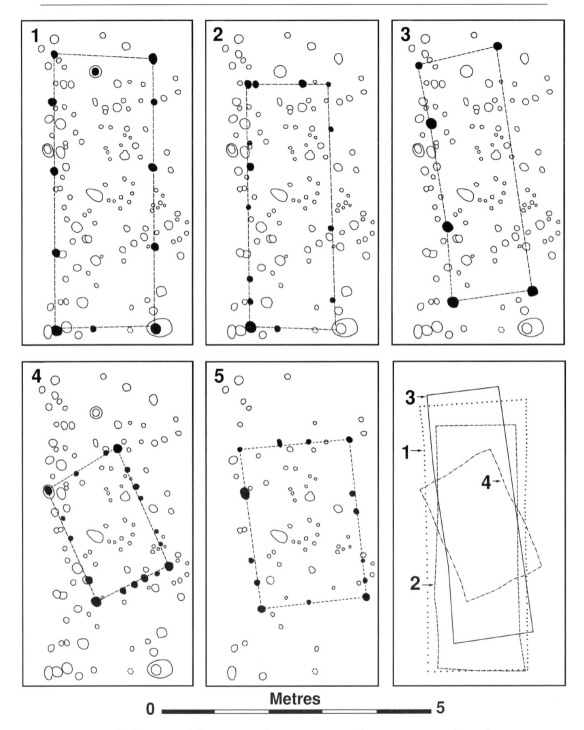

9.6. Yeavering. *The first group of illustrations (a) from Brian Hope-Taylor's excavations at the royal Saxon site of Yeavering in Northumberland demonstrate how careful recording in the field can allow a meaningless mass of post-holes to be unravelled, and reconstructed into individual buildings. The size and fill of each post-hole was carefully recorded and then they were grouped according to the presence or absence of charcoal, different coloured soils, etc. The interpretation suggests six superimposed rectangular buildings, and accounts for almost all the post-holes. The second illustration (b) shows the complex plans of several superimposed plans of timber*

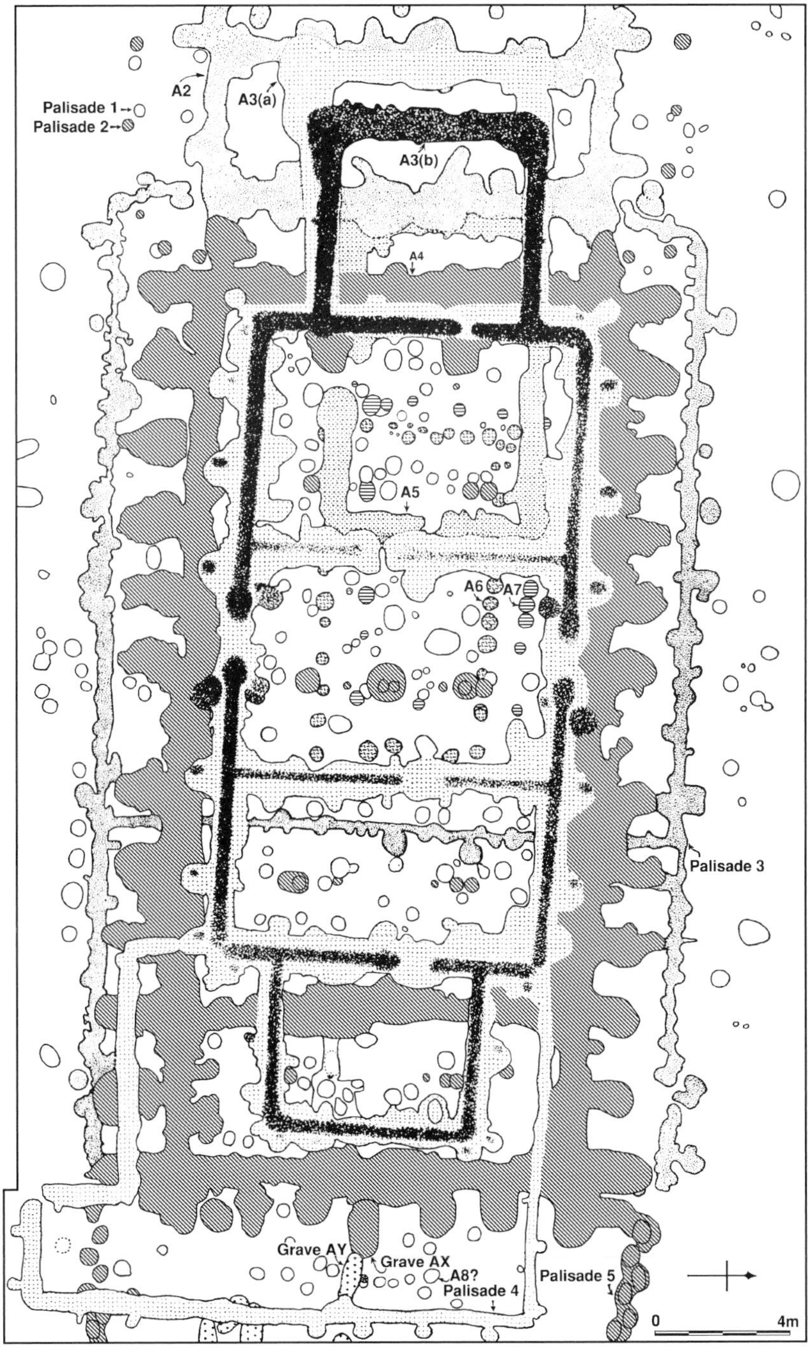

Palisade 1 → ○
Palisade 2 → ◎

A2
A3(a)
A3(b)
A4
A5
A6 A7
Palisade 3
Grave AY
Grave AX
A8?
Palisade 4
Palisade 5

Fig. 9.6b.

0   4m

halls. Though these features showed up clearly on aerial photographs, the details of the plan were only recovered by repeatedly cleaning the site, and noting the plans and relationships under varying weather and lighting conditions. Many of the chronological relationships had already been established before excavation of the individual features was started, so the main task was elucidating the construction methods used. The third illustration (c) shows one of the foundation trenches, which was studied in plan, cross-section and longitudinal section. Alternate posts were sunk deeper than the others, from which Hope-Taylor conjectured that the wall was built of prefabricated vertical timbers, linked together by tongue and groove joints (d) – a more sophisticated method than had ever been suspected in mid-Saxon architecture at the time of the excavation.

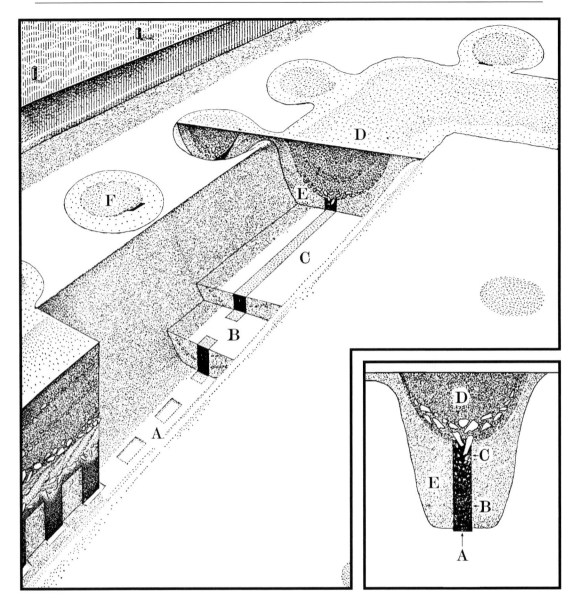

Fig. 9.6c.

sherds to suggest the presence of some sort of fence which had prevented fragments of individual pots from spreading.

OTHER CONSTRUCTIONS

In passing, we should note that other materials were used for building, most notably clay and various mixes with other materials, such as cob (a mixture of chalk, clay and dung). The material can be prepared as bricks in moulds and then dried, like the sun-dried bricks found in the Near East and the Mediterranean, and even in central Europe, on the Iron

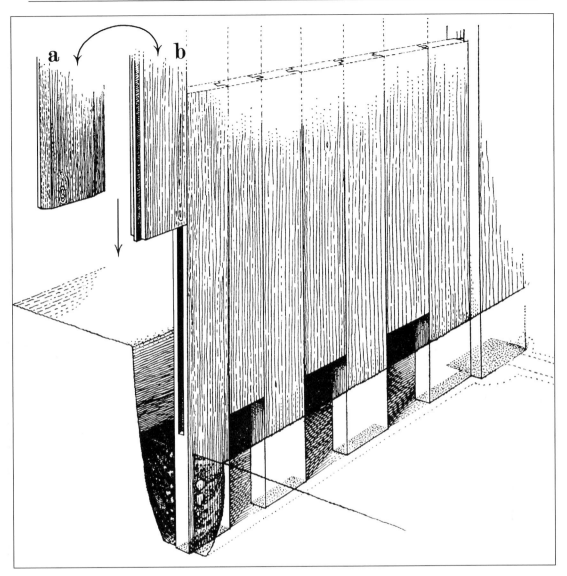

Fig. 9.6d.

Age hill-fort of the Heuneburg, or alternatively it can be gradually built up in layers to form a solid wall. With these methods of construction it is vital to keep out the damp especially if it is an area prone to frost. Thus, the wall at Heuneburg was built on stone foundations, and cob walls in southern England were commonly thatched. These constructions may not always be easy to recognise in the field – it is the regular coursing of the bricks with a different clay between the bricks that helps to differentiate a wall from the collapsed remains of a dried brick building. Cob will very often only leave a scatter of chalk lumps in the soil – the clays will tend to erode away. In another Iron Age context, we can note the cob walls in the final phases of the hill-fort at Hod Hill; where the land is unploughed, the houses can be located by slight mounds of eroded chalk lumps, but it may be impossible to recognise walls on ploughed sites if stone footings were not used. Turf is

*9.7. **Exeter**. This section (a) in the side of a medieval pit shows Roman layers of dark occupation soil with oyster shells. On the left these deposits seem to fade away. It is meaningless in section. The plan revealed that this marked an edge that could be traced for some distance. Where the black soil ends in fact marked the position of a sill-beam laid on the ground surface but not sunk into it. It was the central room of a small building, the rooms on either side having concrete floors (b).*

another material used in housing, but it is most commonly recognised in barrows and fortifications, and will be discussed under 'banks'.

RECONSTRUCTION

Once above the footings, or whatever has survived, of a wall, archaeologists are forced into informed guesswork about the likely reconstruction of their buildings. The presence of second or third storeys may be guessed at by the depth of the footings, or by the identification of a staircase leading up to the next floor. As already mentioned, buildings may have mortared stone footings, but continue up in timber, clay, cob or some other material. If the top of a wall is regular and even, it is a hint that it may have carried a sill-beam, and traces of one should be looked for, but greater certainty will exist if the walls have collapsed and have not been disturbed later. Collapsed rubble should be carefully studied – even if it *is* only collapsed rubble. One interesting case of this was an Iron Age house excavated by Nicholas Thomas on Bredon Hill. It appeared that no stone had subsequently been removed, so Thomas used it to rebuild the walls; this then allowed a good estimate of the original height of the house, and a subsequent reconstruction, to be made.

Fig. 9.7b.

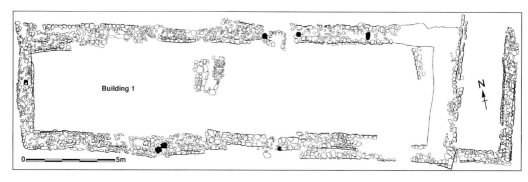

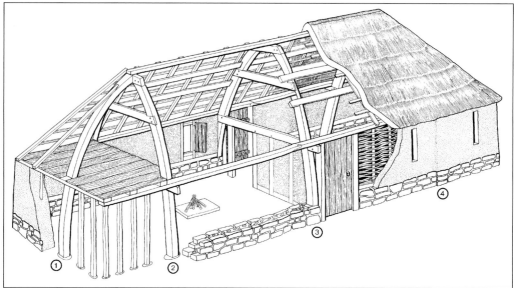

9.8. Wharram Percy. *The excavation of the peasant houses at Wharram Percy proved impossible using traditional methods such as those of Wheeler. Walls were of an ephemeral nature, repeatedly being replaced and reconstructed. The houses, however, were perhaps not as ephemeral as the archaeology at first suggested. Recent work by Stuart Wrathmell, based both on documentary evidence and on surviving buildings, shows that the timber structure, including the roof timbers, was highly valued, and might even be the property of the lord of the manor. Between the beams of the timber skeleton, short lengths of wall were used as infill, and it is these which were continually being rebuilt and replaced. Archaeologists are inclined to think of their buildings being built from the ground upwards, but in some cases it is the superstructure which is put in place first, and the walls added later.*

Sometimes the ephemeral nature of the footings and walls may belie the impressive nature of the original buildings, like the late Roman houses found in the town of Wroxeter by Phil Barker (Fig. 1.8). For many years the patchy lengths of wall of the peasant houses at Wharram Percy were thought to reflect hovels, until it was recognised that they merely filled the gaps between impressive timber crucks (Fig. 9.8).

Roofing materials will sometimes leave a trace, especially slate or tile; their absence may indicate thatch or wooden shingles, which may be held in position by wooden pegs. On one site on the Isle of Man Bersu suggested the use of turf for the roof, a view based on the presence of Mesolithic microliths overlaying the Iron Age levels – these, he believes, may have been in the cut turf. Where there has not been too much disturbance, plotting in

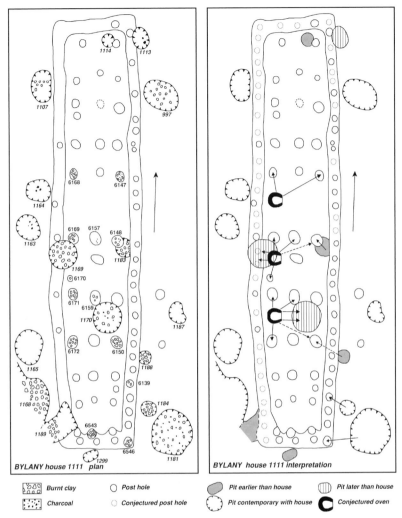

Burnt clay ⬜   Post hole ○   Pit earlier than house   Pit later than house

Charcoal ⬜   Conjectured post hole ○   Pit contemporary with house   Conjectured oven

BYLANY house 1111 plan

BYLANY house 1111 interpretation

9.9. Bylany. The long houses of the Early Neolithic Linearbandkeramik *groups of central Europe date to around 4500–3000* BC, *and show remarkable similarity from France and the Netherlands in the west to Poland in the east. Yet their interpretation is still controversial, in part because in virtually all cases the floor surfaces have not survived. The classic interpretation of these buildings is to be found in authors such as Gordon Childe, who on the basis of ethnographic parallels considered that each one housed several nuclear families, and represented a relatively egalitarian society. Bohumil Soudský, who directed the massive excavations at Bylany in Czechoslovakia, followed this interpretation. Each phase had a large house, interpreted as a clubhouse for the elders, and varying sizes of longhouse according to the size of the different lineages which owned them. Because of the large population, settlements were abandoned every thirty years. Each group would have three or four sites which were occupied in turn in rotation, and they would return to each site about every hundred years, giving the land time to recover from over-exploitation. Soudský tried to demonstrate the number of families in each house from the number of ovens, but as these were destroyed, it had to be done from the concentration of fragments of burnt clay in the post-holes and other features cut into the loess. An alternative explanation emphasises that each building is divided into three parts, and suggests they had different functions. Taking the medieval meaning of a longhouse, the buildings are interpreted as housing only one nuclear family and their cattle. The size of the house is dictated by the number of cattle, and so the wealth of the family, and the big house is the home of the village head – in other words it is a markedly stratified society. The smaller population this model implies makes it less likely that land was exhausted and that the cyclical abandonment of sites took place. One way excavators are trying to resolve the conflict is by looking at the distribution of finds in the houses and within the settlements, and also at concentrations of phosphates to see if these indicate the housing of livestock in the buildings.*

the location of all iron nails may give clues to the timber parts of a house's construction, though wooden pegs were more common on prehistoric and medieval sites.

Where floor levels do not survive there can be major problems in interpreting buildings. This is the case of the round houses of the Iron Age of Britain such as Little Woodbury (Fig. 9.2), or the Neolithic *Linearbandkeramik* houses found over much of central and western Europe (Fig. 9.9), and in this latter case it is fundamental to our whole interpretation of these early farming settlements. Either we have to draw analogies with nearby societies where such information survives (e.g. Iron Age houses in the Hebrides), or extrapolate from the rare examples where the floor does survive. In the latter case the fact that it survives may mean it is atypical (e.g. a *Linearbandkeramik* house with a sunken floor). Alternatively we can look at the fills of the post-holes or of adjacent features. Again there are dangers that this relates to the period of abandonment rather than use.

TEN

PITS, DITCHES AND BANKS

Many sites consist largely of holes in the ground, and even on sites where there are stratified layers, pits and ditches may still prove to be the main source of finds. Sometimes they are nothing but a nuisance, destroying more important stratified layers, but they can equally produce vital information which does not survive anywhere else about the activities, status or environment of the site. In certain respects pits are easy to dig, but in other respects they are extremely difficult – it all depends on the level of information required.

PITS

The first question is always, what was the pit dug for? As with buildings, the contents of the pit may well be very misleading. Just as they are today, in antiquity holes in the ground were seen as a useful means of getting rid of rubbish; some were deliberately filled because they were in the way, in which case the material was usually brought from somewhere else, not necessarily close at hand. Occasionally the shape and structure of the pit will immediately suggest its function – a stone- or timber-lined pit which goes below the water table is likely to be a well. But more often the function is obscure. We should be looking for indications of the use of the pit – was it lined to protect the contents or stop it collapsing (Fig. 10.1); are there signs of wear or weathering which show if the pit has been open for some time or not; has it been deliberately filled or sealed; or perhaps there may be evidence for chemical changes caused by an activity like tanning leather (Fig. 10.2); or they may have the 'bell' shape characteristic of grain storage pits (Fig. 10.3, see pp. 136–7).

(Following pages) *10.1. Timber-lined pit from Exeter. Below the water table (a) the wooden lining of this pit was preserved – in fact, a wooden barrel – and it had been packed behind with clay. The hint that the pit was lined appeared at a high level (b), with a central fill which was clearly of a different colour and nature from a narrow ring around the outside, and the presence of vertical slates in the central part. Presumably this was a well. Careful excavation of the upper part revealed not only the impressions of the decayed staves, but also of the binding around the barrel. This effect of two concentric circles caused by a wooden lining must not be confused with the second situation illustrated in cross-section (c), common with cesspits on urban sites such as Winchester. When the cesspit had finished its useful life, it was commonly sealed over with a thick deposit of clay, both to seal in the smelly organic filling and also to stabilise the ground surface. However, as the organic material decays, it contracts, causing the clay infill to sink. The sinkage reaches its maximum at the centre of the pit, but the organic material tends to hang on to the edges of the pit. In plan the filling of the pit gives the appearance of concentric circles which can be confused with lining, and can cause some difficulty in defining the limits of a pit during excavation. The hollow left by this process may well need further filling, and often the presence of an underlying pit can be detected, long before it is revealed, by the sagging of deposits into its fill – in the case of large ditches their line can sometimes be detected by following cracks in walls of standing buildings caused by sagging foundations.*

Fig. 10.1a.

Fig. 10.1b.

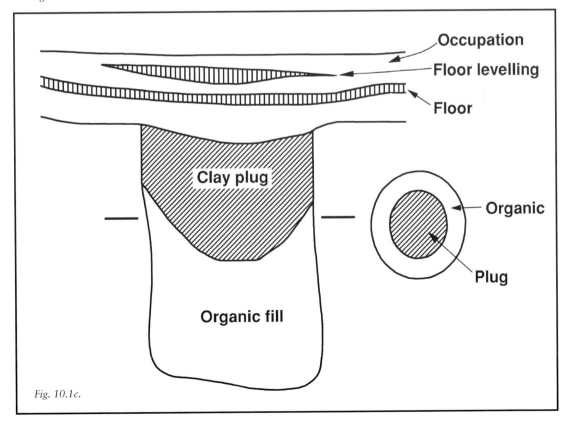

Fig. 10.1c.

10.2. Stone-lined pit from Exeter. This late medieval pit demonstrates some of the problems of interpretation. Though it clearly ran underwater, the shape is wrong for a well. The stone lining suggests it was used over a period of time, and for something industrial. The hollow in the bottom is caused probably by water swirling around in the pit, but implies that is was regularly cleaned out. The filling, however, may be totally irrelevant. The rubbish in it included evidence of metalworking in the form of jets derived from casting pewter objects, and cobblers' wooden lasts, suggesting shoe-making. The environmental evidence was ambiguous – the insects are typical of a dark and dingy place such as a cellar, the pollen implies something more delightful – a pond with water lilies floating on it! In fact, it is likely to have been a pit for tanning leather.

Occasionally the fill is distinctive – cesspits, where the organic material is not preserved under water, often take on a greenish tinge, with a soft, friable fill.

The conflict between plan and section is strongly felt in pit excavation. On the one hand, the cross-section can produce important evidence about the nature and process of the filling – deliberate infill, evidence of turf-lines, and so on. On the other hand, it is important to show from which direction the rubbish has come, as this may define from which part of the site, and perhaps from which building, the rubbish originated; this may even indicate land tenure on an urban site. Usually pits are sectioned, with the section running along the greatest length, or where it will show the relationships with other pits (Fig. 10.4, see pp. 138–9). However, this will not show the direction from which material is dumped, so each layer should be planned with the surface levelled in to show the contours of the deposit.

A common type of pit is the quarry or borrow pit (Fig. 10.5, see p. 140), examples of which are often found on settlements, for instance on Iron Age sites in Wessex (the 'working hollow' at Little Woodbury), and on Neolithic sites in central Europe, where the pits run parallel with the walls of *Bandkeramik* houses. They are dug primarily to recover clay or chalk for use in building houses and other structures on the site. Characteristically they are relatively shallow and totally irregular, consisting of hollows and scoops where material has been removed at various times. Usually they are left open for some time, and every time more material is removed, there is a spread of trampled material adjacent to the area of extraction. This makes excavation in stratigraphical sequence very difficult, as no layers extend over the whole area.

KILNS AND OVENS

These are commonly dug into the ground to conserve heat, though small baking ovens are more usually found above ground. Often they are built of clay, and even if built of brick or stone, clay will be used as bonding and characteristically it will be burnt bright red. Kilns are a specialist interest in their own right, and there is a substantial literature on their structures and experimental firings, and anyone involved in kiln excavation should be familiar with this. Other sorts of ovens turn up commonly on agricultural sites, but their function, like that of the so-called 'corn-drying' ovens on Roman sites, is not always straightforward, and careful sampling of the burnt deposits may be needed to find clues.

DITCHES AND GULLIES

The normal way in which a ditch fills in is for there to be an initial fine silting caused by rain or wind-blown material. This is followed by coarser fill as the weather, especially frost, attacks bedrock exposed in the side of the ditch. Coarse material will roll into the centre of the ditch, including lumps of turf (Fig. 10.6, see p. 141) while finer material will stay at the edge, and the profile will become less sharp. Eventually, a certain amount of stability will develop, and at this stage plants will start to colonise the ditch, further slowing the rate of infill, and making the soil content higher and the rubble content lower the higher one gets up the profile. On a site where worms are present, their activity will eventually create a fine stoneless loam at the top of the fill, with a 'pea-grit' horizon immediately below it. This general pattern provides us with a model for natural infill, and any deviation from it will tell us that some disturbance, either human or animal, has taken place. One complication may be the effect of the weathering of the bank, which may introduce rubble at a more advanced stage of the infilling. On sites where banks have been destroyed by ploughing, the only clue to the location of the bank may be the direction from which rubble comes into the middle filling of the ditch.

Deliberate infill of a ditch which is in an advanced state of infilling is usually fairly easy to identify – by the presence of any large stones and rubble in the top of the fill – but it may be less easy if fine soil has been used (Fig. 10.7, see p. 141). In addition, on sites where worms have been active, a turf-line will have formed – leaving a deposit of fine brown loam – and this is likely to be preserved under the deliberate infill. Where ditches have been filled in at an early stage, the exact point of infill may be less easy to determine, except that the infill will be less 'sorted' than natural infill. Differentiation between deliberate and natural infills is important: the natural infills

10.3. Bell-shaped storage pits. These represent one of the classic studies of pits and their functions (see Fig. 6.5). In Iron Age Britain, before Bersu excavated at Little Woodbury, they were commonly interpreted as underground houses. In fact, even as late as 1943 Wheeler, while recognising most were storage pits, wrote: 'A few, again, were to some extent used as living quarters, or at least as dining rooms; thus the large pit, B1 on site B, had as its original floor a level spread of earth and ash, around the fringes of which, at the base of the sides, was a continuous ring of mutton bones, showing how the eaters had squatted around the centre around the fire and had thrown the gnawed bones over their shoulders.' Shades of Henry VIII and the influence of the cinema on archaeology! Despite the fact that sitting round a fire at the bottom of such a pit would have been both unbearably hot and smoky, the bones around the fringe of a pit form a natural part of the infill of such a pit. Large items tend to roll to the bottom of the slope, and with these pits, the infill tends to start as a cone in the centre of the pit – despite the claim by Wheeler that this filling was flat, his section drawing is not sufficiently well recorded to be sure about the lowest fill (see Fig. 6.5c). Bersu used ethnographic evidence to suggest that they were for storage – such pits in fact have a worldwide distribution among agricultural communities. He carefully observed evidence for the pits remaining open for some time, by the presence of rodent bones in the lower filling – animals that had fallen in, and in some cases had left scratch marks in the chalk where they had attempted to escape – those of us who have dug such pits in a rural context have seen it happen. Bersu assumed that the build-up of carbon dioxide from the germinating grain would preserve the crops for consumption, but not as seed grain as it would lose its fertility. Seed grain, he suggested, was stored in above-ground granaries – the four-post structures mentioned in the previous chapter. It was not until the late 1960s that his view was challenged. On purely functional grounds, I suggested that once such a pit was sealed over, it could not be continually opened and closed without damaging the contents, so pits were likely to be cleared out at one go, and this would be best done at sowing time – grain for daily use would be stored more accessibly in above-ground storage facilities – the reverse of Bersu's suggestion. At the same time, Peter Reynolds' first experiments were showing that over 90 per cent of the grain stored below ground was perfectly fertile the following spring, and could be used for seed corn. These early experiments also showed that Bersu had miscalculated the amount a pit could store – it was in fact about nine times as much as he had assumed! There were also arguments about why pits were bell-shaped. Some had clearly been cut that way – traces of the tools used to dig the pits sometimes survive in the chalk – but Reynolds suggested that in some cases, pits started as straight-sided, and became bell-shaped as they were cleaned out each year for re-use. A pit from Owslebury seems to confirm this – a flint which had been trimmed off at the time of digging was finally left projecting some distance out of the wall (a). The experiments, and simply counting the number of pits and dividing the number by the time a small settlement was occupied, tell us that the average lifespan of a pit was about ten years. This in its turn has implications for calculating the amount of land under cultivation and the number of families living on a particular site. Studies of the build-up of temperature and of carbon dioxide show that the bell shape was more efficient than the straight-sided pit (b). It would also be easier to conceal the pit, something that may have been important in the unsettled conditions of the Iron Age. Another argument concerned whether the pits were lined or not with basketry or hurdles. The projecting stone at Owslebury suggested not. Reynolds' experimental work shows that corn buried underground will develop a protective skin, caused by the outside grains germinating more. This has been confirmed by Martin Jones's observations of coagulated lumps of carbonised grain at Danebury. The study of these pits has thus been developed through a combination of ethnographic parallels, common sense, experimental work and field observation.

may reflect what was happening in the area adjacent to the ditch, and so its purpose; the deliberate infill could come from anywhere, and so there is little point in sampling it for snail or pollen remains. Also deliberate infilling of a ditch implies that it is in the way and cannot be left to fill in naturally, and this reflects the nature of activity in the area.

Ditches are usually meant to be permanent boundaries, so, when they start to fill in, remedial action is often taken by clearing them out. This often means that the initial fill can be dated somewhat later than the original cutting. At Owslebury subtle changes in the layout of the Middle/Late Iron Age ditch system occasionally left small lengths untouched, and the finds from these suggested that the ditches may have been kept clear for a century or more. Small-scale excavation here would have given the wrong impression of the date. Finds in the bottom of a ditch show when it was going

Fig. 10.3a.

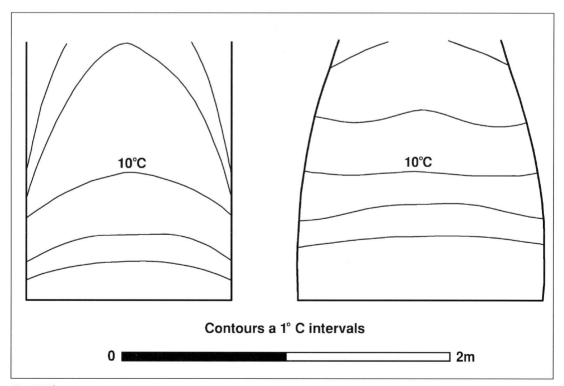

10°C

10°C

Contours a 1° C intervals

0 ▮▮▮▮▮▮▮▮▮▮▮▯▯▯▯▯▯▯▯▯ 2m

Fig. 10.3b.

10.4. Pit excavation. *It is usual to section pits because this can give more information about the processes of weathering and infill. For instance, where the side of a pit has started to collapse from weathering, this may be inevitably removed during excavation, and so not properly recognised or recorded. The most important section is north–south, as this provides the maximum contrast in weathering between the south- and north-facing edges. Also layers are not always particularly easily differentiated. Quadranting, to give four or more sections is best, if the pit is large enough but not too deep, as has been done with the pit from Aulnat (a). Also in this case the shape of the pit has dictated the position of the sections, with the major and minor axes of the pit being chosen for the sections. More normally, however, pits are just half sectioned (b). The problem with this is that, by itself, it does not tell us from what direction the infill came. The third illustration shows a pit at Owslebury which has been deliberately infilled in two distinct phases, with a turf line between (c). This is important in telling us something about the function of the enclosure in which it lay, that even shallow hollows were in the way and had to be filled, rather than being left open and allowed to fill naturally.*

Fig. 10.4b.

Fig. 10.4c.

10.5. Borrow pit excavation. *These are often very complex, with multiple phases of re-use and many localised spreads of trampled material. Multiple sections running down the centre of obvious lobes and pits may help to sort out some of it, as this Roman example from Owslebury shows, in which many phases of reworking were identified.*

Fig. 10.5b. A chalk quarry with deliberate infill, demonstrating how larger pieces of flint and rubble tend to roll to the bottom of the slope.

10.6. The Overton Down experimental earthwork. This ditch was dug to study the effects of erosion of a ditch and bank over a period of a century, and sections are cut across it at regular intervals, after 1, 2, 4, 8 years, etc. In this picture we can see how turves have been undermined by natural erosion, and have then fallen into the ditch, taking with them earlier finds. This, added to the effects of man, animals such as pigs, burrowing animals and especially the activities of earthworms, gives an impression of how confused ditch stratigraphies can be.

10.7. An infilled ditch. The photograph shows a ditch which has been filled in at a developed stage of infill – the high incidence of chalk lumps in the upper fill indicates that it is not natural infill. Underneath it there is a buried surface – a relatively stoneless zone caused by worm activity (turf line).

10.8. A ditch at Aulnat. This was a multi-period (four-phase) ditch, filled with black soil and cut into black soil. The phasing only became clear after excavation was completed, and after the sections had been allowed to weather. The phases were in fact of major chronological significance – the only stratified sequence for the Early to Middle La Tène period (fourth–second centuries BC) in central France, so keeping the finds apart was important. The ditch was dug in spits, with each separate soil in each spit distinguished, and each group of finds confined to a 2-metre square. A plan of each spit was also made so that the observed plan could later be compared with the section. More subdivision was used than thought necessary – groups of finds can always be lumped together afterwards, but they can't be separated later! The ditch was finally phased and the pottery grouped after excavation was completed, with apparently only limited contamination of some groups of finds.

out of use, not when it was dug. Where the bank survives evidence for this may be found in the gradual build-up of the bank, with dumped material interspersed with turf-lines, as was found in the outer, counterscarp, bank at the hill-fort of Danebury. Otherwise it may only be detected by trampled deposits in the very bottom of the ditch.

Occasionally the ditch is allowed to become so infilled that it has to be recut (Figs 10.8, 10.9). If the bank has slumped, it often means that the new ditch is not dug along exactly the same line, and this produces the appearance of a shelf, or perhaps a corrugated effect if the ditch is continually recut on different lines. Alternatively the later ditch may not be so deep, and this can be picked up in a discontinuity in the process of the ditch infill. The terminals of all ditches should always be excavated by means of longitudinal sections, as earlier phases sometimes only survive when a later ditch stopped short of an entrance.

Though I have been digging ditches for years, I still don't know how to dig them properly! Gullies are quite easy as they fill in quickly and have a simple stratigraphy, and

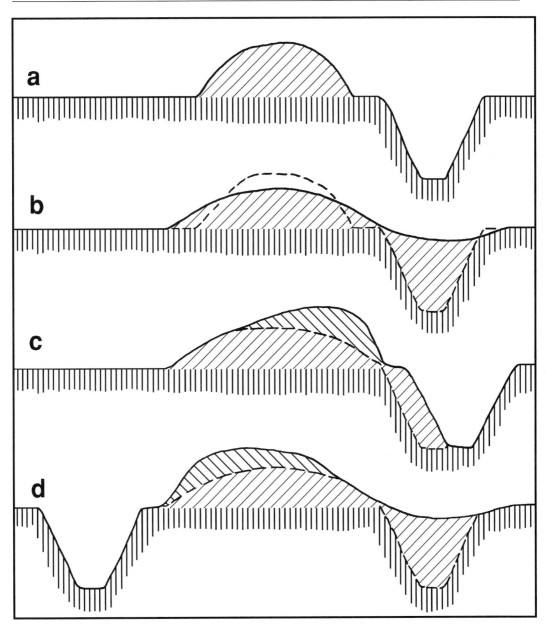

(Above and following page) *10.9. Recut ditches. The diagram shows what often happens when a ditch (a) is allowed to fill in and is then recut. The bank slumps (b), and when the new ditch is dug at its foot, it does not run along the exact line of the old one (c). In an extreme example (d) the ditch is so silted up that the new ditch is dug on the wrong side of the bank. At Owslebury, where the bank had disappeared, this produced the peculiar phenomenon of two ditches of different dates running parallel with each other. The first photograph (e) shows a normal recutting, with two phases (the later, deeper ditch, has been deliberately filled, as stones and chalk in the upper half reveal). The second photograph (f) shows the corrugated effect of multiple recuts covering a couple of hundred years, complicated by the inevitable pits and small chalk quarries; a few metres away all had coalesced into one ditch in which no recut was visible.*

Fig. 10.9e.

Fig. 10.9f.

large defensive ditches are reasonable as their size makes differentiation of the various phases relatively easy – it is the ones in between, 1–2m deep, that present problems. The difficulty is that *at the same time* two or more totally different fills may be deposited. Thus, in the centre of the ditch there may be coarse rubble which grades into fine soil at the edge. The question is whether to ignore the nature of the fill, and to dig the ditch stratigraphically as a series of lenses, or to differentiate between fine and coarse rubble, even though these fade into each other, and each may have been forming over a period of time. A third way is to dig in spits, with the different types of soil differentiated in each spit. Even measuring in every find does not solve the problem, as experimental work has demonstrated the very localised processes that affect ditch filling. Perhaps we should just give up and accept that fine stratigraphy is impossible in ditches, though they are important sources of finds, and so of information.

When digging a ditch, check the stratigraphy first. At Owslebury, because of the complicated stratigraphy, each ditch was divided into 3m lengths; one metre was taken out first, avoiding any obvious complications like the junction with other ditches (see Fig. 1.8). Any later disturbances, such as burials, would usually be identified at this stage, and precautions could be taken to prevent the contamination of the ditch stratigraphy itself. The remaining two metres were then removed (large quantities of finds were required for analysis), but with a baulk 25cm wide left between each 3m length. The section would then be drawn and photographed, and left to weather, because some of the subtleties of the stratigraphy can only be seen after a month or so of weathering. It was also useful to have a series of sections open for comparison; some aspects, such as deliberate infill, may be clear in one section but not in another, and may need the benefit of hindsight to recognise it. For the deeper ditches, a plank laid over the top of the baulk helped ease movement around site – there is nothing sadder than a digger stuck on the wrong side of a deep, completely excavated, ditch when the rush for the tea-break starts!

The intersection of ditches can prove very complicated (Fig. 10.10). Usually it is best to have as much information as possible before the intersection is tackled – excavation of some sections of the ditches involved will give both the date and evidence of any recuts. None the less the intersection should still be investigated, as a ditch which was already largely filled in could still have been functioning as a boundary, perhaps supplemented by a hedge or fence on the bank. It is usually easiest to see what stage of infilling the earlier ditch had reached by sectioning rather than excavating in plan. Where there are multiple ditches intersecting, perhaps with several recuts, the investigation becomes even more complicated, especially as Sod's Law states that large soft areas are also good places to insert burials and other features!

BANKS

Banks and ditches are barriers, and often occur together, though banks can occur by themselves, especially as field boundaries constructed from stones picked off the field and dumped along the line of a pre-existing fence or hedge; others may be formed by the gradual accumulation of soil creeping down a slope due to erosion. For many banks, if all that is required is the profile and some dating evidence, a simple trench will suffice. This will not, however, be satisfactory if information about structure is

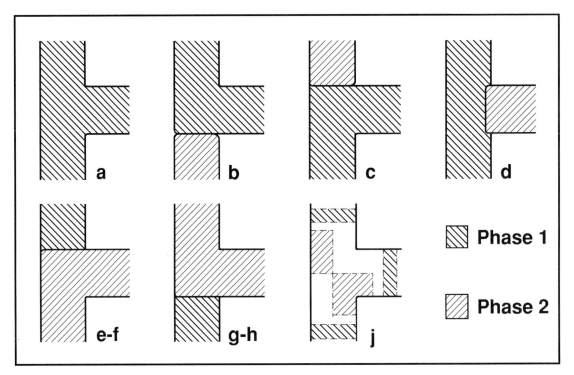

Fig. 10.10a–j.

Fig. 10.10k.

10.11. Moel y Gaer. *The second phase of the defences of this Welsh hill-fort consisted of rows of parallel posts front and back, linked with cross-baulks, and filled with stone and soils. As the bank survived, it was possible to study its internal construction. The spaces between the cross-baulks linking the front and back timbers were filled with differing materials, some well-defined (as here, towards the base of the bank), others identifiable from more subtle variations in the make-up of the earth and stone chippings derived from the adjacent ditch (seen across the top of the picture). The photograph shows part of a 15m length of bank under excavation in plan, as viewed obliquely from inside the hill-fort (a complementary view, along the line of the bank, is seen in Guilbert 1975, Pl. XIIIb). Such evidence would have been totally meaningless if seen within the confines of a narrow trench (scales measure 2m). Photograph G.C. Guilbert.*

(Opposite) **10.10. Ditch intersections.** *This diagram shows that even a simple T-junction need not be all it seems – it could be three contemporary ditches (a), or two phases with one ditch butting on to the earlier (b, c, d); or it could be an early ditch cut by a later one (e-f, g-h) – in either case the early ditch could run straight on or turn a right angle. Diagram (j) shows a suggested sequence of excavation with initial trenches being dug to try to establish the dates and nature of each ditch before the intersection is tackled. Sections are then laid out down the centre of each ditch, and opposing portions taken out to give complete longitudinal sections. The photograph from a ditch junction at Owslebury (k) shows that things are never that simple!*

needed. The section may reveal information about turf-lines and the material from which the bank is made, but little more. A bank may have a timber fence or palisade running along the top, or what may seem to be an irregular pile of stones may prove to have structure when seen in plan, and for these a trench is inadequate – Wheeler's trenches through the defences at Maiden Castle show massive post-holes cut into the top of the bank, but we have little idea what they are. The elaborate timber structures which were commonly used in the defences of the ramparts of Bronze Age and Iron Age hill-forts can only be interpreted if large lengths are opened up, as Graeme Guilbert did at Moel y Gaer (Fig. 10.11).

ELEVEN

BURIALS

Burials, especially human ones, always cause great interest among public and excavators alike. But paradoxically the quality of excavation over the years has been on the whole pretty poor. By the time the bones reach the specialist they may be broken, scraped, sometimes mixed, and the smaller ones lost. Only in the past few years have standards of excavation started to improve as the potential of burials for telling us about ancient societies and populations has been realised. Matters like the age and sex of the dead person are fundamental in understanding ancient burial rites, and in beginning to understand what the grave-goods mean. We have moved on from the simplistic belief that the grave offerings were merely items to accompany the deceased to another place. They are also symbolic, perhaps of the person's status within the society, or of the beliefs of the community, or perhaps of the social organisation. It is, after all, not the dead person who puts the items in the grave – often we are seeing a deliberate destruction of wealth by living people within a funeral context.

We should not think just in terms of human burial, as the status of animals and humans overlap, as they do within our own society with pet animals afforded quasi-human burials with tombstones, etc. Human bones from ancient societies sometimes just turn up with 'normal rubbish' on settlement sites, and some members of society may well have been simply buried in a hole, just as we would bury a pet animal in the garden, and this is especially true of young infants. At Owslebury this was the norm, but conversely a young goat with a broken, but healed, leg was buried with a pot and a coin – more grave-goods than the average adult human on the settlement had at the same period – or was this an early example of *Animal Farm*?

The ethics of excavating human burials is a matter much discussed in a world context, especially if it is contrary to the wishes of the modern population, irrespective of whether or not they are likely to be the genetic descendants of the dead. This is a major problem in Australia and the USA, and in the past archaeologists with western attitudes have not always been diplomatic in their relationships with the wider public. In western society attitudes have changed over the last century as belief in the physical resurrection of the dead has declined, making such burial rites as cremation legal and accepted. Until recently in Britain an Act of Parliament was needed to allow Christian cemeteries to be disturbed, and in Winchester in 1961 this involved all the human remains being placed in a black wooden box ready for reburial – the City Council lorry driver always insisted on driving the bones at 5 miles an hour to the local cemetery. The director was nonplussed when buying trowels in the local ironmongers when the assistant proudly announced that her grandparents were buried on the site! In Britain, in fact, the situation is ambiguous, as there are Home Office guidelines about shielding human remains from the public gaze when they are being excavated. On the other hand, the public are encouraged to visit excavations, skeletons are on display in museums and programmes such as *Meet the Ancestors* rely on public interest. Clearly there is a distinction between the ancient dead and the recent dead (for which the Home Office devised its rules), and perhaps our interest in our predecessors is one way in which we honour them; whatever, there should be respect for human remains, as for all archaeological data.

BASIC PRINCIPLES

The basic aim should be to record as much of the burial ritual as can be recognised in the archaeological record, and secondly to provide as much information as possible to the person doing the bone report. In the latter case, this means making sure that the bones are carefully preserved, with the minimum of loss and damage. For age, the teeth are one of the best diagnostic features. Thus the contents of graves, and especially cremations, should be sieved to make sure that no teeth (or other small bones) are lost. Indeed, in many infant burials, and adult burials in mildly acidic soil, the teeth may be the only thing to survive. For establishing sex, the pelvis is the most important, yet one of the most fragile, parts of the body. Special care is needed in lifting it. Excavation, especially if the bones are soft, should only be done with a wooden or plastic spatula to minimise damage, and when the skeleton is lifted extra care must be taken with disarticulating ball and socket joints not to cause damage. Washing can be done gently if the specialist requests it, and packing should be done in such a way as to minimise rubbing.

INHUMATION

If the presence of a grave is suspected, it should be excavated in such a way as to minimise potential damage to the skeleton. If it is an extended inhumation, avoid digging at the two ends, as one of them will contain the foot and toe bones, which can easily be disturbed if the depth of the grave is unknown; the head end is a favourite place for grave-goods. The grave should be taken down in shallow spits, and cleaned, and perhaps planned at each spit looking for evidence of a coffin or other grave structure. The best place to dig down is on one side of the grave, about a third of the way along – if a bone is encountered, it is likely to be one of the long bones of the arm or leg, and so less likely to be damaged or displaced. With other sorts of burial, such as crouched inhumation, if it is intact, the skull is likely to be the first bone encountered, so care must be taken as the two ends of the grave are excavated.

As the body is exposed, avoid areas where small bones, such as fingers and toes, are likely to be, and define areas with no bones or finds where loose soil can be gathered, or, if the grave is deep, where it may be possible to stand – never stand in a grave until you know the grave layout or you may be crushing delicate bones or objects; it is usually better to excavate lying on the side of the grave or on planks laid across the grave. Once the rough outline of the body is established, you can start excavating the more delicate areas. If the bones are in good condition, try to undermine the long bones so that soil can be removed from under them; the advent of the vacuum cleaner makes picking up soil easier, but be careful not to suck up small bones or finds! Grave-goods are left in position for drawing and photography, but be especially careful if ornaments such as bead necklaces

11.1. Infant burials. *Not all infants are as well preserved as this one from Owslebury. In some cases only the teeth may survive, so care must be taken with any small scoops or pits of the right size. On prehistoric and Roman sites it was normal to bury infants on the settlement rather than in a cemetery. It demonstrates the need to excavate around bones before removing them, to see if there are others in articulation. Sieving is essential to recover teeth and all the epiphyses – the unfused ends of long bones – which can be vital in ageing young people, especially if the body is poorly preserved, as in Fig. 11.1b, showing a Roman burial from Le Pâtural, Clermont-Ferrand.*

Fig. 11.1b.

are present (Fig. 11.1). Infants are less easy to recognise – have a good look at the bones of examples displayed in museums.

On acidic soils the body is likely to have disappeared completely, and its former presence may be detectable only by chemical analysis of the soil, giving a concentration of phosphates. On sand, however, the outline of the body may be preserved in the form of darker-coloured sand; bones tend to be darker than the fleshy parts of the body. This allows the delicate operation of excavating the outline of the body in three dimensions, as was done for the burials recently excavated by Martin Carver around the Saxon mounds at Sutton Hoo.

It is usual to record the position of the body both photographically (the occasional skeleton livens up public lectures and displays) and by drawing. The use of *pro formas* with a drawing of a skeleton to colour in have not proved very satisfactory, other than to record the presence of each bone. At the Saxon cemetery of Raunds, for instance, the incidence and location of coffin burials could only be understood by careful study of the way in which the body had decayed – bodies buried in earth or shrouds retained their anatomical positions better than ones that had decayed in coffins (Fig. 11.2). Therefore the detailed recording of the position of every bone was essential. In some cases, levelling in of the two ends of the long bones may be necessary if it is suspected that the body has been subjected to subsequent disturbance or arrangement.

EXCARNATION

The treatment of bodies is something that varies considerably from one society to another, in the ancient world as well as the modern. We only have to consider the difference in western Europe where religious beliefs and social and economic organisation are similar – in Britain and Scandinavia scattered cremation is becoming dominant, in France the family vault is the norm, in Italy and Spain tower blocks for inhumations have become usual where land is limited. Often archaeologists are excavating the end of a long ritual process, which can involve the exposure of the dead before burial, and may even involve the removal of bones such as skulls for use elsewhere. Bones which have been buried after the body has decayed (excarnation) are quite common, from communal burial in Neolithic tombs (Fig. 11.3, see pp. 155–6), to charnel pits in medieval cemeteries, and even into the present day when cemeteries are

(Opposite and following page) *11.2. Coffins. In compact soils a coffin is likely to show up as a dark stain around the body. As the grave is taken down in spits, plans should be made – though they may not necessarily indicate a coffin (a). In the case illustrated, burial 39 at Owslebury, dated to the mid-first century BC, the layout of the body subsequently showed that there was not likely to have been a coffin (b) – the dark outline is due to differential weathering of the grave fill. This was incidentally one case where excavation one-third of the way along the grave went wrong – it produced a sword rather than a femur! In loose, heavily wormed soils only the presence of coffin nails may indicate a coffin. Each nail should be numbered separately and its position and location noted, as traces of wood preserved in the corrosion may allow the reconstruction of the coffin. In some cases it may only be the layout of the body which will indicate the presence or absence of a coffin, as the Hallstatt burial from Le Pâtural near Clermont Ferrand shows (c). The main bones are in position, but the smaller ones and the ribs clearly show the body collapsed in a void. The disarrangement of the body is partly due to natural collapse, but may have also been caused by a burrowing animal, or, more likely in this case, by the coffin being flooded.*

Fig. 11.2a.

Fig. 11.2b.

Fig. 11.2c.

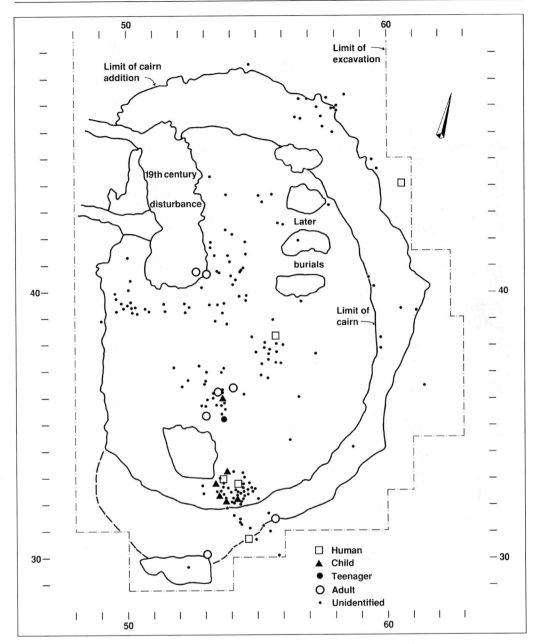

Fig. 11.3a.

cleared out. It can involve burial and exhumation after a period of time, or exposure in the open (in Celtiberian society warriors killed in battle were 'honoured' by being left to the vultures). Usually we find only the end result, in the form of deposits of disarticulated bone, which poses special problems of recording for the archaeologist – the sequence of deposition, the presence or absence of smaller bones – and this may involve the numbering and precise location of every single bone. Rarely do we find the intermediate stages such as the platform from Wigber Low (Fig. 11.3b), where the spread of small bones and teeth and the lack of large bones suggests exposure took place.

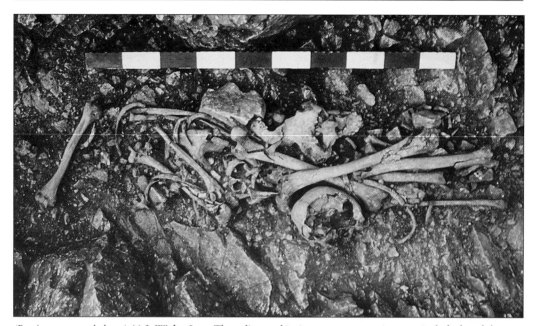

(Previous page and above) *11.3. **Wigber Low**. The policy on this site was to measure in every single find, and the interpretation of the site would have been impossible without this level of recording. The distributions of burnt bone (a), whether identifiable or not, suggested the practice of scattered cremation, a burial rite which, one suspects, was relatively common, but which had never been identified in Britain before. In addition, the mound seems to have been used for the exposure of the dead – skull and long-bone fragments were virtually absent, but there were large quantities of teeth, and toe and finger bones on and in the mound. For deciding which tooth may belong to which body, exact location was of vital importance. Near the mound was a pit with the remains of two individuals who had been excarnated (b). In cases of burials such as these, the process of deposition needs to be understood – whether all at once, or gradually accumulating over time. Megalithic tombs may produce fragments of dozens of individuals all piled up. In these cases each bone can be planned and given an individual number. A stratigraphical matrix can then be prepared to show which bone overlies which, and the location of individual bodies in the heap established. At Wigber we unfortunately did not extend the numbering of individual bones to the complete inhumations, and one adult burial reached the specialist with a number of milk teeth. Was there another burial which had decayed and we had not identified it, or were these teeth grave-goods? I shall not make the same mistake again!*

CREMATION

From the bone specialist's viewpoint, cremation is a disaster as it destroys a lot of potential information – measurements are limited and bones typically disintegrated, and unless the bones have been poorly cremated, sex and age are not easy to determine. It is therefore vital for the archaeologist to find every piece of information – every burnt tooth for ageing. This means that the whole deposit should be carefully sieved. If the cremation is in an urn, it should be removed in layers and each layer kept separate, as there may be some specific ritual in the order in which bones are placed in the urn, or there may be two individuals, and it is important to see if they are mixed, or if one has been put in after the other, and, if there are grave-goods, which body they are associated with.

Often the bones are picked out of the pyre, and there is no charcoal, but if any pyre material survives it should be studied in detail. At the Iron Age cemetery of Dreitsch in Germany males and females were cremated on pyres using different types of wood (males with oak, females with beech), so even in cases where little bone survived the sex could be suggested from the charcoal. A Roman burial from Lussat in France had the remains of the pyre tipped in, including a large number of pots, furniture and other items that had been cremated. All the burnt material was passed through a seed machine, and produced over a thousand grains of cereals and legumes. A cemetery at Alton in Hampshire was systematically sieved, and produced a range of carbonised grass seeds and other materials; these were not deliberate offerings, but they were informative of the circumstances of the burial.

RITUAL DEPOSITS

Anything we don't understand tends to be labelled as 'ritual'. This can include the deposition of bone on religious or settlement sites – in many societies, ritual activity occurs as commonly in a domestic situation as on a special site. For instance, on many Iron Age sites in temperate Europe it is common to find deposits of bone, which may be human, animal or both, articulated or disarticulated. This phenomenon has been studied at Danebury where large numbers of pits with such finds have been excavated, and where some regularity has been suggested, with skulls or articulated limbs at the bottom of storage pits. The only way in which we can see if there is a recurring pattern is to record as many examples as possible – again a plea that bones need to be cleaned round and considered in context before they are removed.

11.4. Palaeopathology. Though it is rare to be able to say what someone died of, some illnesses and traumas do show up on the bone structure – evidence for instance of malnutrition in the form of rickets, or cribra orbitalis (a roughening of the bone in the eye sockets). Broken bones which have healed, osteoarthritis and dental caries are some of the more common items that can be identified in the field – like this individual from Owslebury with both legs broken and healed (the thickening of the bone) and the lipping of the vertebrae, typical of osteoarthritis. Gallstones are rarely identified, probably because excavators do not recognise them!

Twelve

SAMPLING

We cannot dig every site, we cannot walk every field, we cannot record every grain of soil or pollen, and we do not have time to recover and identify every last scrap of pottery or bone. We therefore have to sample. Sampling is a technique which can be used to tell us what we are missing; it is a way of using expensive time- and labour-consuming techniques economically to recover vital information although such techniques can only be applied to a small amount of what we are excavating. If we are to use sampling in a meaningful way, we must be clear what it is we want to know, why we are doing it, and how best to preserve the sample so that the information survives. We must also be clear about what method of sampling we are using, and it must be clearly stated on the labels, in our site records and in the excavation report. Different sorts of sampling can tell us different things.

SAMPLING STRATEGIES

There is now an extensive literature on sampling techniques as used in specific circumstances, but in all cases the technique used should be discussed with the relevant specialist, who must also be made aware of the implications of the sampling technique in terms of cost in time and money. Sampling techniques were discussed in Chapter 2, especially for sampling the terrain. Here I will only give examples of how each type may be used for soils and other deposits, especially for environmental information. The methods most relevant to excavation are:

Bulk sampling. This is when an isolated quantity of soil is taken from a deposit of whatever size is deemed necessary, and placed in a bag. Care should always be taken that the soil is not contaminated by other deposits falling in, and also it should be double-bagged, and the label not left in direct contact with the soil.

Column or core sampling. This is when soils or deposits overlying one another are sampled as a continuous sequence. There are three main ways of doing this. First, if there is an exposed section, blocks of soil are taken out at defined intervals, say every 2cm, and bagged separately. Start at the bottom of the column to prevent contamination, as material from the top samples will naturally fall on to the lower deposits. Secondly, a deep baking tin or a half-section of plastic drainpipe can be banged into the deposit, in the case of the pipe usually behind an exposed section which allows the pipe to be removed (not always easy! – I usually try to hold a piece of wood against the section to prevent it crumbling). When the sample has been taken, it can then be bound up with plastic clingfilm, both to hold the sample in position and to prevent contamination. Don't forget to mark which is the bottom and which the top of the core! This method has the advantage that sample intervals can be changed in the laboratory. A sample, say, for pollen, is removed by cutting through the film, and this can be sealed up again, so the core can be used several times. The stratigraphy will also be visible through the film. Thirdly, where sections are not exposed, a corer must be used – there are various types according to the soil type, depth, etc. The core can be removed with a knife and stored in a half drainpipe sealed with cling film. Care may be needed in the storage of cores – some may need to be kept in cold conditions to prevent the contents from rotting, as bacteria will inevitably enter with exposure to air.

Judgement or purposeful sampling. This is very common on excavations because certain types of information will only survive in special conditions. Thus, samples for intestinal eggs will be taken from cesspits; samples for organic material will be taken from waterlogged deposits; column samples for pollen or molluscs may be taken from the place where the stratigraphy is preserved best in a surviving section. In this way time is not wasted on deposits which are not likely to yield the required information.

Haphazard sampling. At Aulnat, sampling was decided by whether we had the seed machine, whether there was water available, whether we were at the beginning or end of a season, or whether there was someone whose standard of recovery I did not trust (ie, who only found large pieces of pottery or bone) – especially someone 'experienced' who was clearly not aware that their standards were not mine! I do not recommend haphazard sampling as few statistical inferences can be drawn.

Systematic sampling. We used this technique on a deposit of burnt grain at Montarrenti, probably from a granary that had caught fire. In each 1 metre square of the grid a block 10 × 10cm was taken from the south-west corner of the square (a 1 per cent sample – but it still yielded about eighty samples to be studied!). This could then be used to reconstruct the approximate total amount of burnt grain, and also to compare the relative importance of different grain types in samples across the site. The seed expert himself then had to sample our samples, as there was too much material for all of it to be identified.

Random sampling. There is a tendency to go for the samples which look rich, or the ones which have goodies sticking out of them, but this could mean that features of a certain period or function may be missed. So if it is not possible, for instance, to excavate all the pits on a site, the pits can be numbered, and random number tables consulted to decide which should be examined. This method is often used in conjunction with a judgement sample, so that in addition to the random sample other features may be excavated. The random sample for instance may miss one rare type of pit. The results of the two sorts of sampling must be strictly distinguished. On Iron Age and Roman sites in north-eastern England every feature was sampled, but the seed specialist, Marijke van der Veen, then had to select the number of samples she could deal with, which was done using random number tables. Deposits with large amounts of grain visible only represent certain types of activity, and it is necessary to see the full range of variation, as some activities (e.g. winnowing) will produce more debris than others (e.g. baking).

SIEVING

Sieving is carried out for two reasons: first to find things; and secondly to estimate what is being missed. Though superficially these might seem to be the same thing, they are in fact fundamentally different, and require very different sampling strategies. Finding things can take place at different levels: at Wigber Low we decided to go for a policy of as complete recovery as we could manage, which meant sieving *everything* that came out; items found in sieving were so marked on the labels, and they were measured in to approximately where they were found (each excavator sieved their own buckets, so approximate positions could be guessed at). On more complex sites, sieving to find things may be confined to deposits which are especially rich, or which are likely to produce useful returns in the form of small coins, beads or small human bones which are otherwise likely to be missed.

Sieving to calculate what is missed is concerned with statistical analysis of the finds, and therefore requires a well-formulated policy, perhaps with a statistical basis such as random sampling. It is concerned to define, for instance, to what extent small bones such as fish, or sheep's teeth are under-represented in the material that is being collected by normal digging methods, so that figures can be adjusted at the finds analysis stage. The sampling strategy employed must be worked out beforehand with the finds analysts. In fact, it is best if a combination of both sieving techniques can be used, but they must be carefully differentiated in the labelling – the data from a deposit which is chosen for sieving because it may have a lot of fish bones in it cannot be used to extrapolate to the rest of the site. One problem with extrapolation is to persuade people to dig as normal – there is a tendency for people to dig more carefully if they know their soil is to be sieved, so as not to be shown up for their poor recovery rate. Conversely, one of the early sieving experiments was biased for the opposite reason – the excavators thought it was not necessary to pull out all the finds at the digging stage if the soil was to be sieved later!

There are two main methods of sieving: wet and dry. Water sieving is best, because it washes the objects and makes them more visible, but it is not always feasible. There may be an inadequate water supply, and techniques which involve the importation or recycling of water may prove too time-wasting for the returns. Sandy and other light soils being dug under dry conditions may not require water. It is not always easy to deal with large quantities of material. In York the speed of the process has been improved by mixing the soil with water in a cement mixer – the amount of damage to finds seems to be unexpectedly light!

The size of the mesh of the sieve will be varied according to what information is required. A site with large numbers of fish, and especially otoliths (the highly distinctive 'ear' bones of fish), may require fairly fine meshes, but on sites where recovery mainly concerns artefacts, coarser meshes may suffice. Various devices for easing the back-breaking work have been devised, such as 'shakers' on bendy iron bars, and some have even been mechanised! Sieving is hard work, but great fun for those who like to get wet and muddy.

Flotation. The other main sampling process often carried out on site is flotation to recover seeds, charcoal and other materials that float (Fig. 12.1). Various systems have been devised to maximise recovery – such as pumping air through the water, or adding

12.1. Flotation. Various machines have been developed to separate charcoal from soil. The Cambridge model, here being used by the author at Aulnat in the 1970s, relies on the charcoal floating to the surface, overflowing into a pipe, and then passing though sieves to catch the charcoal, using two different sizes of mesh to prevent the sieves from blocking. Always keep a close eye on the sieves – soil particles can block them causing an overflow which will ruin the sample. The soil can be washed out of the bottom of the machine through a larger pipe, which has a simple sealing device to keep the water in. It can suffer from constipation, so massaging of the pipe and stirring with a stick will help. The soil is sieved as it goes in to the machine to remove larger items, and the residue can be water sieved. The amount of soil sieved needs to be measured to calculate densities, which is important for interpretation.

chemicals – but most seed specialists accept that some denser items, for instance olive stones, may not float, and so will be under-represented. Some of the soil residue is also therefore searched. At Owslebury, one of the first sites to use flotation, we had found one seed in three years before flotation was introduced – the first bucket of soil to be floated in 1967 produced thirty seeds! Since that time recovery has greatly improved, including weed seeds and other debris from crop processing which are vitally important for interpretation. Sampling is usually a combination of rigorous statistical sampling to encompass a range of the activities and contexts, plus some judgement sampling of deposits which may look extra-rich – but usually these deposits are heavily biased in their content.

ENVIRONMENTAL SAMPLING

Pollen will survive in waterlogged or acidic conditions, and so is sampled by judgement and in columns. Where individual samples are used, great care must be taken not to contaminate – the deposit must be carefully cleaned before the sample is taken, but only a small polythene bag of soil needs to be taken.

The equivalent on alkaline soils for reconstructing the local environment is molluscs. These require a 5kg deposit for a good sample, though smaller samples are sometimes necessary, especially if taken as a column, which is the normal method. The majority of molluscs are so small that they need to be sieved out and identified under a microscope, but I also ask my excavators to keep any shells they may find – marine molluscs such as oysters were commonly eaten, and we have found examples of cockles and *Pecten* ('ash trays') in Iron Age contexts in central France – they must have been traded from the coast as ornaments. Some of the larger snails may well have been eaten.

Under waterlogged conditions macrofossils are likely to survive, such as grasses, twigs, leaves and insects, and large samples of several kilograms may need to be taken. They must be carefully double-bagged so no moisture can escape, and the bags kept out of the sun. We are also beginning to recognise that under some conditions phytoliths may survive – these are the silicate skeletons of plants such as grasses, and they are certainly identifiable in waterlogged conditions and in acidic soils where there has not been too much worm activity. These need samples of about a kilogram.

In cesspits, helminth (intestinal parasites such as tape-worms) eggs may survive. These are good things from the public interest point of view, but in fact are less important archaeologically, as it seems that everyone, at least on urban sites, had intestinal worms; they can, however, tell us which deposits are genuine cess deposits. They may also be preserved in burials in lead coffins. Helminth eggs in other animals such as pigs are of a different size, and this can be useful in identifying the presence of animals on a site, and the interpretation of a building such as stables or sties. But waterlogged cess deposits can yield up other information, such as pollen, fibres from the diet, etc.

Phosphates can be measured in two ways, either chemically in the laboratory or by a pulsed induction metre (concentrations of phosphates affect the magnetic properties of the soil). In either case small samples of a few grams suffice. If one is dealing with a building, perhaps to decide if it was used for stalling animals, systematic sampling is usually required.

Samples of soil may be taken for a variety of reasons, perhaps to study its chemical composition, or to look at the grain size to see under what sort of conditions it was laid down. The usual policy is to take more than one thinks one will require – a kilogram bag suffices for most purposes.

With all these forms of sampling, it essential that labels are not placed in direct contact with the deposit, or the labels will rot!

SAMPLES FOR DATING

On prehistoric sites C14 dating is still important. Contamination must be carefully avoided, so no smoking on site! Charcoal for C14 dating should be collected along with a sample of the surrounding soil, including obvious contaminants such as roots, though with the advent of accelerator dating, only small samples are needed, and so species such as cereals with a short life are preferable to a piece of oak charcoal which can be several hundred years old when the tree was felled, and so give a misleading date. I usually wrap up the sample in aluminium foil before placing it in a polythene bag – again double-bagging is essential, with the label in the *outer* bag.

Dendrochronology is potentially the most accurate dating method – even to the season of the year in which the tree was cut down. In Britain at present there is little hope of an absolute date with species other than oak, or with less than fifty years of rings, but short runs of other woods, for instance hazel, can give relative dating – e.g. to show if two samples are likely to be contemporary or not. For wood, the sample needs to be kept damp, well wrapped and sealed in polythene, perhaps with some fungicide added to prevent decay. Carbonised pieces of wood will require careful wrapping, perhaps in clingfilm, or expanded polyurethane foam to hold them together. Special care must be taken with the outer rings, as these are the key to accurate dating, and must not be lost.

Archaeomagnetic dating relies on measuring the orientation of iron particles in clays and soil – the position of the north pole has tended to shift through time, and a curve has been established into which samples can be fitted with some accuracy. For dates from the first millennium BC onwards, it is potentially more accurate than C14. The particles become oriented if clay has been fired, as in hearths or kilns, and this can even happen in naturally forming silts, in the bottom of ditches or in lakes, but clearly the deposits must have remained undisturbed, for instance by worms. Samples need to be taken by the specialist.

THIRTEEN

SUMMARY

I hope this book will help to do two things. First, for those who are going on their first excavation, be it as student or amateur volunteer, I hope it will give them some confidence in knowing what is going on around them, what is likely to happen, and that they will not necessarily cause some disaster by failing to react to some unexpected discovery. Over-confidence can be disastrous; too little confidence can cause delay and indecision, which, especially on sites where there is pressure of time to finish, can also be destructive, in that important discoveries will not be made if the pace of work is too slow. Secondly, I hope it will influence site directors, to remind them of best practice, especially in their duties in training their staff (and indeed themselves), and also to show them the range of different excavation traditions and practices that exist across Europe.

DOS AND DON'TS

On all excavations there is a certain level of discipline which is essential to the running of the excavation. The director or supervisor should lay these down the minute you step on site, but there are many rules which all sites share in common.

Communication. Open area excavation, like open-plan offices, are ideal for communication. So know what is happening around you; watch and learn from other diggers; if you don't understand something, ask – first the nearest experienced worker, then the supervisor, and if necessary the director – they should be circulating around the site regularly to deal with queries and to make sure things are going smoothly, but don't harass a director if someone else can deal with it. If you have special skills or interests, make them known; it may be possible to make use of them.

Cleanliness. Do not wander around the site on areas which other people have been cleaning up; do not trample loose soil into undisturbed deposits or leave litter around; do not dig things out of sections or the surface unless instructed to do so; keep your own spoil under control; and leave your area looking cleaner than when you started.

Discipline. Fill in labels and forms exactly as you are told to: the data will have to be entered on to databases, so will have to comply with a fixed format. Short-cuts in recording always come unstuck – so stick to the system as laid down, but do contribute ideas for improving it. It is one of the unwritten rules of recording that one minute saved in taking a short-cut on site will lose someone an hour at the post-excavation stage. Take nothing off the site unlabelled.

Archaeology is enjoyable, but it is also a discipline. I hope that those who read this book will share some of the pleasure I have had in the last forty-odd years. But it is only worth doing if it is done well.

RECENT TRENDS: PROFESSIONALISATION

It was at the beginning of the 1970s that a great change came over British archaeology. The major shift was in the professionalisation of the subject. Though professional archaeologists had been around for many years, in the museums, universities and government agencies such as the Ministry of Works, the Royal Commissions on Historical Monuments and the Ordnance Survey, most of these saw excavation and fieldwork as only a small part of their brief. The first professional field archaeologist was probably W.F. ('Peter') Grimes who was employed to excavate sites threatened by wartime construction work, and subsequently in bomb-damaged London. By the 1950s there was a small group of freelance workers directing rescue excavations on a fairly full-time basis; the major breakthrough came with the establishment of the Winchester Unit under Martin Biddle, and soon afterwards the York Unit under Peter Addyman at the end of the 1960s.

The larger funds that became available from both central and local government in the 1970s saw a proliferation of such units, mainly based in local government but occasionally in universities or as independent trusts. Most of these professionals came from a small number of universities where it was possible to study archaeology, or had come via fieldwork, and were people either with degrees in other subjects such as History, or with no full-time higher education. This period of expansion, however, also saw a proliferation of new degrees being set up in a range of universities, and the number of graduates in archaeology quickly outran the number of jobs available. Archaeology through exposure on television proved a popular general degree for those who did not have a clear vision of what they wanted to do in life, and it took over from subjects such as Classics as it gave a broader background, with practical fieldwork and laboratory skills, and a broad basis in the Humanities, Sciences and Social Sciences. There is no information on how many of these new students ended up in archaeology, but probably it was somewhere between 15 and 20 per cent. In the 1980s an additional influx both of funds and of people came from government-funded job-creation schemes, though some of these people subsequently went on to university as mature students.

The next major change came with the publication of PPG16, which greatly increased the funding for archaeology, and so produced a further expansion in professional archaeology. A recent survey gives a estimate of about 4,600 professional archaeologists working in Britain, including those in museums and universities. With commercialisation of archaeology the government demanded privatisation, and this led to a four-way split in the groups involved with field archaeology:

Planning and Development. In the 1980s greater emphasis was placed on the planning process, in order to avoid costly delays on sites where unexpected major finds might delay redevelopment – the Temple of Mithras and the Rose Theatre are the two most notorious cases. A centralised National Monument Record had been set up under the Royal Commission on Historical Monuments, and now similar county-based records were established in planning departments, the Sites and Monuments Record (SMR). A member of staff, often a County Archaeologist (the 'curator'), was charged with maintaining these records, advising on planning matters and, with developer funding, to arrange excavations where necessary, and ensure standards were maintained.

Archaeological Units. These could no longer be under local government control, as there was an ideological rejection by the government of the notion that there should be a monopoly system whereby local government units would instruct developers about what needed to be done, and then demand the money to do it. Competition was introduced by privatising the fieldwork side of the Units, who would then compete for work put out to tender by the County Archaeologist.

Consultants. Developers were naturally not always happy at the financial demands that were being made of them and though some have built up special relationships with certain Units, others have decided to employ their own archaeological consultants to give them advice.

Freelance archaeologists. With the loss of local government income, and no guarantee that local archaeological projects would come to them by right, many Units decided to shed specialist staff, such as finds specialists, geophysicists, etc. Many of these individuals became self-employed, and now earn their living by short-term contractual arrangements with various units.

These changes are in many ways peculiar to Britain. Under the same Valetta Convention, France has gone for an entirely centralised system, in which the *Association pour les Fouilles Archéologiques Nationales* (AFAN) has a virtual monopoly in carrying out excavations, overseen by regional offices of the Ministry of Culture (*Service d'Archéologie*). The system gives greater freedom in concentrating money on specific projects, and within AFAN, the largest archaeological employer in Europe, conditions of employment are good. There are also national themes of research, such as 'The City' or 'Mines and Metallurgy', into which much rescue excavation is integrated. However, the teaching of archaeology at universities is highly undeveloped in comparison to other countries in Europe, with no first degree. In Germany the situation varies from one *Land* to another, some following the commercial model, while in others the *Denkmalpflege* has retained the monopoly both in dealing with the problems of Planning and Development, and in running the excavations. University training is longer than in Britain (usually seven years), but still concentrates mainly on traditional approaches to archaeology such as artefact identification. Field projects are directed by people with academic training, but much of the day-to-day running of a site is carried out by trained field technicians with no academic training, and workmen are employed to do the digging, though this situation is gradually changing.

RECENT TRENDS: COMPLEXITY OF PARADIGM

Though in the first chapter I suggested the dominance of certain types of paradigm at certain periods of archaeology's development, none the less there has never been only one approach, and many paradigms can co-exist; indeed, in the 1950s schools of archaeology developed around the economic approach of Grahame Clark, or the Culture-Historical approach of Christopher Hawkes, or the Marxist approach of Gordon Childe. The rejection of the Culture-Historical approach in the 1960s does not mean that we were no longer interested in matters such as linguistics or population change, merely that we looked for different ways of approaching the question, for instance using the genetic possibilities of DNA.

Much of the methodology and theory of the New Archaeology of the 1960s and 1970s is still very much with us. Regional surveys, using aerial photography and field-walking, the study of settlement hierarchies and other socio-economic questions, such as trade and exchange, have not disappeared. Archaeologists still look upon open area, large-scale excavation as the only way in which to solve some of the problems such as intra-site variability; it is the emphasis which has changed from purely functional interpretations, as advocated by writers such as Louis Binford and Mike Schiffer, to one in which ideology is allowed to play a more important if not dominant part.

Medieval archaeology still has major concerns with art, art history and architecture, as it did in the nineteenth century. But it now has wider interests derived from socio-economic questions, such as the origin of towns and villages, indeed of landscapes. In Britain medieval archaeology tends to be more thematic than the study of other periods, for instance in looking at subjects like moated settlements, church archaeology or potteries; in part this may reflect the complexity of the period, and the extensive documentary evidence.

Conservation is a major problem for organisations such as English Heritage, which has led on to a number of surveys such as that made of the Fenlands or of the environs of Danebury. The result is a bewildering range of approaches to the past, with many small groups looking at specialist problems. Excavations, and especially landscape studies, because of the range of evidence that is produced, are the points where all these interests can coincide and cross-cut. The modern archaeologist needs a wide education in archaeology.

RECENT TRENDS: METHODOLOGY

Alongside this increase in scale and theoretical complexity, there is also a more and more complicated methodology which needs to be, if not mastered, at least understood. We have seen how the paradigms demand ever-increasing detail of recording and analysis, for which concepts like the context, the Harris matrix and computer technology supply some of the answers. The latter demands greater systematisation of the way in which data are collected and analysed. At the same time there has been an enormous increase in both the quantity of excavation which is being carried out, and the scale, with the shift from the trench archaeology of the 1930s–1950s to the massive open area excavations of both urban and rural sites. There is now a wider range of questions – Wheeler, for example, did little with animal bones, and nothing with seeds. Sourcing of pottery and metals was unknown then, as were many of the dating techniques now used by archaeologists.

These developments mean that we need full-time teams to be running archaeology – for monitoring, planning, excavation, analysis of finds and publication. This has to be done within a legal framework, which of necessity has become more rigorous. Training needs have become more complex, and in recent years the undergraduate course has no longer been seen as adequate for an archaeological career. More and more students are coming back to do more specialist Taught Master courses, and following more specialist careers than in the past. In brief, archaeology has become more complex.

CONSERVATION OR EXCAVATION

The Valetta Convention lays great stress on the conservation of archaeological sites, which is an important principle in dealing with sites threatened by development, but it has started a debate in Britain about how far this principle should be extended. Does it mean that excavations which are carried out on unthreatened sites, for research or social purposes, should likewise be treated as threats to our rapidly diminishing archaeological heritage, and so discouraged, if not banned? A slightly different view argues that certain sites such as Stonehenge should be put aside as sacrosanct, unless there is some burning academic reason for excavating, and that generally sites should be preserved for the future when there will be better techniques, perhaps even non-destructive techniques, of finding out all we need to know. It does not, however, exclude research on other more common sorts of site.

The reverse argument, put forward strongly by Martin Biddle in a recent lecture, is that many of the measures taken to reduce destruction on sites, such as piling for foundations, are in fact extremely destructive in themselves and do not leave the sites intact. He also argues that rescue excavation is of necessity second best to research excavation as there are inevitably pressures of time and money, and if rescue excavation only takes place in the future, it means that no sites will ever be excavated up to the highest standards. So, there should be a continuing programme of research work, raising the standards in rescue excavation and widening the range of questions asked. This is a debate which will certainly continue for some time!

THE FUTURE

Though we are unlikely to return to the situation in Britain in the 1960s, when large-scale excavations were very much the domain of student volunteers, who might be paid some subsistence for a stay of a few weeks, none the less there are still many opportunities for students and others to participate in excavation. Indeed, it may well continue developing as a leisure activity, giving professional opportunities to carry out detailed projects which are beyond the capabilities and financial possibilities of a purely professional discipline. The conflict which has developed in some areas of Britain, where professionals have tried to exclude the volunteers, are to no one's advantage, as archaeology depends on public support; furthermore, archaeology is not there just to keep a few professionals employed, and to let them indulge in their hobby at someone else's expense.

The professional needs to be adequately paid, with reasonable working conditions, and these should not be undermined by volunteers providing cheap labour. The sort of conflict that can emerge where professionals and volunteers are working together is typified by the matter of working hours. Professionals who have been working at a job throughout the week reasonably want weekends off to be with their families, or to do something which is not archaeology, whereas this is the time when volunteers want to indulge in their hobbies and use their leisure time, including taking part in archaeological activities. But accommodation can be made between the two requirements. In any case, most professionals themselves started off as volunteers, or at least as students taking part in field projects organised by their universities. Somehow, despite the professionalisation of archaeology in Britain, the majority of students entering university to study archaeology already have some experience of field projects. We have fortunately not reached the Swedish Catch-22 situation, in which all archaeology is done by professionals, and naturally only those with field experience are likely to be employed, as it is not cost-effective to employ the inexperienced. The problem is how to get experience, so that one is employable, if there are no opportunities open for the inexperienced.

In Britain, there has been a long tradition for local amateur groups to carry out their own excavations; the problem with this is that standards of post-excavation work are now much more rigorous, with detailed studies needed for animal bones, environmental reports, pottery studies and so on, which lie beyond the scope and funding of most amateur groups. Such groups are open to the criticism that they are destroying the archaeological record by using techniques that are not up to the standards required. Where professionals are using volunteer groups, there are often complaints that the volunteers are expected to do the mundane and boring work, and they are not given much responsibility or opportunities to use their initiative. However, many of these conflicts often come down to clashes of personality; amateurs who do not see their own limitations and professionals who have an overblown sense of their own ability and importance. But it is not something confined to the professional/volunteer interface; it is a complaint levelled at the profession by the ordinary diggers at the bottom of the professional ladder.

In Britain there are two major non-governmental organisations which are trying to deal with these problems. The first is the Council for British Archaeology, set up just after the Second World War by the leading professional archaeologists as an organisation to represent the archaeological world, but with a special remit to provide support to amateur groups by setting standards, providing training and generally developing archaeology in this country by initiating new legislation, establishing new organisations where they were needed, encouraging education initiatives, etc. It set the agenda in the 1960s which led to the establishment of the first archaeological units; it laid the foundations for the pressure group Rescue in the early 1970s; it set up the committee which developed into the Institute of Field Archaeologists in the early 1980s. Other initiatives, such as the Young Archaeologists Club, it has continued to maintain in-house. Initially all organisations concerned with archaeology were invited to become members, not only the county societies and smaller research groups, but also national societies, the universities and even government bodies such as English Heritage. It thus became a major talking-shop for archaeologists, and a major disseminator of information. Times have changed, and though it is still the main meeting point for archaeological organisations in Britain, as well as a major publisher, it has now decided to make more direct contact with the wider public by having individual as well as institutional membership, and issuing a monthly newsletter, *Archaeology in Britain*. It provides information about university courses, and has also set up an information desk on training opportunities and careers in archaeology.

The other organisation is the Institute of Field Archaeologists. It is concerned with the maintenance of professional standards in Britain, though 'professional' does not mean the exclusion of amateur archaeologists; indeed, the Institute recognises that there are many 'non-professionals' who have skills desperately needed by the profession, and who are encouraged to join. The importance of such professional organisations is that they set up 'Codes of Practice', aimed at establishing and maintaining standards. High standards are of advantage to everyone, and are essential for the belief that what one is doing is worth doing. So, how does one stop people who do not reach these standards from operating?

This question concerns not only amateurs but also professionals themselves, trying to exclude the 'cowboys' whose work is not up to professional standards. In most countries in the world, this has been addressed by the issuing of permits to carry out fieldwork; the experience, however, in countries where this has been introduced is that it does not in fact guarantee high standards. Indeed, it often stifles initiative, and some of these permits are more connected with whom one knows rather than with one's abilities.

In Britain we have been more concerned with 'Codes of Practice' and 'Codes of Conduct'. These voluntary codes by common agreement end up becoming compulsory, because without the stamp of approval of, say, the IFA, those who are paying for the excavation will not be willing to enter into contracts, as there is no guarantee of high quality and no means of redress after the event. For the IFA, the first concern has been with the professional units, and we are now well advanced down this path; the standards are policed by the professionals themselves. Similar moves are under way in dealing with volunteers as well. There is already an IFA Code of Practice in how to integrate and treat both volunteers and students. The next stage will be to guarantee standards of training (see Appendix), and to provide the professional training needed.

This brings us on to a major concern of the volunteer, the student and the young professional – the groups at which this book is aimed. How can one get training of an adequate standard? Increasingly there are advertisements to take part in 'Training Excavations'. These can be quite expensive, and at present there is no Code of Practice to guarantee the standards, though it is a matter high on the agenda of the Professional Training Committee of the IFA. Most students studying archaeology at university will have the opportunity to take part in university-sponsored projects. Though many of these projects are of a very high standard, indeed some are at the cutting edge, there is also no guarantee that any particular university lecturer has the necessary skills to teach practical techniques in the field; again, standards need to be guaranteed, either through the IFA or through the Quality Assurance Agency in Higher Education (QAA), a body set up by the government to monitor standards of teaching and research in British universities.

There is also a major need for properly organised professional training, which can be linked with career and personal development. There is a very clear gap between the training given in universities (very important for areas like the theory and history of archaeology, as well as giving a wide general background), and the specific needs of the young professional (excavation skills; relevant knowledge of the organisation of archaeology in Britain; Health and Safety). Some of these professional areas are better not taught at university, as the majority of archaeology graduates do not go on to become professional archaeologists, and university lecturers are not necessarily the best people to teach such matters. In any case, with changing technology, ideas and knowledge, there is a need for everyone to undergo life-long learning or Continuing Professional Development (CPD). To meet these needs the IFA is setting up a system for accrediting courses and training, which can then be recorded in 'log-books' which will be inspected at intervals by the IFA, and which increasingly employers will demand to see when appointing or promoting staff. But such concerns affect the whole of the archaeological world. For England, English Heritage has initiated the establishment of an Archaeology Training Forum which includes all the interested bodies, such as the CBA, the IFA, universities, local government and archaeological units, to oversee the development of training schemes; the hope is that these will be open to everyone wishing to improve their skills, professionals, students and volunteers alike. The European

Association of Archaeologists is taking on some of the roles of the IFA and the CBA at a European level, setting up Codes of Practice over a wide range of activities, including training excavations (see Appendix 1).

The future is thus, I think, quite bright, with new opportunities opening up and with better guarantees of adequate standards. We can expect an expansion of formal training excavations organised through both Continuing Education Departments in universities, and perhaps independent groups. English Heritage has started giving funds for rescue projects so that trainees can be taken on to the excavation team. There is also an increasing European market, and in some countries, such as Russia, this could expand considerably. I would recommend that people try to get some experience in Britain before working abroad; as I have already pointed out, traditions are very different in Europe, and you will get much more out of the experience if you can compare and contrast techniques. I had comments from two readers on the draft of this book; one commented, from a British perspective, that I did not emphasise Single Context Recording enough as the main way in which excavations are recorded; the other, from a European perspective, said I spent too much time on what is mainly a British phenomenon! However, you should scrutinise what is on offer: is there a detailed programme of training advertised, including lectures and training with specific types of equipment such as dumpy levels, and does the project state that it is following specified Codes of Practice?

FINDING EXCAVATIONS AND FIELD PROJECTS

In Britain the Council for British Archaeology traditionally advertises excavations where volunteers are needed, and its monthly newsletter, *Archaeology in Britain*, comes free to members. It also produces factsheets on various topics, including excavation and employment, as well as publishing information on university courses, and runs a free job information service, the British Archaeological Jobs Resource (www.bajr.co.uk). The CBA also provides the central organisation for the many local Young Archaeologists' Clubs. Details can be obtained from:
The Council for British Archaeology
Bowes Morell House
111 Walmgate
York YO1 2UA
Tel. no. [0904] 671417
Fax. no. [0904] 671384
E-mail 100271.456@compuserve.com
Website: www.britarch.ac.uk

As previously mentioned, English Heritage is now providing opportunities for students and younger professionals to take part in rescue excavations. Information can be obtained from:
English Heritage
Inspectorate of Ancient Monuments
Fortress House
23 Savile Row
London W1X 2HE

Projects abroad, especially in Europe, are advertised by the Archaeology Abroad Service, which produces two issues a year, for which a small subscription has to be paid. Its address is:

Archaeology Abroad Service
31–4 Gordon Square
London WC1H 0PY

The major source of information about excavations will be more local. Most parts of Britain have county societies; though few of them are now engaged in archaeological work, they provide a good point of contact with local workers. Museums and some archaeology units are involved in projects with the wider public, on Community Archaeology projects and the like. But keep an eye on your local newspaper: I started my digging career when a local project was advertised as in need of workers. I was deposited by my mother on the excavation, and put into a trench by the director, equipped with a trowel and a tray for finds. To put it mildly, it changed my life!

APPENDIX

The following is a draft recommendation to those running practical training projects such as excavations. It was prepared at a gathering at the Annual Meeting of the European Archaeologists' Association in 2000, and it is being recommended to the EAA as the basis of a Code of Practice or Advisory Note which the EAA can adopt. It is also likely to form the basis for an IFA Code of Practice, as well as laying down the principles on which English Heritage will be providing funds for training projects. I advise volunteers and students to check to see how far the information they are given measures up to the criteria in this document if they are choosing a training project.

Practical training should only be undertaken by those competent to provide the particular training offered (e.g. field survey, excavation, geophysics, or laboratory expertise). Where possible they should have recognised professional documentation of their competence.

Documentation provided to participants and potential participants should state clearly:

1) the names of the competent people running the project and their professional and training qualifications;

2) what specific training will be on offer (e.g. fieldwalking, excavation, finds processing, drawing, etc.), and to what level (where this can be defined, e.g. under the Institute of Archaeologists proposed levels of competence);

3) the date of the site and its nature;

4) which categories of student or volunteer are being catered for. (This can vary from people for whom the project is a working holiday with an educational aim, school children wondering whether to study archaeology at university, students fulfilling requirements for courses, or young professionals seeking professional training. All these groups have very different needs.)

5) what kinds of students or volunteers are being catered for (e.g. the level of previous experience, those with disabilities, age restrictions, etc.);

6) the way in which teaching will be carried out, preferably with a defined programme (e.g. lectures, on-site training, site documentation, mentoring by competent workers, etc.);

7) the ratios of competent staff to students;

8) a statement of the methods to be used, where possible with specific reference to manuals and textbooks;

9) a guide on the intended duration length of the excavation;

10) clear advice on living conditions, personal insurance, hazards, equipment to be provided, etc.

The project must be fully insured for accidents, professional indemnity and so on. It should maintain legal standards of Health and Safety, e.g. in working conditions, protective clothing, first aid training and provision of first aid kits. Every member of the team should know what to do in an emergency, and where to find the nearest doctor or hospital.

Field projects should conform to the legal requirements of the country in which they are carried out (e.g. for permits, legal access to land, deposition of finds and archives, publication, etc.). This will also normally involve carrying out an official 'Risk Assessment'.

There should be concern for the local social and political environment in which work is being carried out (e.g. students should not be seen to have privileged access to historical sites from which local people are excluded). It is the responsibility of the participants to enquire what are the working languages for the course, and ensure that they have sufficient command to participate fully.

Given the limited nature of the archaeological resource, due concern should be given to its preservation, and it should not be destroyed merely to provide training. Sites which are threatened or where there are pressing research interests should be chosen in preference to unthreatened sites.

Sites should be chosen that are suitable for the level of training being given – for example beginners should not start on complex and difficult deeply stratified sites. Students should not be exploited. Training excavations should not be used merely as a way of financing research; equally they should not be used as a means of undermining professional activities, for example by offering cut-price rescue excavations where these should be properly funded under state and European planning legislation.

Any certificates given out should be endorsed by a recognised institution, such as a university, museum, or other professional body. Participants should be asked for feedback on their experiences, and proper consideration should be taken of complaints and suggestions. Where possible these should be passed on to the relevant institution overseeing the standards.

Any participants should be told how they can make formal complaints if they are dissatisfied with their training and treatment.

BIBLIOGRAPHY

The bibliography is divided up into general reading in part according to chapters. For the different types of excavation technique, I have given examples of sites which have been excavated using those techniques, and, where they exist, critical or historical reviews of the methods or individuals who use them.

Complementary reading

Barker, G. (ed.) 1999. *Companion Encyclopaedia of Archaeology*. London, Routledge.

Barker, P. 1993. *Techniques of Archaeological Excavation*. London, Batsford, 3rd edition.

Carver, M. 1987. *Underneath English Towns: interpreting urban archaeology*. London, Batsford.

Coles, J.M. 1972. *Field Archaeology in Britain*. London, Hutchinson.

Drewitt, P.L. 1999. *Field Archaeology: an introduction*. London, UCL Press.

Hodder, I. 1999. *The Archaeological Process: an Introduction*. Oxford, Blackwell Publishers.

Renfrew, C. and Bahn, P. 1991. *Archaeology: Theory, Methods and Practice*. London, Thames & Hudson.

Roskams, S. 2001. *Excavation*. Cambridge, Cambridge University Press.

Previous books on excavation techniques

Alexander, J. 1970. *The Directing of Archaeological Excavations*. London, John Baker/New York, Humanities Press.

Atkinson, R.J.C. 1946. *Field Archaeology*. London, Methuen, 1st edition (2nd edition 1953).

Browne, D.M. 1975. *Principles and Practice in Modern Archaeology*. London, Teach Yourself Books.

Kenyon, K.M. 1952. *Beginning in Archaeology*. London, Phoenix House, 1st edition (2nd edition 1964).

Thomas, D.H. 1989. *Archaeology*. Fort Worth, Holt, Rinehart & Winston, 2nd edition.

Webster, G. 1963. *Practical Archaeology*. London, Adam & Charles Black, 1st edition (2nd edition 1974).

Wheeler, R.E.M. 1954. *Archaeology from the Earth*. Harmondsworth, Penguin Books.

Specialist manuals

Barber, J.W. (ed.) 1992. *Interpreting Stratigraphy*. Edinburgh, AOC (Scotland) Ltd.

Harris, E. 1989. *Principles of Archaeological Stratigraphy*. London, Academic Press, 2nd edition.

Harris, E., Marley, R. *et al.* (eds) 1993. *Practices of Archaeological Stratigraphy*. London, Academic Press.

Molas 1994. *Archaeological Site Manual*. London, Museum of London Archaeology Service, 3rd edition.

Schiffer M.B. 1987. *Formation Processes of the Archaeological Record*. Albuquerque, University of New Mexico Press.

Watkinson, D. and Neal, V. (ed.) 1998. *First Aid for Finds*. Hertford, Rescue, 3rd edition.

Rescue Archaeology

Jones, B. 1984. *Past Imperfect: the story of rescue archaeology.* London, Heinemann.

Rahtz, P. (ed.) 1974. *Rescue Archaeology.* Harmondsworth, Penguin Books.

History of Archaeology

Daniel, G. 1975. *A Hundred and Fifty Years of Archaeology.* London, Duckworth.

The early antiquarians

Original sources

Bateman, T. 1861. *Ten Years' Digging in Celtic and Saxon Grave Hills in the Counties of Derby, Stafford, and York from 1848–1858.* London, privately printed.

Colt Hoare, R. 1810. *Ancient History of North and South Wiltshire, I.* London, W. Miller.

Colt Hoare, R. 1822. *Ancient History of North and South Wiltshire, II.* London, W. Miller.

Reappraisals

Annable, F.K. and Simpson, D.D.A. 1964. *Guide Catalogue of the Neolithic and Bronze Age Collections in Devizes Museum.* Devizes, Wiltshire Archaeological and Natural History Society.

Evolutionists

Original sources

Pitt Rivers, A.H.L.F. 1887. *Excavations on Cranborne Chase.* Vol. 1. Privately printed.

Pitt Rivers, A.H.L.F. 1888. *Excavations on Cranborne Chase.* Vol. 2. Privately printed.

Pitt Rivers, A.H.L.F. 1892. *Excavations on Cranborne Chase.* Vol. 3. Privately printed.

Pitt Rivers, A.H.L.F. 1898. *Excavations on Cranborne Chase.* Vol. 4. Privately printed.

Reappraisals

Barrett, J., Bradley, R., Bowden, M. and Mead, B. 1983. 'South Lodge after Pitt Rivers', *Antiquity* 57: 193–204.

Bowden, M. 1991. *Pitt Rivers: the life and archaeological work of Lieutenant Augustus Henry Lane Fox Pitt Rivers, DCL, FRS, FSA.* Cambridge, Cambridge University Press.

Clarke, A. and Fulford, M.C. 1997. *Silchester Roman Town: the Insula IX 'Town Life' project; first interim report.* Reading University, Department of Archaeology.

Coles, J.M. and Minnitt, S. 1995. *Industrious and Fairly Civilised: the Glastonbury Lake Village.* Exeter, Somerset Levels Project and Somerset County Museums Service.

Hawkes, C.F.C. and Piggott, S. 1947. 'Britons, Romans and Saxons around Salisbury Plain and in Cranborne Chase', *Archaeological Journal* 104: 150–335.

Thompson, M. 1977. *General Pitt Rivers.* Bradford upon Avon, Moonraker Press.

Environmentalists

Original sources

Clark, J.G.D. 1954. *Excavations at Star Carr: an early mesolithic site at Seamer, near Scarborough, Yorkshire.* Cambridge, Cambridge University Press.

Reappraisals

Andreson, J.M. *et al.* 1981. 'The deer hunters: Star Carr reconsidered', *World Archaeology* 13: 31–46.

Clark, J.G.D. 1972. *Star Carr: a case study in bioarchaeology.* Addison Wesley module in anthropology 10.

Legge, A.J. and Rowley-Conwy, P. 1988. *Star Carr revisited: a re-analysis of the large mammals.* University of London, Birkbeck College.

Mellars, P. and Dark, P. 1998. *Star Carr in context: new archaeological and palaeo-ecological investigations at the early Mesolithic site of Star Carr, North Yorkshire*. Cambridge, Macdonald Institute for Archaeological Research.

Culture Historical: grid
Original sources
Wheeler, R.E.M. 1943. *Maiden Castle, Dorset*. Oxford, Reports of the Research Committee of the Society of Antiquaries of London, no. 12, Oxford University Press.
Wheeler, R.E.M. 1954. *The Stanwick Earthworks, North Riding of Yorkshire*. Oxford, Reports of the Research Committee of the Society of Antiquaries of London, no. 17, Oxford University Press.
Reappraisals
Sharples, N. 1991. *Maiden Castle*. London, English Heritage/Batsford.
Wheeler, R.E.M. 1955. *Still Digging: interleaves from an antiquary's notebook*. London, Michael Joseph.

Culture Historical: Schnitt
Original sources
Bersu, G. 1940. 'Excavations at Little Woodbury, Wiltshire. Part I: the settlement revealed by excavation', *Proceedings of the Prehistoric Society* 29: 206–13.
Bersu, G. 1977. *Three Iron Age Round Houses in the Isle of Man: excavation report*. Glasgow, Robert MacLehose and Co.
Krämer, W. 1957. 'Zu den Ausgrabungen in dem keltischen Oppidum von Manching', *Germania* 35: 32–44.
Krämer, W. 1958. 'Manching, ein vindelikisches Oppidum an der Donau', *Neue Ausgrabungen in Deutschland*, 175–202.
Krämer, W. 1960. 'The Oppidum of Manching', *Antiquity* 34: 191–200.
Reappraisals
Evans, C. 1989. 'Archaeology and modern times: Bersu's Little Woodbury 1938 and 1939', *Antiquity* 63: 436–60.
Evans, C. 1998. 'Constructing houses and building contexts: Bersu's Manx round-house campaign', *Proceedings of the Prehistoric Society* 64: 183–201.

Open Area: barrows
Collis, J.R. 1983. *Wigber Low, Derbyshire: a bronze age and Anglian burial site in the White Peak*. Sheffield, J.R. Collis Publications.
Grimes, W.F. 1960. *Excavations on Defence Sites 1939–1945. I: mainly neolithic – bronze age*. London, Her Majesty's Stationery Office.
Waterman, D. 1951. 'Quernhow: a Food Vessel barrow in Yorkshire', *Antiquaries Journal* 31: 1–24.

Open Area: complex sites
Barker, P. 1969. 'Some aspects of the excavation of timber buildings', *World Archaeology* 1–2: 220–35.
Barker, P. and Higham, R.A. 1982. *Hen Domen, Montgomery: a timber castle on the English–Welsh border*. London, Royal Archaeological Institute Monograph.
Beresford, M. and Hurst, J.G. 1990. *Wharram Percy: deserted medieval village*. London English Heritage/Batsford.

Biddle, M. 1964. 'Excavations at Winchester 1964: second interim report', *Antiquaries Journal* 44: 188–219.

Biddle, M. 1975. 'Excavations at Winchester 1971: tenth interim report', *Antiquaries Journal* 55: 96–126, 295–337.

Open Area: simple sites

Cunliffe, B.W. 1983. *Danebury: anatomy of a hillfort*. London, Batsford.

Collis, J.R. 1968. 'Excavations at Owslebury, Hants: an interim report', *Antiquaries Journal* 48: 18–31.

Collis, J.R. 1970. 'Excavations at Owslebury, Hants: a second interim report', *Antiquaries Journal* 50: 246–61.

Guilbert, G. 1976. 'Moel y Gaer (Rhosemor) 1972–3: an area excavation in the interior', in D.W. Harding (ed.) *Hill-forts: later prehistoric earthworks in Britain and Ireland*, pp. 303–17, 465–73.

Hope-Taylor, B. 1977. *Yeavering: an Anglo-British Centre of Early Northumbria*. London, Her Majesty's Stationery Office, Archaeological Report no. 7.

Wainwright, G.J. 1979. *Gussage All Saints: an Iron Age settlement in Dorset*. London, Department of the Environment, Archaeological Reports no. 10.

Experimental Archaeology

Bell, M., Fowler, F. and Hillson, S. 1996. *The Experimental Earthwork Project, 1960–1992*. York, Council for British Archaeology.

Coles, J.M. 1973. *Archaeology by Experiment*. London, Hutchinson.

Coles, J.M. 1979. *Experimental Archaeology*. London, Academic Press.

Jewell, P. 1963. *The Experimental Earthwork on Overton Down, Wiltshire, 1960*. London, British Association for the Advancement of Science.

Reynolds, P. 1979. *Iron Age Farm: the Butser experiment*. London, British Museum Publications.

Burials

Brothwell, D. *Digging up Bones: the excavation, treatment and study of human skeletal remains*. London, British Museum (Natural History).

Chamberlain, A.T. 1994. *Human Remains*. London, British Museum Press.

Garratt-Frost, S. with Harrison, G. and Logie, J.G. 1992. *The Law and Burial Archaeology*. Birmingham, Institute of Field Archaeologists, Technical Paper no. 11.

McKinley, J.I. and Roberts, C. 1993. *Excavation and Post-Excavation Treatment of Cremated and Inhumed Human Remains*. Birmingham, Institute of Field Archaeologists, Technical Paper no. 13.

Official publications

English Heritage 1991. *Planning Policy Guidance 16: archaeology and planning* (PPG 16). London, English Heritage.

English Heritage 1991. *Management of Archaeological Projects*. London, English Heritage.

English Heritage 1991. *Exploring our Past: strategies for the archaeology of England*. London, English Heritage.

Miscellaneous

Atkinson, R.J.C. 1957. 'Worms and weathering', *Antiquity* 31: 219–33.

Biddle, M. 1994. *What Future for British Archaeology? The opening address at the Eighth Annual Conference of the Institute of Field Archaeologists, Bradford, 13–15 April 1994*. Oxbow Lecture 1. Oxford, Oxbow Books.

Clark, A. 1988. *Scientific Dating Techniques*. Birmingham, Institute of Field Archaeologists, Technical Paper no. 5.

Collis, J.R. 2000. 'Towards a national training scheme', *Antiquity* 74: 208–14.

Gero, J.M. 1988. 'Socio-politics and the woman-at-home ideology', *American Antiquity* 50-2: 342–50.

van der Veen, M. 1992. *Crop Husbandry Regimes: an archaeo-botanical study of farming in northern England 1000BC–AD500*. Sheffield Archaeological Monographs 3. Sheffield, J.R. Collis publications (1992).

Sources of illustrations

Barker, P. 1969. 'Some aspects of the excavation of timber buildings', *World Archaeology* 1–2: 220–35.

Beresford, M. and Hurst, J.G. 1990. *Wharram Percy: deserted medieval village*. London English Heritage/Batsford.

Bersu, G. 1940. 'Excavations at Little Woodbury, Wiltshire. Part I: the settlement revealed by excavation', *Proceedings of the Prehistoric Society* 29: 206–13.

Clark, J.G.D. 1954. *Excavations at Star Carr: an early mesolithic site at Seamer, near Scarborough, Yorkshire*. Cambridge, Cambridge University Press.

Collis, J.R. 1983. 'Review article of G.J.H. Wainwright: Gussage All Saints: an Iron Age Settlement in Dorset' (including a discussion of the Little Woodbury house), *Germania* 60: 625–8.

Collis, J.R. 1983. *Wigber Low, Derbyshire: a bronze age and Anglian burial site in the White Peak*. Sheffield, J.R. Collis Publications.

Dimbleby, G. 1965. 'Overton Down Experimental Earthwork', *Antiquity* 39: 134–6.

Frankovitch, R., Hodges, R., Parenti, R. and Barker, G. 1983. 'Il Progetto Montarrenti (SI): relazioni preliminare', *Archeologia Medievale* 10: 317–39.

Grimes, W.F. 1960. *Excavations on Defence Sites 1939–1945. I: mainly neolithic – bronze age*. London, Her Majesty's Stationery Office.

Guilbert, G. 1975. 'Moel y Gaer, 1973: an area excavation on the defences', *Antiquity* 49: 109–17.

Harris, E. 1989. *Principles of Archaeological Stratigraphy*. London, Academic Press, second edn.

Hope-Taylor, B. 1977. *Yeavering: an Anglo-British Centre of Early Northumbria*. London, Her Majesty's Stationery Office, Archaeological Report no. 7.

Krämer, W. 1957a. 'Zu den Ausgrabungen in dem keltischen Oppidum von Manching', *Germania* 35: 32–44.

MoLAS, 1994. *Archaeological Site Manual*. London, Museum of London Archaeology Service, third edn.

Musson, C. 1970. 'House plans and prehistory', *Current Archaeology* 21: 267–75.

Redman, C.L. 1986. *Qsar es-Seghir: an archaeological view of medieval life*. London, Academic Press.

Reynolds, P.J. 1974, 'Experimental Iron Age storage pits: an interim report', *Proceedings of the Prehistoric Society* 40: 118–31.

Richmond, I.A. 1961. 'Roman timber building', in E.M. Jope (ed.) *Studies in Building History; essays in recognition of the work of B.H. St.J. O'Neil*. London, Odhams Press, pp. 15–26.

Soudský, B. 1966. *Bylany: osada nejstarších zemědělců z mladší doby kamenné* (a settlement of the oldest farmers in the late Neolithic). Prague, Akademia.

Wheeler, R.E.M. 1943. *Maiden Castle, Dorset*. Oxford, Reports of the Research Committee of the Society of Antiquaries of London, no. 12. Oxford University Press.

Wheeler, R.E.M. 1954. *The Stanwick Earthworks, North Riding of Yorkshire*. Oxford, Reports of the Research Committee of the Society of Antiquaries of London, no. 17. Oxford University Press.

INDEX